Angela Carter

16.99
13/10/06

Angela Carter

The rational glass

AIDAN DAY

MANCHESTER
UNIVERSITY PRESS

Manchester and New York

Copyright © Aidan Day 1998

The right of Aidan Day to be identified as the author of this work has been asserted by him in accordance with the Copyright, Designs and Patents Act 1988.

Published by Manchester University Press
Oxford Road, Manchester M13 9NR, UK
and Room 400, 175 Fifth Avenue, New York, NY 10010, USA
www.manchesteruniversitypress.co.uk

Distributed exclusively in the USA by
Palgrave, 175 Fifth Avenue, New York NY 10010, USA

Distributed exclusively in Canada by
UBC Press, University of British Columbia, 2029 West Mall,
Vancouver, BC, Canada V6T 1Z2

British Library Cataloguing-in-Publication Data
A catalogue record for this book is available from the British Library

Library of Congress Cataloging-in-Publication Data
A catalog record for this book is available from the Library of Congress

ISBN 0 7190 5316 1 paperback

First published 1998

First digital, on-demand edition produced by Lightning Source 2006

Til min datter Asta

Contents

Acknowledgements

I first came across Angela Carter's work in 1979, when a friend gave me a copy of *The Sadeian Woman*. Many years later I read more of her writing and started teaching her fiction on English Literature courses at the University of Edinburgh. I owe a debt to the stimulus and debate provided by the students on those courses. I am also extremely grateful to Kath Burlinson, John Gillies, Elaine Jordan, Betsy Ermarth and Tom Vargish, who read the typescript or parts of the typescript in one form or another. Their criticisms were always offered in a spirit of academic generosity and, even though I may sometimes have disagreed with their disagreements, I have benefited profoundly from their careful and perceptive readings. I want to thank Matthew Frost at Manchester University Press for all his help, and I would also like to thank Denyse Presley who typed a fair copy of the book with extraordinary speed. Lastly, I want to thank my partner, Charlotte Jacobsen Day, with whom I had long, detailed and illuminating discussions about post-modernism and about Carter's work, and who put up with me spending so much time at my desk.

Aidan Day
Edinburgh, August 1997

INTRODUCTION

'I'm a *socialist*, damn it! How can you expect me to be interested in fairies?'

Angela Carter (1940–92) was nothing if not versatile. She wrote children's stories, radio plays, film scripts, poetry, journalism and criticism of various kinds. But she was principally a writer of fiction and it is with her fiction – nine novels and four collections of short stories between 1966 and 1993 – that this book is mainly concerned. The book does not significantly take up biographical matters, though it does pay heed to Carter's own observations about her writing. A biographical sketch of Carter is available in Lorna Sage's excellent 1994 Writers and their Work booklet, *Angela Carter*.

Carter's fiction is a bit extreme. She explores aspects of Western sexuality through a series of strange fables: about a doctor who invents reality-distorting machines, a man who is surgically transformed into a *Playboy* centrefold, a woman who grows wings, and so on. Her style is vivid, highly wrought. Some readers flinch from this manner, though I happen to find it thrilling. Thrilling and – very often – amusing. In a perceptive review of *Shaking a Leg*, Carter's collected journalism, Blake Morrison noted that 'Her power as a feminist writer is that she's funny and derisive' (Morrison 1997: 31). Carter's mocking and subversive humour can be felt throughout her fiction, where she frequently uses it against the most unhumorous of objects. Humour directed towards sometimes deadly serious ends is a Carter forte. It is an aspect of the zeal that drives her style. In an interview published in 1985 John Haffenden said to Carter: 'I think it's true that you do embrace opportunities for overwriting.' To which Carter replied: 'Embrace

1

them? I would say that I half-suffocate them with the enthusiasm with which I wrap my arms and legs around them' (Haffenden 1985: 91). Though this book is not about her style of writing, I must say I sympathise with Carter's unashamed endorsement of her own manner. Sympathetic readers have found many different ways of describing the special character of Carter's work. 'Undecorous, overripe and mocking tales in which nothing is sacred and nothing natural', says Nicci Gerrard (Gerrard 1995: 20). Lorna Sage writes that Carter's fictions

> prowl around on the fringes of the proper English novel like dream-monsters – nasty, erotic, brilliant creations that feed off cultural crisis. She has taken over the sub-genres (romance, spies, porn, crime, gothic, science fiction) and turned their grubby stereotypes into sophisticated mythology ... she writes aggressively against the grain of puritanism-cum-naturalism, producing adult fairy tales. (Sage 1977: 51)

Marina Warner has observed that Carter's

> imagination was one of the most dazzling this century, and through her daring, vertiginous plots, her precise yet wild imagery, her gallery of wonderful bad–good girls, beasts, rogues and other creatures, she causes readers to hold their breath as a mood of heroic optimism forms against the odds. (Warner 1992: 25)

'Tales in which nothing is ... natural', 'dream-monsters', 'daring, vertiginous plots': the anti-realism of Carter's dominant style has generated a rash of more technical labellings. Carter is a 'magic realist' or she is a 'postmodernist'; she is a writer of 'speculative fiction' or she is a writer of 'fantastic fiction'. More on this kind of terminology later: for the moment I must note that Carter's anti-realism has also provoked a special form of mythologising, a mythologising that confounds author and work.

This mythologising is especially apparent in some of the obituaries and other retrospective pieces written after Carter's death on 16 February 1992. Many of Carter's obituaries were deeply felt and deeply moving. Margaret Atwood, for example, in a piece that acutely registers her sense of loss, observed that the 'imagination at work' in Carter's writing 'was mercurial, multi-sided, and more than faintly Gothic' (Atwood 1992: 61). But she also spoke of Carter's appearance and personality, if not in terms of the Gothic, then at least in those of the fairy tale:

The amazing thing about her, for me, was that someone who looked so much like the Fairy Godmother ... should actually *be* so much like the Fairy Godmother. She seemed always on the verge of bestowing something – some talisman, some magic token ... There was something of *Alice*'s White Queen about her, too. (Atwood 1992: 61)

In a comparable vein, the presenter of a BBC2 television memorial to Carter (*The Late Show*, 18 February 1992), spoke of her as the 'white witch of English Literature'. Some three years after Carter's death Nicci Gerrard was to observe, in an appreciation in *The Observer*, that Carter

has achieved a cult status: the good witch, the fairy godmother, the Gothic fabulist of English fiction. And she looked a bit like a fairy godmother, with her large-boned height, prematurely white mane of hair, pink skin and far-seeing, blinky, ever-so-knowing eyes. (Gerrard 1995: 22)

The problems with this cult were highlighted, not long after Carter's obituaries appeared, by Merja Makinen: 'this concurrence of white witch/fairy godmother mythologising needs watching; it is always the dangerously problematic that are mythologised in order to make them less dangerous' (Makinen 1992: 2). There is a particular irony about Carter and her work being mythologised. She was herself so anti-mythic. 'A lot of my conscious energy', she observed in 1984, 'is devoted to demythologising things' (Harron 1984: 10). A year earlier, in an essay entitled 'Notes from the Front Line', she had written:

I become mildly irritated (I'm sorry!) when people, as they sometimes do, ask me about the 'mythic quality' of work I've written lately. Because I believe that all myths are products of the human mind and reflect only aspects of material human practice. I'm in the demythologising business. (*SL* 38)

Carter expanded a little on this in a 1988 interview with Anna Katsavos:

AK: In 'Notes From the Front Line' you say that you are not in the remythologising business but in the 'demythologising business'. What exactly do you mean?

AC: Well, I'm basically trying to find out what certain configurations of imagery in our society, in our culture, really stand for, what they

mean, underneath the kind of semireligious coating that makes people
not particularly want to interfere with them.

AK: In what sense are you defining myth?

AC: In a sort of conventional sense; also in the sense that Roland
Barthes uses it in *Mythologies* – ideas, images, stories that we tend to
take on trust without thinking what they really mean. (Katsavos 1994:
11–12)

Not thinking what Carter's own stories really mean, not thinking
about their demythologising energy, may apply also to some of the
readers of those stories. Nicci Gerrard writes: 'I remember a
colleague of mine' – who was idealising or mythologising Carter
'as a New Age role model, an earth mother' – 'once asking Carter
to write something on the summer solstice and Stonehenge; Carter
looked at her pityingly and said in her soft, reedy voice: "You just
haven't got me, have you dear?"' (Gerrard 1995: 22). Carter's view
was that myth functions to console people – not least, women –
for deprivation and dissatisfaction in the actual world:

All the mythic versions of women, from the myth of the redeeming
purity of the virgin to that of the healing, reconciling mother, are
consolatory nonsenses; and consolatory nonsense seems to me a fair
definition of myth, anyway ...
    Myth deals in false universals, to dull the pain of particular circum-
stances. (*SW* 5)

To mythologise Carter and her writing is indeed to neutralise
the dangerous relevance to life of her life's work. Given the flam-
boyance and sheer outrageousness of much of her writing, it is
perhaps not surprising that Carter and her work have been mythologised. Even so, Marina Warner's obituary *was* able to keep a
steady eye on the referents of Carter's fantasies. Warner's obituary
makes the one move that the mythologisers do not when she points
out that 'For a fantasist, Carter kept her feet on the ground ...
For her fantasy always turns back its eyes to stare hard at reality,
never losing sight of material conditions' (Warner 1992: 25).

The idea that Carter uses fantasy to investigate the material
conditions of reality demands some definition of the nature of her
fantasy. In popular usage the term fantasy may be taken to mean
an insubstantial, even 'escapist' kind of writing that has very little
to say in terms of the real world. Carter herself seems to have

reacted against just this connotation. In 1995 Paul Barker observed that Carter's 'fiction is now often seen as pure fantasy. To her annoyance, Gollancz invented a new category, "Fantasy and Macabre", when they published the novel she said was her own favourite, *The Passion of New Eve*, in 1977' (Barker 1995: 14). But if Carter wasn't writing merely escapist 'fantasy' literature, then perhaps what we should say is that she was writing 'fantastic' literature, something which can be claimed as altogether more respectable.

The seminal theoretician of the fantastic as a literary genre is Tzvetan Todorov. Todorov defined the literary fantastic as a genre which exists between two other genres: the marvellous and the uncanny. These are genres associated with different kinds of worldview. The marvellous refers to a view of the world in which strange events are explained in terms of supernatural, superhuman or magical forces. The uncanny is associated with a rationalised and secularised view of the world in which strange events are no longer explained by reference to forces outside of human reality, but according to the idea that strangeness is the product of a subjective disturbance in the mind of a perceiver. The strange event has a psychologically natural rather than a supernatural explanation. For Todorov, the fantastic is the realm a person occupies when they hesitate between a supernatural and a psychologically natural explanation of an event:

> In a world which is indeed our world ... there occurs an event which cannot be explained by the laws of this same familiar world. The person who experiences the event must opt for one of two possible solutions ... The fantastic occupies the duration of this uncertainty. Once we choose one answer or the other, we leave the fantastic for a neighbouring genre, the uncanny or the marvelous ... The possibility of hesitation between the two creates the fantastic effect. (Todorov 1973: 25–6)

For Todorov, literature is fantastic so long as it leaves its reader in a state of hesitation between a supernatural and a natural explanation of the events described in the text; it is a kind of writing that refuses to put its reader at ease through declaring whether or not it endorses a supernatural or a natural explanation. The literary fantastic ends at the moment when hesitation and ambiguity are resolved in favour of either a supernatural or a natural explanation of the events recounted in the text. Fantastic literature, Todorov observes, 'requires the fulfilment of three conditions':

> First, the text must oblige the reader to consider the world of the characters as a world of living persons and to hesitate between a natural and a supernatural explanation of the events described. Second, this hesitation may also be experienced by a character ... and at the same time the hesitation is represented, it becomes one of the themes of the work ... Third, the reader must adopt a certain attitude with regard to the text: he will reject allegorical as well as 'poetic' interpretations. (Todorov 1973: 33)

Carter's work does not satisfy Todorov's criteria for the fantastic. There is, it seems to me, no possibility that the supernatural could be an explanation for anything in Carter's writing. The supernatural in Carter's work is neither generously entertained nor even provisionally validated. When it appears in her fiction it is only ever mocked and dismissed. One term of Todorov's polar tension is absent in Carter's fantastic, so that the principle of hesitation in the sense that Todorov defines it is also missing. If Carter does not write crass fantasy literature, then neither does her writing inhabit the fantastic in the sense given by Todorov.

In a refinement and extension of Todorov's ideas, Rosemary Jackson introduces psychoanalytic terms of reference: she sees in fantastic literature a kind of return of the repressed. Whatever cannot be fitted into the norms and codes of established culture, whatever is taboo according to those norms and codes, finds expression in the fantastic. Fantastic literature, Jackson writes, 'characteristically attempts to compensate for a lack resulting from cultural constraints'; it 'traces the unsaid and the unseen of culture: that which has been silenced, made invisible, covered over and made "absent"' (Jackson 1981: 3–4). Specifically, for Jackson, fantastic literature seeks to articulate what has been repressed, and hence it articulates the unconscious: that field of the individual mind, and of the culture composed of individual minds, which lies outside the conscious, day-to-day dimension that is regulated through norms and codes and which is inseparable from language. 'The fantastic', writes Jackson, 'is a literature which attempts to create a space for a discourse other than a conscious one' (Jackson

1981: 62). Overall, Jackson argues that the fantastic is a politically subversive form to the extent that it challenges institutional orders with whatever those orders have banned or repressed:

> The modern fantastic, the form of literary fantasy within the secularized culture produced by capitalism, is a subversive literature. It exists alongside the 'real', on either side of the dominant cultural axis, as a muted presence, a silenced imaginary other. Structurally and semantically, the fantastic aims at dissolution of an order experienced as oppressive and insufficient. (Jackson 1981: 180)

The idea that the fantastic as a literary form has 'social and political implications' (Jackson 1981: 6), that it is subversively concerned with things excluded from mainstream culture, is an idea that, up to a point, fits Carter's use of the fantastic as a means of exploring aspects of sexuality that are not allowed for in dominant patriarchal ideology. But it is only a partial fit. Jackson does not specify in any detail what kinds of connection there are between the formal textual features of fantastic literature and actual political practice. Subverting established order alone, without re-establishing grounds for alternative political practice and agency, is at most a negative politics. And if this is Jackson's idea of the political implications of fantastic literature then it does not parallel Carter's use of the fantastic in her writing, because Carter's use of fantastic elements in her work is politically far from negative. These elements are invoked in the service of a positive and highly directed feminism. In my reading, the fantastic elements in Carter's fiction do not anarchically disrupt established orders; they do not introduce liminal possibilities which veer off into the rationally unaccountable and unrecoverable. Fantastic features in Carter's fictions do not engage at a fundamental level with the surreal. Her fantastic is entirely under conscious, rational control and is deployed in order to articulate issues concerning sexuality that occur in the actual, day-to-day world. The elements of fantasy or of the fantastic in Carter's work may be understood more on a par with Jacqueline Rose's understanding of the nature of fantasy in her 1996 book *States of Fantasy*. Rose, too, draws on Freud, but she is concerned to analyse the constitutive relation between fantasy and the construction of national identities in the real world. She observes that:

> Fantasy is not ... antagonistic to social reality; it is its precondition or
> psychic glue ... you don't have to buy into Freud's account of hidden
> guilt to recognise the force in the real world of the unconscious dreams
> of nations ... there is no way of understanding political identities and
> destinies without letting fantasy into the frame. More, that fantasy –
> far from being the antagonist of public, social, being – plays a central
> constitutive role in the modern world of states and nations. (Rose 1996:
> 3–4)

One of the objectives of her book, Rose declares, 'is to place fantasy
at the heart of our political vocabulary' (Rose 1996: 4). Politics is
not fantasy, but fantasy is politics. The elements of fantasy in
Carter's fictional writing possess a feminist political vocabulary
that connect them directly and positively with the real world. For
this reason I understand Carter's fiction, with its fantastical
features, as operating more in the manner of traditional allegory
than anything else; in the manner of a traditional 'allegory of ideas'
where, as M. H. Abrams has put it, 'the literal characters represent abstract concepts and the plot exemplifies a doctrine or thesis'
(Abrams 1993: 4). Carter herself, thinking back to the medieval
literature she studied intensively during her Bristol University
degree in English Literature, used the term allegory to describe
what she was doing in her fiction, though she was slightly wary of
the word:

> I do put everything in a novel to be *read* – read the way allegory was
> intended to be read, the way you are supposed to read *Sir Gawayne
> and the Greene Knight* – on as many levels as you can comfortably cope
> with at the time ...
>   As a medievalist, I was trained to read books as having many layers.
> Using the word 'allegory' may make it all too concrete ... it does seem
> a bit of an imposition to say to readers that if you read this book you
> have got to be thinking all the time; so it's there only if you want it.
> From *The Magic Toyshop* onwards I've tried to keep an entertaining
> surface to the novels, so that you don't have to read them as a system
> of signification if you don't want to. (Haffenden 1985: 86–7)

As a description of Carter's literary form, 'allegory' may indeed
'make it all too concrete'. At the same time, however, as Carter
points out, her novels do have a 'system of signification', and the
term allegory does at least hold out possibilities of multiple levels
of meaning. It is a term which, for all its traditionalism, may be
taken to subsume the kinds of sub-genre that Lorna Sage spoke of

as inhabiting Carter's fiction: 'romance, spies, porn, crime, gothic, science fiction'. In Carter's case it may be taken to subsume generic terms such as the fantastic and even, for that matter, magic realism. At any rate, for all its limitations, it is the term I shall use here to describe the nature of Carter's fantastical fiction. Certainly that fiction is a fiction of ideas. Here again, Carter has made the point in various ways. In 1988, Anna Katsavos asked her 'What is your definition of speculative fiction, and do you consider yourself part of such a tradition?' To which Carter replied:

> Well, I have had some following in science fiction. I didn't read a lot of science fiction when I was younger, but there was a whole group of science fiction writers in Britain in the sixties, who really were doing very extraordinary things with the genre. They weren't writing about bug-eyed monsters and space at all. One of them, J. G. Ballard, coined this phrase, 'inner space.' I was quite profoundly affected by them. They are all still working, and Ballard is, I suppose, the most important ... It seemed to me, after reading these writers a lot, that they were writing about ideas, and that was basically what I was trying to do.
>   Speculative fiction really means that, the fiction of speculation, the fiction of asking 'what if?' It's a system of continuing inquiry. (Katsavos 1994: 14)

Comparably, Carter has said that 'a narrative is an argument stated in fictional terms' (Haffenden 1985: 79). Which brings us back to the matter of allegory. Todorov observed that one of the conditions of the fantastic text is that in reading it 'the reader ... will reject allegorical ... interpretations' (Todorov 1973: 33). Such interpretations are, however, the very *raison d'être* of Carter's stories and what I will be doing in this book is reading her fiction precisely for its system of signification.

The cornerstone of that system is Carter's materialism. This is a metaphysical position which Carter outlined in 'Notes from the Front Line' when she said that the 'investigation of the social fictions that regulate our lives – what Blake called the "mind-forg'd manacles"' is what she had concerned herself with in her writing (*SL* 38). That concern, she went on to say, is

> the product of an absolute and *committed materialism* – i.e., that *this* world is all that there is, and in order to question the nature of reality one must move from a strongly grounded base in what constitutes material reality. (*SL* 38)

Carter's metaphysic grounds her politics. Her conviction that *'this* world is all that there is' drives her social concern – her concern with the excluded, the oppressed and underprivileged. Carter's social concern was shaped by the particular social and historical circumstances of her own childhood and early adulthood. She was one of those of an age and economic background to benefit profoundly from the Welfare State established by the Labour government of 1945. Carmen Callil wrote in 1992 that:

> She was a child of the austerity age, and she thanked the postwar welfare state every day of her life for the good things it gave her.
> In her view Thatcher's Britain had plunged *her* Britain to the bottom of the sea. ('We're going to hell in a handbasket' were her invariable words on the subject). In this, as in much else, she was the prime representative of a British personality that has not been privatised away. Tom Paine and Shakespeare lived on in her, and in her political opinions and integrity. (Callil 1992: 6)

I'm going to have more to say on Carter's view of Shakespeare later in this book. Here, I would emphasise the importance of Callil's observation that Carter was working within the tradition of English radical writing exemplified by Tom Paine. Carter herself was always keen to insist that her writing, contrary to the way it might sometimes appear, was not disengaged from social reality. In her interview with John Haffenden, for example:

> JH: I know that you find it fundamentally important to have an intelligent awareness of society, and yet the highly stylized and decorative apparatus of your novels might appear to be disengaged from the social and historical realities you want to illuminate.
>
> AC: Yes, this is a very real risk, really tricky. Obviously the idea that my stories are all dreams or hallucinations out of Jung-land, or the notion that the world would be altogether a better place if we threw away our rationality and went laughing down the street ... that's all nonsense. I *can* see how it must look to some readers.... (Haffenden 1985: 85)

Or, again, interviewed in 1984 by Mary Harron of *The Guardian*:

> 'I'm a very old-fashioned kind of feminist', she says, and her preoccupations are with social justice: 'abortion law, access to further education, equal rights, the position of black women' ... The current feminist preoccupation with mysticism and Mother goddesses is smartly

slapped down: 'I'm a *socialist*, damn it! How can you expect me to be interested in fairies?' (Harron 1984: 10)

Carter's materialist metaphysic also conditioned her attitude to the philosophical and theoretical issues of her times. She was well read in the cultural, political and literary theories of writers like Barthes, Theodor Adorno and Michel Foucault. Lorna Sage has noted that:

> Her closest affinities earlier on had probably been with Roland Barthes, but in the 1970s it was, I suspect, Michel Foucault who counted most. She lists his early book *Madness and Civilization* (1961) in [*The Sadeian Woman*'s] bibliography, but she was also thinking very much along the same lines as he had in *La Volonté de savoir* (1976), translated as Volume I of *The History of Sexuality* in 1978 ... like her, he's concerned to question the notion that sex is outside history: 'what was involved ... was the very production of sexuality. Sexuality must not be thought of as a kind of natural given which power tries to hold in check, or as an obscure domain which knowledge tries gradually to uncover. It is the name that can be given to an historical construct: not a furtive reality that is difficult to grasp, but a great surface network in which the stimulation of bodies, the intensification of pleasures, the incite-ment to discourse ... are linked to one another, in accordance with a few major strategies of knowledge and power.' Carter's 'Flesh comes to us out of history' (*The Sadeian Woman*, p.11) makes the same move. (Sage 1994b: 14)

Carter's reading of people like Barthes and Foucault can be felt throughout her stories ('my fiction is very often a kind of literary criticism', she observed to John Haffenden; Haffenden 1985: 79). But her materialism and her political engagement led her to be suspicious of some of the avant-garde tendencies of thought which came to the fore in the 1960s and after. She came to be uneasy with the postmodern idea that authors have no unmediated access to a reality outside of language and texts. At the heart of that unease lay the vexed question of the relations between postmodern thought and political engagement. For several years, Carter told Kerryn Goldsworthy in 1985:

> I thought that writing, all fiction, really, was about other fiction. That there was no way out, really, of this solipsism; that books were about other books ...
>
> But then I began to ask myself, if all books are about other books, what are the other books about?... What's the Ur-book, then? And one

is forced to answer, after a while, of course the Ur-book is really Life, or The Real World ...

One of the things that really made me feel that a whole lot of the post-modernists were sort of tap-dancing on the edge of the abyss was reading Christina Stead, which I did very recently, three or four years ago. I read almost all her novels at a gulp. And I thought – my goodness me, there's an awful lot of life left in the old horse yet ...

All the interviews I've read with her in her old age are so equivocal. I mean she really isn't interested in telling everybody – she's lying all the time. She seems to have acute paranoia about most of her past ... She was blacklisted in Hollywood ... And you get absolute idiots asking her things like, 'Were you interested in politics?' (Goldsworthy 1985: 5–6)

There are many ways of reading Carter. This book recognises that major aspects of Carter's metaphysical materialism are her empiricism and her passion for reason. Carter's exploration, throughout her fantastic allegories, of 'Life, or The Real World' is primarily an exploration of the politics of Western heterosexual identity. But the argument of this book is that this exploration is conducted through an engagement with the discourses of reason. Carter's wild fables and the pungency of her style may disguise the extent to which her feminism is grounded in the values of reason. 'Reason' is not, of course, a neutral term and, in tracing Carter's commitment to reason, I shall be examining the way in which her vision significantly modifies the Enlightenment structuring of rationality. As Elaine Jordan has acutely observed, Carter 'is ... great in re-thinking the fables of Enlightened modernity' (Jordan 1994: 196).

This study also sees that, in her rationality, Carter stands at odds with an extreme postmodernism: not postmodernism as defined simply by formal textual features such as pastiche, inter-textuality or reflexiveness (some, at least, of such features arguably appear in modernist and earlier texts as well as in Carter); but postmodernism as defined also in a more philosophical sense. As I shall attempt to show, Carter stands at odds with this latter sense of postmodernism because the relativising impulse of such post-modernism threatens to undermine the grounds of a liberal-rationalist, specifically feminist politics. Susan Rubin Suleiman has described Carter as a 'feminist postmodernist' (Suleiman 1994: 100). My study sees Carter's fiction, principally because of its rationalist feminism, as fundamentally anti-postmodern.

This study discusses Carter's fiction in chronological order, and takes up the issues of reason and postmodernism at relevant points in the sequence of her work. In my reading, Carter's themes are fairly consistent throughout her writing. But consistency of theme is not the same thing as repetition. There are continually new angles and new emphases. These are developed partly out of Carter's immersion in the changing intellectual debates of her times and, concurrently, out of the books she was reading at different stages of her life – from the medieval and later literary texts of her undergraduate days to the theoretical writings of, say, Foucault in the 1970s. Sometimes the new angle marks a significant shift in Carter's way of figuring her themes. In this book I see the most important of such shifts occurring with the publication of her fourth novel, *Heroes and Villains*, in 1969. *Heroes and Villains*, the first of Carter's post-1968, second-wave feminism books, addresses the issue of reason directly for the first time in her work. Carter once commented on the way in which the atmosphere of the late sixties, and specifically 1968, conditioned the maturing of the feminism she had incipiently demonstrated in her first three novels:

> towards the end of that decade there was a brief period of public philo-
> sophical awareness that occurs only very occasionally in human history;
> when, truly, it felt like Year One, that all that was holy was in the
> process of being profaned and we were attempting to grapple with the
> real relations between human beings. So writers like Marcuse and
> Adorno were as much part of my personal process of maturing into
> feminism as experiments with my sexual, and emotional life ... I can
> date to that time and to some of those debates and to that sense of
> heightened awareness of the society around me in the summer of 1968,
> my own questioning of the nature of my reality as a *woman*. How that
> social fiction of my 'femininity' was created, by means outside my con-
> trol, and palmed off on me as the real thing. (*SL* 37–8)

Carter's first three novels, *Shadow Dance*, *The Magic Toyshop* and *Several Perceptions*, lay the ground for a great deal of her later work and I survey these three works in Chapter 1 before going on, in the second chapter, to consider *Heroes and Villains* as the earliest of Carter's mature reconfigurings of her subject matter.

ONE

Shadow Dance,
The Magic Toyshop and
Several Perceptions

Carter's first three novels show her establishing, in embryonic form, many of the themes and orientations that were to recur throughout her writing career. Above all, the novels display her early preoccupation with the destructive effect of patriarchal culture on both women *and* men. The novels invoke – each in its own distinct way – claustrophobia.

Shadow Dance (1966) reads like a clearing operation. A clearing away of the past and its darknesses of attitude and outlook. In 1988 Carter observed that 'towards the end of the sixties it started to feel like living on a demolition site' (Carter 1988: 211). *Shadow Dance*, written and set in the 1960s, reads in many respects like a dramatisation of such feeling. The two principal male characters, Morris and his partner Honeybuzzard, who live in a provincial English city, scratch a living plundering Victoriana and the like from condemned houses and by selling the fragments on as *"Observer* Design-for-Living Gear"' (*SD* 90). Morris, we are told,

> loved junk. He loved to nose questingly among the abandoned detritus of other people's lives for oddments, fragments, bits of this and that ... The best times of his life were the dark nights when, in Honeybuzzard's van, they went secretly to the deserted, condemned old houses which the city council planned shortly to demolish and, by the light of guttering candles, would sort over and pick about in all their dead flotsam. (*SD* 23–4)

The thing about all this 'dead flotsam' is that it is not innocent. Like the metaphoric 1960s demolition site Carter spoke of in 1988, the ruins and junk of *Shadow Dance* are symbolic of old, outdated cultural values. But while the Victorian buildings are shattered, the values they symbolise retain a power sufficient to devastate contemporary lives.

The story opens with Morris accosted by a young woman, Ghislaine, who had been, until recently, a familiar amongst his circle of friends. Ghislaine has just returned from hospital. Formerly stunningly and sexually beautiful, she now wears a revolting scar down the length of her face. This is the result of a slashing apparently given her by Honeybuzzard. Morris, after a night of failed lovemaking with Ghislaine, had said to Honey-buzzard 'Take her and teach her a lesson' (*SD* 34). It seems that, although the assault is blamed on a gang of teenage boys, he did just that. Morris recoils from Ghislaine, who for the rest of the story haunts his imagination, provoking disgust, guilt and fear. Shortly after Ghislaine has reappeared, Honeybuzzard, who has also been away, returns to the provincial scene with a new girl-friend from London, Emily. The plot traces the continuing junk-hunting forages of Morris and Honeybuzzard and gradually builds towards a climax where Honeybuzzard murders Ghislaine, and leaves Emily pregnant with their child.

A touch histrionic – it is, after all, a first novel – the story nevertheless sketches a view of the workings of patriarchy. These workings are perhaps most succinctly captured in the description of a series of pornographic photographs of Ghislaine taken by Honeybuzzard with Morris's co-operation. In the account of these photographs, the objectification of the female in old-world values is symbolised by the 'masculinism' of the junk-objects that Honey-buzzard uses to frame Ghislaine as she displays herself to the masculine eye of the camera:

> Tirelessly, Ghislaine contorted herself, spread herself wide, arrayed herself in a bizarre variety of accessories. Honey would disappear at intervals to the shop and return with his arms full of new toys. Military boots and brocaded hat; rhino whips; clanking spurs; a stag's head. (*SD* 16–17)

The masculinism of the old world is again symbolised by the baronial chair with its martial insignia that Honeybuzzard offers to Emily when she first visits his and Morris's junk shop. Here the

religious dimension of traditional patriarchy is hinted at through
the leather-bound volumes of sermons that spill out as Emily sits
down:

> Honeybuzzard invited her to sit upon an Abbotsford oak chair, all
> wooden curlicues and snarling lions and martial but non-heraldic coats
> of arms, and a heap of calf-bound, late eighteenth-century sermons
> slithered out from under her as she did so. (*SD* 68)

The religious dimension of patriarchy is also emblematised in
one of Honeybuzzard's fantasies as he and Morris hunt for junk in
a condemned house that had once been home to a religious community. In one of the rooms of this house the two men find a large
crucifix that has fallen from a wall. Honeybuzzard imagines bringing Ghislaine to the house and having sex with her as she lies on
the figure of Christ: 'We would take it in turns to lay her on that
chap there ... And we could take pictures and sell them to the
colour supplements' (*SD* 132). This act of apparent profanation
does not, in fact, contradict the religious meaning of the crucifix.
For, in this novel, a part of the religious meaning of the crucifix is
precisely the demeaning of women that Honeybuzzard indulges in.
Even though Honeybuzzard has no active religious faith, his cast
of mind has been formed by a culture oppressive to women which
is shot through with the attitudes of religious patriarchy: 'chaining
her to that symbol of her father over there and raping her – now,
that would be really something' (*SD* 132).

Ghislaine, envisaged in this scene of Honeybuzzard's fantasy as
the female victim sacrificed on the altar of patriarchy, is characterised by Carter as cooperating in her own victimisation. She is one
of the first examples of Carter's fictional studies of the feminine
mind that has been colonised by a masculine view of the feminine.
Even after he (apparently) has mutilated her, Honeybuzzard is still
committed to asserting his dominance over her, and she continues
to accept her subservience. After she has returned from hospital,
Ghislaine writes Honeybuzzard a letter:

> The letter contained three lines of self-abasing scribble, forgiving
> Honeybuzzard enormously and giving an address ...
> 'She's coming back crawling to me!' whispered Honey. 'Oh, my God,
> ain't it a gas? What do you make of that! I could marry her for that,
> almost – but she's going to have to crawl much farther than that for

me, first; she'll have to crawl till her knees are all bloody, poor little girl!' (*SD* 72–3)

Ghislaine does crawl farther. Towards the end of the book she finds Honeybuzzard and abases herself completely: 'I've learned my lesson, I can't live without you, you are my master, do what you like with me' (*SD* 166). The problem is that with this confirmation of his power behind him, Honeybuzzard tracks the power to its logical end. The ultimate confirmation of his absolute authority over Ghislaine comes with his obliteration of her.

Ghislaine, in her complicity with the masculine power that dominates and finally destroys her, has a metaphorical sister in the novel in the form of Morris's wife Edna. Edna, like Ghislaine, displays a female internalisation of the masculine sexist values symbolised by the junk that clutters Honeybuzzard's and Morris's imaginations. The significant difference is that Edna has never needed to be taught a lesson. She has always accepted the authority of men:

> She was a Victorian girl; a girl of the days when men were hard and top-hatted and masculine and ruthless and girls were gentle and meek ... and laid their tender napes beneath a husband's booted foot, even if he brought home cabfuls of half-naked chorus girls ... Or, drunk to a frenzy, raped the kitchen-maid before the morning assembly of servants and children and her black silk-dressed self (gathered for prayers) ...
>
> Husbands were a force of nature or an act of God; like an earthquake or the dreaded consumption, to be borne with, to be meekly acquiesced to, to be impregnated by as frequently as Nature would allow ...
>
> Edna thought marriage was for submission and procreation. When she said, 'love, honour and obey' in the watered-milk light of the church where they had been married, her face glowed with such unearthly splendour that the brass pots on the altar holding a few late chrysanthemums were put to shame. (*SD* 45)

I shall have more to say on Carter's treatment of the question of female complicity in patriarchy when I discuss her later treatments of the same subject. Here, I want briefly to consider Honeybuzzard as the prototype of numerous male figures in Carter's writing. Honeybuzzard is distinguished by the instability of his identity. That is to say, he endlessly puts on masks of identity. He is entirely self-conscious about his play-acting:

'I like,' he said obscurely, 'I like – you know – to slip in and out of me.
I would like to be somebody different each morning. Me and not-me.
I would like to have a cupboard bulging with all different bodies and
faces and choose a fresh one every morning ... There was a man, last
night; we were in a club and there was this man, singing blues, and he
had a red rose stuck in his shirt. It was red as a cap of liberty ... I
would like to wear him, tomorrow morning.' (*SD* 78)

The irony in this passage rests with the allusion to the red cap of
liberty. Honeybuzzard is fashionably free in his capacity to adopt
different personae. But his freedom is a freedom which mocks the
spirit of the blues. The story of his treatment of Ghislaine itself
calls in question the nature of his freedom. The story implies that
it is a false, self-serving and dangerous freedom; a freedom that
spells captivity for others and empties all meaning out of the word
truth. 'Believe what you want to believe', he advises Morris at one
point in the novel. 'What you want to believe is the truth' (*SD*
125). Carter stands against such an idea in a world where
Ghislaine's face has literally been cut open. Honeybuzzard's freedom to be anybody he likes and to make the world in his own
image are seen in the novel as symptoms of an egocentricity which
takes no account of others. It is an egocentricity which refuses
even reality to others. When Morris tells him that he feels sorry
about the bad things that have happened to some of their circle of
friends, Honeybuzzard replies: '"They are all shadows. How can
you be sorry for shadows?" Honey's voice was harsh' (*SD* 86).
Honeybuzzard's egomania dehumanises people, rendering them
objects to be manipulated at his will: '"I should like", said Honey
dreamily, "to have a floor set out in chequers and to play chess
with men and women. I would stand on a chair and call out my
moves from a megaphone and they would click their heels and
march forward"' (*SD* 117).

Carter does not argue – in *Shadow Dance* or in any of her later
books – for some essential human nature which may stand against
the exploitations of someone like Honeybuzzard. Throughout her
work she argues the contrary: that human beings are the products
of historical and cultural circumstance and that they *may*, therefore, find themselves in positions where they can reinvent themselves. But changing identity is only acceptable in her writing when
it is done with due recognition of the rights of others, when it is

done as part of an economy not of domination and subservience but rather of relationship, exchange and reciprocity. Honeybuzzard is seen as dangerous because the shape-shifting of his own identity is conceived only at the expense of others. His patriarchy is an act which sees all others as objects for him to manipulate and overwhelm. Carter's portrayal of Honeybuzzard signals what turned out to be a recurrent fictional interest in figures modelled on the Marquis de Sade. She was also to explore this interest theoretically in her 1979 study, *The Sadeian Woman*.

It is Emily and Morris who discover the body of the murdered Ghislaine. At the outset of their acquaintance, Morris had regarded Emily as a woman with nothing in her head. Later, she had surprised him as she began to articulate her reservations about Honeybuzzard in terms of the story of Bluebeard and his murdered wives. In this first of Carter's novels lies a premonition of her reworking of the Bluebeard story in the 1979 tale 'The Bloody Chamber'. Emily tells Morris how, in one of Honeybuzzard's pockets, she had found a key to a locked room in the junk shop:

'I found this key in one of his trouser pockets, see, and I thought, you know, of Bluebeard.'
    'Bluebeard?'
    'Bluebeard. And the locked room. I don't know him very well, you know.' (*SD* 103)

Emily's unease about Honeybuzzard is subsequently confirmed when Ghislaine visits him and abases herself in front of him. Emily is present at that meeting, and she later tells Morris that she has realised that it was Honeybuzzard who slashed Ghislaine. Morris learns that it is this realisation which, in part, has provoked Emily to destroy the paraphernalia in Honeybuzzard's room in the junk shop. The destruction signifies her rejection of the past and its patriarchal perversities (Honeybuzzard kept a foetus pickled in a jar):

The bedroom was a scene of total devastation. The corset advertisements were ripped and torn from the walls and so were all the photographs and drawings ... Broken in half, the bust of Queen Victoria rolled in the grate ...
    'What happened to the foetus?' [Morris] asked. It was gone from the windowsill.

'I flushed it down the lavatory,' she said harshly ...
He followed her back down the stairs ... In the backyard, she stuffed
two frilled shirts and a string vest into the dustbin and stirred the fire.
'What are you doing, Emily?' he asked.
'Burning him, the bastard. Burning him all up.' (*SD* 164)

And so Honeybuzzard and all he represents are fired from Emily's
mind. She tells Morris that she is pregnant by Honeybuzzard, a
fact which causes Morris to query Emily's intent to separate herself from Honeybuzzard. The query is occasion for Emily to display her strength and independence:

'He could whistle for me for ever but I wouldn't come.'
'But you say you're pregnant – '
'That's my affair, isn't it?' ... 'It's inside *me*, not inside him, isn't
it?' ...
'Do you want an abortion?' He spoke more barely and cruelly than
he intended. She stiffened as if he had slapped her.
'No, I do not! I called my piper, so I'll pay for my tune, thank you
very much.' ...
She had decided to love her baby. That was all. (*SD* 168, 180)

Emily's recognition of Honeybuzzard's character and her self-
sufficient decision to have her baby mark her as a type that Carter
was to treat again and again in her fiction. She represents the new
order that displaces the old reality. Morris, at one level, would like
to go with her. He has been haunted by Ghislaine ever since she
returned. The form she takes in this haunting of his mind is itself
a symptom of the way in which his mind cannot free itself from
archaic images of women. The thought of Ghislaine modulates in
his imagination into an image of her as succubus, as a witch-like
siren drawing him to destruction:

[W]hen he came back to the café out of his dream, he found himself
trapped inescapably in the town, in a private circle of hell, locked to
the memory of Ghislaine like Paolo to Francesca in Dante. There was
the memory of her, waiting for him, and he left the café and, invisible
old woman of the sea, all ugly and piteous, she went with him, clutching
him with her white legs and her long, slender arms. Ghislaine ...
... all the spring, she went about with him, weighing him down,
although he never saw her in the real world. In the night, she laid her
wet, invisible mouth on his and he woke up, choking. (*SD* 36–7)

Morris would like to leave this realm of nightmarish stereotyping
of the female. He is attracted by Emily's staunch exorcism of

Honeybuzzard. As they leave the junk shop after Emily has burned Honeybuzzard's possessions:

> Emily walked in a disciplined ... stride and her arms swung to the rhythm of her walk. Her sleek hair bounced on her nape and her large breasts moved steadily up and down. She walked as if she had a destination ahead of her of which she was quite sure ... Morris felt less shadow-like the more they went on together. (*SD* 174)

But Morris cannot escape the dark orientations and values of a past which impairs his own life, which mutilates and destroys Ghislaine, and which will ultimately catch up with and ruin Honeybuzzard himself. The very last line of the novel informs us that 'Morris vanished into the shadows' (*SD* 182). He turns back to the unreconstructed and destructive world of Honeybuzzard, whom he feels he 'cannot betray' (*SD* 181). Neither of the principal male characters in this novel can make themselves anew. Yet, just prior to Morris's vanishing, we see Emily kneeling 'in a pool of vomit' (*SD* 182). This is, as it were, against all appearances, joyful vomit. For it is the vomit of a pregnancy that emblematises, as pregnancies always will in Carter's works, new hope.

Marc O'Day has characterised *Shadow Dance*, along with *Several Perceptions* and Carter's fifth novel *Love*, as generically different in kind from most of Carter's other work, to which he attaches the label 'magical realism', (Sage 1994b: 24). He speaks of *Shadow Dance*, *Several Perceptions* and *Love* as 'The Bristol Trilogy' (Sage 1994b: 25) and says that the novels 'invite readings in terms of quite traditional literary realism' (Sage 1994b: 24):

> The Trilogy novels offer realist representations of the 1960s 'provincial bohemia' which Carter herself inhabited. They deploy a similar motley array of characters, plot structures which can be read as variants of one another, comparable forms of narration, and a wide variety of themes and motifs concerning the sixties counterculture in which Carter moved ...
>
> How do these books produce their reality effects? ... the events of the Bristol Trilogy 'happen' ... where art and life mingle so that life itself is often a form of art – in a variety of everyday, local private and public spaces. These include bedsits, flats and houses (derelict as well as occupied), cafés and coffee bars, pubs and shops, auction rooms, museums, libraries, hospitals, the Zoo and the Labour Exchange, and outdoor locations like the streets, the park and the Down. (Sage 1994b: 25)

Important as these points are, I don't accept the clear generic distinction Marc O'Day draws between these three novels and the rest of Carter's work. Certainly the three novels are packed with everyday detail, and the men and women in them do not grow wings. But the everyday detail of the junk shop, say, and the stories or fables of all the novels as well as the principal characters in them, do not relate to the real world in a primarily reflectionist or mimetic way. They relate in an essentially figurative way. These three novels, for all their surface realism, function as allegories of the nature of sexual identity in a manner comparable to Carter's other fiction.

The fundamental connection between the modes of *Shadow Dance* and of *The Magic Toyshop* – the first example of Carter's supposed 'magic realist' mode – may be illustrated by pointing out the way in which a detail of Honeybuzzard's life connects centrally with the presentation of a major character in *The Magic Toyshop*. At one stage in *Shadow Dance* Honeybuzzard makes a puppet – a Jumping Jack – that has the face of Morris. The scene parallels that where Honeybuzzard imagines playing chess with women and men, figuring the way in which Honeybuzzard plays with people as toys:

> Morris turned on the light. Honey held up the object he had been making and pulled a string attached to it. Cardboard legs and green cardboard arms shot out, collapsed, shot out. He had been making a Jumping Jack. The Jumping Jack jumped. The Jumping Jack had a large black head and a small black beard. Morris swallowed; his mouth was full of bitter saliva. The Jumping Jack was Morris. Honey pulled the string once more and Morris's cardboard self convulsed in its St Vitus' dance.
>   'Isn't it pretty? Isn't it funny?' said exuberant Honey. 'I saw them in London, in a shop full of toys, lovely toys, old toys. I thought I might be a toy maker and make Jumping Jacks and Jacks-in-Boxes and paper dolls and tigers with big teeth that bite when you press down a lever and singing birds!' (*SD* 80)

The idea of a man who reduces others to the level of playthings directs the presentation of Uncle Philip in *The Magic Toyshop*.

The Magic Toyshop (1967) tells of three children – Melanie, Jonathan and Victoria – whose liberal, educated middle-class parents are killed in an air crash while in the United States. The orphaned children have to move from their safe home in the country to the South London house of their mother's estranged brother, Uncle Philip. Philip Flower is a toymaker who sells his work in a shop on the premises. He is married to an Irish woman, Margaret, and these two live together with Margaret's brothers, Finn and Francie Jowle. The material conditions of life change for the children, from bourgeois comfort to something much less prosperous. But it is the change in spirit that Carter is interested in. Of the three children, Melanie is the focus of attention. Victoria is barely more than a baby, and Jonathan is a little boy. Melanie is a pubescent girl, having to change homes and guardianship at the most critical transitional age in life. Her encounter at this age with the psychic world of Uncle Philip and his toyshop is a major preoccupation of the novel. But it is only one of the two main preoccupations. The second is Carter's exploration of a young man's – Finn's – confrontation with the psychic world of Uncle Philip. *The Magic Toyshop* introduces Carter's persistent interest in the way in which men as well as women may be negatively affected by patriarchy and seek to resist it.

Uncle Philip is almost a caricature of the patriarch. Having met him, Melanie decides that, like a god of the sky, like Jove, 'he was hewn or cut out of thunder itself' (*MT* 92). Shortly before she met him, Finn had warned her of his tastes:

'He can't abide a woman in trousers. He won't have a woman in the shop if she's got trousers on her and he sees her. He shouts her out into the street for a harlot.'...
   'Is there anything else like that I ought to know about him?'
   'No make-up, mind. And only speak when you're spoken to. He likes, you know, silent women.' (*MT* 62–3)

We hear that, at the head of his dining table, Uncle Philip

sat in shirt-sleeved, patriarchal majesty and his spreading, black waist-coat ... was strung with an impressive gold watch-chain, of the style favoured by Victorian pit-owners ... His authority was stifling. Aunt Margaret, frail as a pressed flower, seemed too cowed by his presence even to look at him. She had only the tiniest portion of porridge ... but she took the longest to eat it ... She had not finished it when Uncle Philip crashed down his own spoon on an empty bowl.
   'Finn change plates! Pronto!' (*MT* 73)

But Uncle Philip doesn't just rule the dining-table. As the personification of patriarchy he rules the world. The imperiousness of his patriarchy is emblematised in the power relations between himself, as Englishman, and the Jowles, who are Irish Catholics. He dominates the Jowles as the English, historically, dominated Ireland. The connections between patriarchy and imperialism and the dominance they exert are put figuratively in a scene where the entire household has to go down to the basement of the house to watch a performance of Uncle Philip's puppets. The figurative message is that patriarchal power in the world turns people into puppets, deprives them of autonomous life:

> Melanie had not been down to the work-room since her very first morning; she tried not to look at the partially assembled puppets, hanged and dismembered, on the walls ... They took their seats with some ceremony, arranging their good clothes around them ... On the wall was a poster in crude colours announcing: 'GRAND PERFORMANCE – FLOWER'S PUPPET MICROCOSM,' with a great figure recognisably Uncle Philip by virtue of the moustache and wing collar, holding the ball of the world in his hand. (*MT* 126)

Uncle Philip does his utmost to treat Margaret as if she were an object like his puppets. He made her a wedding present of a necklace that constrains the natural movement of the human body, and he derives pleasure from observing this constraint when, on Sundays, she wears the necklace, or collar, a token of being owned:

> [W]hen she was dressed and ready, she took her necklace out of some box or cupboard and clasped it round her throat, to complete her outfit.
> The necklace was a collar of dull silver, two hinged silver pieces knobbed with moonstones which snapped into place around her lean neck and rose up almost to her chin so that she could hardly move her head. It was heavy, crippling and precious ... Uncle Philip broke the armour off a pink battalion of shrimps and ate them steadily ... while gazing at her with expressionless satisfaction, apparently deriving a certain pleasure from her discomfort, or even finding that the sight of it improved his appetite. (*MT* 112–13)

Philip's objectification of Margaret is highlighted when, in the puppet-performance, we are told of a 'historical sequence' (*MT* 129) which has a puppet of Mary Queen of Scots enjoying a 'secret rendezvous' (*MT* 129) with Bothwell:

> The Queen turned slowly and sat down. She wore a collar like Aunt Margaret's but it could not chafe her neck because she was made of wood. Aunt Margaret surreptitiously ran her finger round her own silver choker as if the sight of the Queen's collar had reminded her how much her own one hurt. (*MT* 129)

Reduced in Philip's eyes to being little more than a manikin, Margaret symbolically lost her voice the day she was married. When, at the end of the story, Philip and his authority are finally thrown over, Margaret's voice returns: 'Struck dumb on her wedding day, she found her old voice again the day she was freed' (*MT* 197).

Melanie the adolescent does not lose her voice. But she goes through a gruelling rite of passage into the state of being a woman. Whatever way she might once have grown up is simply cancelled after she has arrived at Uncle Philip's. In the uncompromisingly patriarchal world of his house, Melanie's adolescence is at first directed, as Sue Roe has put it, by a 'mythology of awakening in which women blossom into shuddering subordination' (Roe 1994: 69). In Uncle Philip's house Melanie, like Margaret, is reduced to an automaton. On one occasion, as Margaret and Finn are embracing in sibling solidarity, Melanie

> separated herself from their intimacy by putting the forks precisely away in a drawer, where other forks were. Then she dried and put away knives, and spoons, also. She was a wind-up putting-away doll, clicking through its programmed movements. Uncle Philip might have made her over, already. She was without volition of her own. (*MT* 75–6)

Somewhat later in the book we hear that Uncle Philip resents Melanie 'because she was not a puppet' (*MT* 144). His attempt to subordinate her into being one reaches its zenith in a scene towards the end of the novel when he has her take part, in one of his puppet-shows, in a dramatisation of a scene from classical mythology. The scene is that where the sky-god Jove (or Zeus) – the father of gods and men, the supreme ruler, the originator of law and order – rapes the mortal woman Leda, in the form of a swan. Uncle Philip has made a model of a swan and he has the thing mount Melanie as Leda. To begin with, Melanie thinks the model swan is silly: 'It was nothing like the wild, phallic bird of her imaginings. It was dumpy and homely and eccentric. She nearly laughed' (*MT* 165). But, as Melanie discovers, the swan's dumpiness increases its grotesque menace. As it threateningly nears her she copes by dissociating herself from herself:

> 'Well, I must lie down,' she thought ... Like fate or the clock, on came the swan, its feet going splat, splat, splat. She thought ... if she did not act her part well, a trapdoor in the swan's side might open and an armed host of pigmy Uncle Philips, all clockwork, might rush out and savage her. This possibility seemed real and awful. All her laughter was snuffed out ... she felt herself not herself, wrenched from her own personality, watching this whole fantasy from another place. (*MT* 166)

Melanie's attempt to survive her objectification and humiliation by standing outside herself does not carry her through the entire scene which, at its climax, is darkly disturbing:

> 'Almighty Jove in the form of a swan wreaks his will.' Uncle Philip's voice, deep and solemn as the notes of an organ, moved dark and sonorous against the moaning of the fiddle. The swan made a lumpish jump forward and settled on her loins. She thrust with all her force to get rid of it but the wings came down all around her like a tent and its head fell forward and nestled in her neck. The gilded beak dug deeply into the soft flesh. She screamed, hardly realising she was screaming. She was covered completely by the swan but for her kicking feet and her screaming face. The obscene swan had mounted her. She screamed again. There were feathers in her mouth. (*MT* 166–7)

This obscene episode confirms Melanie in her hatred of Uncle Philip. It is a hatred she had conceived much earlier when, putting away cutlery in one of the drawers, she hallucinated something in the drawer:

> a freshly severed hand, all bloody at the roots.
> It was a soft, plump little hand with pretty tapering fingers the nails of which were tinted with a faint, pearly lacquer ...
> 'I am going out of my mind,' she said aloud. 'Bluebeard was here.'
> (*MT* 118)

Paulina Palmer has observed that this fantasy of the severed hand 'advertises to the reader the elements of violence at the heart of the patriarchal family unit' (Palmer 1987: 184). Certainly it initiates Melanie's decision to side with Margaret and her brothers against Uncle Philip's tyranny:

Uncle Philip never talked to his wife except to bark brusque commands. He gave her a necklace that choked her. He beat her younger brother. He chilled the air through which he moved. His towering, blank-eyed presence at the head of the table drew the savour from the good food she cooked. He suppressed the idea of laughter. Melanie chose her side the night she thought she saw the hand; she began to hate Uncle Philip. (*MT* 124)

Yet, as this passage emphasises, it is not only Margaret and Melanie who suffer under Uncle Philip's authority. It is also Finn.

Finn is endlessly physically abused by Uncle Philip: 'Sometimes he fell in a landslide on Finn ... Often, Finn emerged from the workroom with a bruise on his cheek-bone or a swollen eye, the result of a disagreement over some detail of the work in hand' (*MT* 92). When Finn makes a mistake with the puppets in one of the puppet-shows, Uncle Philip causes him to fall from the puppeteer's gallery down to the stage. The action takes the natural life out of Finn's body in a manner that parallels the constraining collar which Margaret wears on Sundays:

still he never moved. His eyes were open and staring ... All his lovely movement was shattered. Melanie tried to grasp how dreadful it would be if Finn were dead but she could not think coherently because of the terrible sound of Aunt Margaret's silence. Uncle Philip, huge and sombre, came onto the stage, straightening his bow tie, which was askew. He brusquely kicked Finn's stomach but Finn did not move. (*MT* 132)

Everyone seems to be aware of Uncle Philip's murderous thoughts towards Finn, including Uncle Philip himself. At the denouement of the novel, which finds Uncle Philip raging at Francie for reasons we shall discover, Finn declares: 'I thought it would be me he would kill' (*MT* 196). He adds: 'And so did he' (*MT* 196). 'He'll murder you', Melanie has told Finn a little earlier (*MT* 172). In some respects this picture of a patriarch harbouring vengeful, murderous feelings towards a younger man prefigures a point made by Carter in a Channel Four television programme, *The Holy Family Album*, which she wrote and narrated, that was broadcast on 3 December 1991 (the programme was produced by John Ellis and directed by Jo Ann Kaplan). In *The Holy Family Album* Carter deconstructs visual images of the life of Christ. When it comes to representations of Christ's torture and agony, Carter says of God the Father: 'He was a cruel God. He was a cruel father. Remember he planned all this.' She goes further when she says:

> Perhaps we read Oedipal conflict the wrong way. Perhaps men don't want to kill their fathers. Surely not, or how could Christianity have lasted all this time. But deep down they want to kill their sons. Just like God did. To get rid of the rival.

Although Uncle Philip is not literally Finn's father, his treatment of his wife's youngest brother nevertheless bears the mark of such a rereading of the competition between a father figure and a young male.

Finn the young man is objectified in Philip's gaze in a manner comparable to the women of the household. It is a dehumanisation which he resists. He resists playing a part in Uncle Philip's game when he resists Philip's suggestion that he have sex with Melanie. Finn uses the word 'fuck', which disconcerts Melanie in her romantic fantasy about sex. Even so, Finn still resists Uncle Philip's imperative:

> 'You see,' he said, 'he wanted me to fuck you.'
> She had only read the word before, in cold and aseptic print ... She had never connected the word with herself; her phantom bridegroom would never have fucked her. They would have made love. But Finn, she acknowledged with a sinking of her spirit, would have ...
> 'It was his fault,' he said ... 'He's pulled our strings as if we were his puppets, and there I was, all ready to touch you up just as he wanted.' ...
> 'Well,' said Finn ... 'I'm not having any, see? I'm not going to do what he wants even if I do fancy you. So there.' (*MT* 151–2)

The vehemence of Finn's reaction against Philip's domination is apparent in one of Finn's paintings:

> Then she saw the horrible picture. It was a hell of leaping flames ... Uncle Philip was laid out on a charcoal grill like a barbecued pork chop ... His flesh was beginning to crack and blister as his fat bubbled inside it ... His mouth was a black, screaming hole from which issued a banner with the words: 'Forgive me!' (*MT* 154)

Covert resistance turns into direct rebellion when Finn destroys Uncle Philip's puppet swan. He buries the pieces of the swan in a derelict park that had been established in 1852 to house and celebrate the achievements of Victorian capitalism. A fallen statue of Queen Victoria herself, snapped in two, lies in the park. The park and the fallen statue symbolise the old order of values that still sustains Uncle Philip's patriarchy. Appropriately enough, Finn, having rebelled against that power and broken its emblematic swan, buries the remains of the puppet near the fallen Queen Victoria. But his sense of transgression is strong enough for him momentarily to imagine that Victoria and all she stood for have reasserted themselves:

> 'I buried the swan near the queen,' he said conversationally in this dimensionless voice he now had. 'Do you think that was kind of me? I suppose I thought they'd be company for one another.'
> 'Well,' she said, 'it is as good a place as any.'
> 'I'm not really sure why I went to the pleasure garden when I could have put the bits of swan in the dustbin ... Do you know, though, I was almost delirious in the pleasure garden? ... the queen was upright on her pedestal. That gave me a turn, I must say. I saw her from a distance but she must have seen me coming and gone and lay down again quickly. She was lying down, all right, when I got up to her. The bitch.' (*MT* 172–3)

With his casting off of Victorian values, Finn can come into his own, become himself rather than dangle at the whim of Uncle Philip. When Uncle Philip is away from home, Finn sits in his chair at the head of the table. It is not a gesture of usurpation and perpetuation of Philip's authority but rather a parodic inversion of that authority:

> Uncle Philip's ominous chair stood empty, the shell of a threat, the Siege Perilous.
> 'Sod it,' said Finn. 'I'm going to sit in his chair.'
> Aunt Margaret's hand flew to her aghast mouth.
> 'Don't fret, Maggie. It can't engulf me.'
> He sat at the head of the table like the Lord of Misrule, feeding the dog marmalade sandwiches, which it appeared to relish. (*MT* 183)

Uncle Philip is described at one point in *The Magic Toyshop* as being 'heavy as Saturn' (*MT* 168). Saturn was the Roman deity who was counterpart to the Greek titan Cronos, the governor of time, the devouring father who eats his children. When Finn has destroyed Uncle Philip's swan and parodied his headship of the family, he also figuratively revokes devouring, murdering patriarchal time:

> Finn thoughtfully took Uncle Philip's very own mug from its hook on
> the dresser ...
> 'Jesus, Mary and Joseph,' he said, 'I come of age today.'
> He raised his arm, took aim and flung the mug at the cuckoo clock
> ... The stuffed cuckoo belted out thirty-one calls and then jerked back
> into the clock. The door slammed behind it with a dithering shudder.
> The ticking stopped.
> 'There goes the time,' said Finn ...
> The day stretched before them with nothing to do. It was like the
> first day of the holidays. (*MT* 185)

The time that has been revoked is the patriarchal time that had
governed the puppet swan's threatening, rape-intending approach
to Melanie: 'Like fate or the clock, on came the swan, its feet
going splat, splat, splat' (*MT* 166).

If Finn so rebels against Uncle Philip and all his works, there
has been all along another form of subversion. It turns out that
Margaret and Francie have been conducting an incestuous relationship right under Uncle Philip's nose. Little could be more directly
calculated to violate the patriarchal family unit maintained by him.
When he returns and accidentally discovers the affair, he goes
mad. He sets fire to the house, intending to burn his wife and her
brother, as well as Finn and Melanie, to death. We are given to
understand that Francie and Margaret escape, and we know that
Finn and Melanie, who have become lovers, get free. Paulina
Palmer objects to the presentation of Melanie and Finn running
away as lovers. She sees their relationship in the closing pages of
the novel as itself a symptom of the continuing power of patriarchy: 'As is typical of woman in a patriarchal society, [Melanie] is
pressured to seek refuge from one man in the arms of another'
(Palmer 1987: 187). But it really isn't necessary to read the conclusion like this. As Palmer herself cogently points out, Melanie
has not been presented as subservient to Finn. There is, for
example, the matter of the peephole into Melanie's bedroom which
Finn uses to spy on her. Once Melanie discovers this peephole,
however, she turns the tables:

> [Carter's] description of the peephole which Finn constructs in the
> wall of his room in order to spy on Melanie while she is undressing,
> introduces the theme of voyeurism. It draws attention to the power
> exerted by the male gaze. The gaze is a practical means for men to
> impose control on women, as well as a symbol of sexual domination.

However, the fact that Melanie responds with indignation to the intrusion on her privacy and retaliates by using the peephole to spy on Finn
back (p. 109), complicates the meaning of the image. On peering in it,
she catches sight of him walking on his hands. This results in a
momentary instance of role-reversal. She becomes the observer and he
the observed. She represents the norm while he, in his odd position,
becomes the freak and 'spectacle'. These are roles which, in a patriarchal society, are generally reserved for women. Thus, in her treatment of both motifs Carter indirectly reveals that, despite appearances
to the contrary, the roles adopted by men and women are, in fact,
flexible. They are open to change. (Palmer 1987: 185)

Exactly. And changing the role prescribed for himself as a man is
precisely what Finn does in the story. It seems to me that it is
possible to pay insufficient attention to the way in which Finn is
presented as actively rejecting patriarchy and reinventing himself.

It is possible to see Melanie and Finn, when they escape from
the burning house, as examples of a different kind of human being
– a kind where relationship is defined not in terms of oppression
and subservience but in terms of equality. They have passed
through an initiation rite into adulthood of a different kind to
normal. They can mature in a new world because they have *both*
resisted and thrown off the sexist oppressiveness of the old. In a
1992 interview Carter observed that 'The shop in *The Magic
Toyshop* gets burnt down, the old dark house, and adult life begins'
(Sage 1992: 190). Throughout *The Magic Toyshop* there have been
allusions to the biblical fable of the Garden of Eden, and the fall
of humankind and its expulsion from Eden. When, at the very
end of the novel, Melanie and Finn stand ready to leave the garden – the metaphoric garden – of a neighbour's house, they are
not about to leave as the sinful children of a wrathful, patriarchal
God. The mythology of sin has been purged. The fire in Uncle
Philip's old house has consumed him, leaving the young adults
free on the threshold of a world that will not be constrained by
an archaic mythology. The toyshop was not divinely ordained.
Neither was it magic. It was – like Uncle Philip's swan, which
Melanie at one point described as 'a ludicrous thing' (*MT* 174) –
a ludicrous *representation* of the way things are, not the essence of
the way things are. In adulthood, Melanie as a woman is not to be
treated as a child. The fire, not unlike Emily's burning of Honeybuzzard's possessions in *Shadow Dance*, has purged both Uncle

Philip and the childhood – represented by Melanie's toy bear –
that he ruled over:

> A floor caved in inside the house with a gush of fire. All burning,
> everything burning, toys and puppets and masks and chairs and tables
> and carpets ... Edward Bear burning, with her pyjamas in his stomach.
> 'All my paintings,' said Finn faintly. 'Such as they were.'
> 'Even Edward Bear,' she said.
> 'What?'
> 'My bear. He's gonę. Everything is gone.'
> 'Nothing is left but us.'
> At night, in the garden, they faced each other in a wild surmise.
> (*MT* 200)

That wild surmise – that wild imagining of a new future – alludes
to Keats's picture, in 'On First Looking into Chapman's Homer'
(1816), of the sixteenth-century Spaniards' first sight of the Pacific
Ocean. Carter's imagination seems to have been caught by Keats'
poetic evocation of the glimpsing of a new world, a new order of
being:

> Then felt I like some watcher of the skies
>   When a new planet swims into his ken;
> Or like stout Cortez when with eagle eyes
>   He stared at the Pacific, and all his men
> Looked at each other with a wild surmise –
>   Silent, upon a peak in Darien.
>   (11.9–14; Allott 1970: 62)

Several Perceptions (1968) continues Carter's early experimentation
with themes that were to become characteristic of her work as it
envisages a world that has broken with paternalistic order. The
novel's 'hero' is a young man, Joseph, who inhabits 'a desultory,
shiftless world in which hippies and vagrants, tramps and a whore
whose family were "fairground people" ... form a drifting counterculture' (Sage 1994a: 16–17). It is the counterculture of the 1960s.

This sub- or counterculture is characterised, in the first place
and not surprisingly, by appearances. One of Joseph's acquaint-
ances, for example, the bisexual Kay, is described as wearing

> Levi jeans and jacket weathered to the beautiful blue of very old and
> often handled five pound notes. On his head he wore a khaki forage

cap and golden ear-rings glinted in his ears. The rest of his outfit comprised: a flannel shirt ... dyed a cheerful orange in the communal spaghetti saucepan ...

A veteran of numerous forlorn hopes such as art school ... Kay was now content to live at ease among theatrical relics, sell a little pot from time to time and keep open house for friends who came and went like ships that pass in the night. (*SP* 10–11)

Another of Joseph's friends, Viv, the son of a 45-year-old prostitute, Mrs Boulder, is cast in terms of a different type of 1960s alternative appearance: 'He was the glass of fashion and the mould of form in a pin-striped suit of navy blue, a Mafia-style shirt of rough black silk and a fatly knotted lilac satin tie' (*SP* 23). The reviewer for the *Times Literary Supplement* of 1 August 1968 noted that Viv is 'cheerfully dapper on unemployment benefit' (p. 817). In the novel he is described as 'well-adjusted and sweet tempered' (*SP* 23).

But if these friends of Joseph are defined by a kind of driftless contentment, then Joseph occupies the same world without the same peace of mind. Joseph's room, in the attic of a crumbling period terrace-house, is the epitome of bohemian squalor overlaid with a 1960s topicality:

> There was a narrow mattress on the floor; his tumbled sheets were grey with dirt and smelled of flesh ...
>
> There were some pictures tacked to the wall. Lee Harvey Oswald, handcuffed between policemen, about to be shot ... A colour photograph, taken from *Paris Match*, of a square of elegant houses and, within these pleasant boundaries, a living sunset, a Buddhist monk whose saffron robes turned red as he burned alive. (*SP* 14–15)

For Joseph, these circumstances of his life are associated not with freedom from the conventions of ordinary society but with being desperately cut off from social norms of any kind. A little later in the book he is described as being 'shipwrecked in time' (*SP* 40). His room, we are told, 'had the feel and smell of a waiting-room at a railway station where few if any trains stop. Joseph was entirely surrounded by the banal apparatus of despair' (*SP* 16). Joseph's despairing sense of shipwreck leads him, at the close of the novel's first chapter, to a suicide attempt that just manages to fail. So groundless and, in Joseph's case at least, essentially depressing do the lives of these young people seem that one

commentator has said that *Several Perceptions* 'satirise[s] aimless-
ness in British youth' of the 1960s (McDowell 1991: 180). But the
novel is not satirising these people. It is, in the end, celebrating
them.

Like his room itself, Joseph's sense of shipwreck is characterised in historically very specific terms. His alienation is from a
governing order that sanctions the atrocities of the Vietnam War:

> On the way home, Joseph ... saw a photograph which distressed him
> very much. It showed an American soldier holding a child in his arms
> although the child itself appeared to have no arms left. The face ... of
> the soldier was broad, freckled and not very bright. When he was the
> age of the child he held, he would have been the image of the arche-
> typal American schoolboy ... who grins from hoardings: 'Gee, mom,
> what a swell dessert.'... Now, at less than Joseph's age, betrayed into
> murder, he accused the camera with a horrid surprise. (*SP* 82–3)

Betrayed into murder. The betrayers of this young American, as
indeed of Joseph, are the men and the fathers who control society's
power structure. Joseph's sense of alienation, his sense of shipwreck, is cast not just in historical but in gendered terms. The
young people in this novel are, in the first place, seen as distanced
from or, indeed, entirely lacking their parents. Joseph is beyond the
command of his lower-middle-class mother and father and their
nightmare of a home with its 'plaster ducks' on the wall (*SP* 105):
'His bewildered father surveyed a son who was hardly there at all
and said from time to time: "But we've always done the best for
you, I can't understand it"' (*SP* 7). But he shouldn't criticise what
he can't understand, for the times are changing and Carter characterises the new order of the counterculture as one that is free, not
simply of parental but specifically of paternal authority. Kay's father,
for example, is dead, killed at the end of the Second World War.
On the mantelpiece in Kay's home there 'was a photograph of the
late Mr Kyte, the fighter pilot' (*SP* 129). Kay resents his father's
war history and, it appears, maintains his contentment by carefully
containing the memory of his father and all he stood for:

> 'Do you see him?' asked Kay, indicating the photograph of his father,
> the war hero. 'Mr Kyte the fighter pilot. He also took part in the fire
> raids over Dresden. I read all the books about them, for years I was
> obsessed with it and thought I lit those flames myself; he was my father
> and I keep him, now, where I can keep an eye on him.' (*SP* 142)

A little later, Kay, momentarily losing his cool, expresses still greater disgust at the image of his father:

> 'My father,' said Kay, 'who aren't in heaven. I hate your lousy face and always have.'
> He seized the photograph from the mantlepiece and pitched it bodily into the fire; the glass broke in two. (*SP* 145)

The connection that is made in these passages between the figure of the father and war is something that has various parallels throughout the novel. Another of Joseph's familiars, for instance, Anne Blossom, is an orphan. Joseph, in his antagonism towards the Vietnam War, at one point asks her what she thinks of that war:

> 'I've got sorrows of my own.'
> 'But which side are you on?'
> 'Don't bother me with wars in foreign places,' she said petulantly. 'I lost a father in the last one. Or,' she added in a voice more hesitant than Joseph had ever heard from her, 'I may have lost a father, I mean, I, may have, I mean, it's possible and seems likely.' (*SP* 86)

War is seen in *Several Perceptions* as the expression of a destructive masculinism which deprives many young people of their fathers and which, in the case of Vietnam, as we have seen, betrays other young people into acts they can only be aghast at. Joseph himself recoils not just from the war pursued by the US president, Lyndon Johnson, but from the ravaging masculinism in his own psyche:

> This was one of his dreams. It was spring and he was walking in a formal garden. Tulips and children's heads were arranged like apples on a shelf in a store, in neat rows. The tulips swayed and the children smiled with red mouths. Innocent sunlight shone on everything. Along came a man in heavy boots and trampled down the flowerbed, both tulips and children; juicy stalks and fragile bones went snap. Blood and sap spurted on all sides. Joseph flung himself on the man and tried to choke him or gouge out his eyes but his hands made no impression for his body was, in the dream, insubstantial as smoke. When the last child's head was irrevocably smashed, the murderer turned his face to Joseph and Joseph realized he was looking at his own face. (*SP* 3)

Between revulsion at the Vietnam War and at the violence within himself, Joseph feels trapped. He identifies strongly with the extreme frustration of a badger caged in the local zoo (he manages eventually to break into the zoo and set the animal free). Joseph's sense of outraged entrapment had led him to his suicide-attempt. Having survived that he remains alienated, out of kilter with himself and his times. He seeks help from a psychiatrist, a man named Ransome. But Ransome has little empathy with his patient's feeling of displacement and his diagnosis is merely formulaic: 'A good deal of your sickness is merely a failure to adjust to the twentieth century', he helpfully informs Joseph (*SP* 63). It is not until Joseph has an encounter with Mrs Boulder in the penultimate chapter of the novel that he gains any real insight into his own condition and a direction out of his unhappiness. Viv, Mrs Boulder's child, is a further example of a son who does not have a father. When he is visiting Mrs Boulder and after he has had sex with her, Joseph asks her about Viv's father; it is her response that enlightens him. He has been appalled by the negative energies of war and by the negative energies within himself. He now sees that the very means by which he sought to cure himself of those energies, by consulting Dr Ransome, were part of the problem. He had been looking to a father figure to solve the problems of a culture determined by father figures. In an exchange whose symbolic resonances will reverberate throughout all of her subsequent work, Carter has Mrs Boulder profoundly question the value of paternalistic culture:

> 'Who was Viv's father? I've often wondered, Viv is so unnaturally happy. He must have a good hereditary.'
> 'I'll never know for certain,' she said collectedly. 'In fact, it's in rather bad taste of you to ask.'
> 'Come off it,' said Joseph ...
> 'Anyway, what does it matter?' she said. 'Father is only a word at the best of times but mother is a fact.'
> 'You mean, Father is only a hypothesis?' suggested Joseph.
> 'It was hard going at first but my boy, my Vivvy, made it all worth while.'
> 'You mean, Father is a kind of wishful thinking,' pursued Joseph.
> 'Screw you, Ransome, my father figure.'
> 'Mother knows best,' said Mrs Boulder obscurely. (*SP* 116–17)

Being able to identify Ransome the psychiatrist as a father figure and being able, now, to reject that figure, Joseph is at once able to inhabit his revulsion against the violence of the times with equanimity. He is no longer caught between rejection of an old order and a continuing dependence on that order. Mrs Boulder, we are told, 'had hurled him into the interior of the earth, where up is down' (*SP* 122).

Once Joseph's mental horizons have been turned thoroughly inside out and upside down by Mrs Boulder, we are led into the concluding chapter of the novel. If the realism of the preceding chapters has had an allegorical dimension in its gendered emblematising of cultural forces, then this last chapter pretty much leaves realism behind for the sake of a dominantly figurative mode. The scene is a Christmas Eve party given at Kay's house. There is a Christmas truce in Vietnam and the chapter, in which a number of special things happen, is composed in a comic spirit – in the spirit, that is, of Shakespeare's comedies: the kind of comedy where alienation and division are finally largely overcome and positive feeling reigns.

The entire alternative or drop–out community in the novel gathers at Kay's house: 'in the hall, the walls were covered with mirrors which distortedly reflected the party-goers in their gypsyish clothes of so many colours that ... they seemed fragments in a giant kaleidoscope' (*SP* 126). The clothes of many colours are a reminder of Joseph, who is named after the dreamer of the Book of Genesis who wore a 'coat of many colours' (37.3). Joseph in *Several Perceptions* describes himself as 'colourful but mixed up' (*SP* 123). Joseph in the Bible was a dreamer, but his dreams came true. In the last chapter of *Several Perceptions* Joseph loses his mixed-up-ness as a symbolic new world of generosity comes into being.

Mrs Boulder, the wise if increasingly derelict prostitute, finds love with an African man who is going to carry her off, as if she were the White Queen from *Alice in Wonderland*, to the romantic Ivory Coast: 'The Black King and the White Queen were gone' (*SP* 138). A man called Sunny, whom everyone has known as a tramp who always played an imaginary violin and claimed – notwithstanding Joseph's and Anne Blossom's scepticism – to have once been a successful violinist, turns out to be able to play a real violin proficiently:

> Rosie, who had slipped into the room unnoticed as he played, rushed up to him, kissed his withered cheeks and embraced him.

'I never heard such music, grandad,' she said. 'That's what I call a tune.' ...

'I bet you played really great when you were young, just like you said,' Anne told him. She was stiffly apologizing for her previous rudeness. 'I bet you played like a real maestro.' (*SP* 141)

Anne Blossom, who has always walked with a limp, is persuaded by Kay that she can walk normally. Her limp had been a symptom of the guilt she felt at having once given away her illegitimate baby. Now she is renewed in a spirit of forgiveness:

'I'm alright again,' she said. 'It wasn't a punishment for what I did.'

'Did you think that, Anne?' asked Joseph, shocked he had not guessed.

'Oh, yes,' she said, 'I thought they made me lame to punish me ... I thought they'd punished me for that.'

She continued to run backwards and forwards for several minutes ... Kay came slowly back to Joseph ...

'She had hysterical paralysis,' he said. 'Anybody could have cured her, anybody who said to her in a firm enough voice, "Nonsense, you don't really limp at all".' ...

Anne continued to run up and down, now rippling with laughter. Like a quiet brook. (*SP* 144–5)

It is after his intervention on Anne's behalf that Kay destroys his father's photograph. This forgiving, creative world of the Christmas Eve party has no place for an image associated with the destructions of war.

After Anne has walked without limping, Joseph himself declares that he is 'friends with time again' (*SP* 146). At the party he loses the discontent that had set him apart from the likes of Viv and Kay: 'Now Joseph could find it in his heart to forgive' Kay 'for being happy' (*SP* 142). But Joseph is not rejoining conventional society here. He is finding solidarity with the counterculture from which he had distanced himself, even as he had distanced himself from mainstream culture. The special happenings recorded in this concluding chapter of *Several Perceptions* take place within the 'floating world' (*SP* 128) of the counterculture. Generosity and creativity in human relationships are figured as the key to the counterculture, which is celebrated as an alternative model of human relationships to that of the old order of fathers and wars. The counterculture of the 1960s – in its general opposition to the Vietnam War and specifically, in this novel, through Joseph's instruction by Mrs Boulder on the irrelevance of father figures – is being identified by Carter as anti-paternalistic in character and hence as creative and regenerative. At the very end of the novel Joseph imagines seeing his father figure Ransome's face. He dismisses it as an hallucination. The old order of paternalistic authority is finally exorcised and the novel ends with a vignette of new life as Joseph wakes to find his cat has given birth to five fresh kittens:

> Dr Ransome's ... face immediately began to fade away. Then Joseph clambered back over his windowsill, gave his cat food and milk, lay down on his bed and fell into a profound sleep. When he woke again it was the violet dawn of another morning and a tremendous purring was going on at the foot of the bed; his cat sat smiling and purring like an aeroplane about to take off giving suck to five kittens all as white as snow and beautiful as stars. (*SP* 147–8)

Many years after *Several Perceptions* was published, Carter commented on the 1960s and on the peculiar significance that the Vietnam War then held for many in the West:

> Wars are great catalysts for social change and even though it was not specifically *our* war, the Vietnam war was a conflict between the First World and the Third World, between Whites and Non-Whites and, increasingly, between the American people, or a statistically significant percentage thereof, and Yankee imperialism. And the people won, dammit. Whatever happened afterwards, however much they rewrite that war and whatever else the U.S. does, it was the first war in the history of the world where the boys were brought back from the front due to popular demand from their own side. But why should Britain have been so caught up in the consequences of U.S. foreign involvement? The more I think of it, the odder it seems ... that so much seemed at stake in Vietnam, the very nature of our futures, perhaps. (Carter 1988: 211–12)

However odd the effect of the Vietnam War may still have seemed in 1988, Carter, in her comedic figurative conclusion to *Several Perceptions*, had already sought to point to a future whose nature would be radically different from that envisaged by the powers who were perpetrating the war. Though she never returned in her fiction to the specific matter of the Vietnam War and what it symbolised, she returned again and again to imagining futures that would escape the dead and destructive weight of the past. Quite often her fiction is set actually *in* the future – which doesn't mean that the future setting necessarily has escaped the dead past. Carter's future settings usually provide, in fact, an arena in which she can freely consider the problems of a present which is still distorted by the attitudes and outlooks of an old world. The futures that are envisaged at the ends of her narratives, even narratives that are themselves set in the future, are the projected futures of a renovated world. The first of Carter's stories to be set in the future is her fourth novel, *Heroes and Villains*, and it is to this that I now turn.

TWO

Heroes and Villains and *Love*

In her book *Strangers to Ourselves* Julia Kristeva writes:

> Strangely, the foreigner lives within us: he is the hidden face of our identity ...
>   The foreigner is within us. And when we flee from or struggle against the foreigner, we are fighting our unconscious – that 'improper' facet of our impossible 'own and proper'. Delicately, analytically, Freud does not speak of foreigners: he teaches us how to detect foreignness in ourselves. That is perhaps the only way not to hound it outside of us. (Kristeva 1991: 1, 191)

Angela Carter's *Heroes and Villains* (1969) is, in many respects, a fictional exploration of the kind of point Kristeva is making. As Lorna Sage has observed, the novel undertakes a 'sceptical exploration of the whole mystique of Otherness' (Sage 1994a: 18).

Heroes and Villains takes a trope from the Cold War world of the 1960s and is set in a post-holocaust future. In this richly described world of ruin and rank natural growth, three groups of human being survive. There are the Professors, who have preserved many, not all, of the features of pre-holocaust 'civilisation'. They live in ordered communities which are fortified from attack by the Barbarians, who live 'savage', nomadic lives in the lands outside the Professors' communities. Then there are the Out People, the radiation mutants who live beyond the pale even of the Barbarians. The protagonist of the novel, Marianne, is a Professor's daughter who is at once bored with the ordered life of her Professors' community and attracted by the romantic colour and energy of the Barbarians.

Following an attack by a group of Barbarians, Marianne helps one of their number, Jewel, who has been wounded in the attack, to escape the Professors' village. She leaves with Jewel who immediately pronounces her his 'hostage' (*HV* 18), notwithstanding her protest. The two meet up with Jewel's Barbarian tribe. This tribe is formally governed by Jewel and his brothers but behind them lies the tutelary authority of a renegade Professor, Donally. Marianne fairly quickly tries to escape the Barbarians but is caught by Jewel, who rapes her, brings her back to the settlement, and arranges that she marry him. The Barbarians then uproot themselves and head south to winter by the sea. Donally is expelled from the tribe after a quarrel with Jewel. But having expelled Donally, Jewel then goes on a mission to rescue his old tutor, who has sent a message saying he has been captured by the Professors' soldiers. On that mission Jewel is killed. Donally, too, does not return. The novel ends with Marianne deciding that *she* will rule the Barbarian tribe. This is the basic plot, but not the meaning of Carter's allegory. To touch on something of that meaning I want first to look at Carter's characterisation of the Professors.

The Professors' communities are certainly disciplined. They are, in contrast with the Barbarian tribes, self-sufficient and technologically sophisticated. They seek to preserve what they think of as the best elements of the advanced societies of the pre-holocaust world. In the first chapter Marianne's father explains to her that

'Before the war, there were places called Universities where men did nothing but read books and conduct experiments ... some Professors were allowed in the deep shelters with their families, during the war, and they proved to be the only ones left who could resurrect the gone world in a gentler shape, and try to keep destruction outside, this time.' (*HV* 8)

The attempt to exclude the principle of destruction embraces also the attempt to exclude the principle of the Barbarian. In chapter six, Jewel imagines making peace with the Professors but Marianne warns him that no accommodation with them is possible. They would subject him to scientific tests that would only highlight the fact that his animal vitality – symbolised here by his 'coat of fur' – was unassimilable to their reality:

'They would put you in a cage so everyone could examine you. You'd be an icon of otherness.' ...

'They'd walk around you carefully in case you bit them ... They'd take away your coat of fur and dress you in a dark suit and set you intelligence tests where you had to match squares with circles and circles with squares. And give you aptitude tests ... And many other tests. And everything you did or said would be observed and judged ... to see how you revealed your differences, every word and gesture studied and annotated until you were nothing but a mass of footnotes with a tiny trickle of text at the top of a page. You would be pressed inside a book. And you'd be lodged probably with psychologists and all the time you'd be a perfect stranger.' (*HV* 123–4)

With their sheer cerebralness the Professors have sought to deny or exclude the instinctual forces that are associated with the Barbarians. Sexual intercourse, in all its animal compulsion, is something that Marianne, the Professor's child, cannot imagine in the context of the Professors' world. In the nuptial chamber after her marriage to Jewel, Marianne finds herself drawn to him and she contrasts the sensation with what she had grasped of sex in her father's world:

He was a curiously shaped, attractive stone; he was an object which drew her. She examined the holes pierced in his ears to contain earrings. She had read such cool words in the books in her father's study ... she had heard her father's gentle voice speaking of happenings between men and women that, in spite of her affection she could not associate with happenings between the hairless old man and her mother's ghost; now she lay far away from his white tower with a beautiful stranger beside her and he stark naked. (*HV* 82–3)

If Jewel would remain a stranger to the Professors, so Marianne, brought up in the abstract Professors' world, is a stranger to all the basic drives which Jewel the Barbarian epitomises: 'he's *id*', Carter commented, using the Freudian term for the primordial instincts which root human behaviour (Sage 1977: 56). On Marianne, Carter also observed, in a letter to Elaine Jordan: 'she *is* very much a stranger to her own desire, which is why her desire finds its embodiment as a stranger' (Jordan 1994: 198). To the extent that Marianne is drawn by Barbarian energy she is impelled by energies within herself that are repressed in the Professor's world. On the matter of repression, Carter also said, in 'a long parenthesis, prickly as well as apologetic' that she attached to her letter to Elaine Jordan:

> If you *teach* 'Heroes and Villains', that is, and haven't been put off by that distinctly ideologically dodgy rape scene, which I put into the novel in the first place for reasons of pure sensationalism and which I can't defend on any other grounds except that 'H and V' is *supposed* to share a vocabulary with the fiction of repression, i.e. 'The sheikh' – this isn't defending it, it's explaining it. Note, however, that it doesn't make Marianne feel degraded – it makes her absolutely *furious*. And, in common with all the rape-fantasies to which some women used to admit, the aggressor is a man of compulsive allure and unnatural beauty. A 'demon lover' who absolves the woman of all responsibility for her own desire, so she can continue to maintain her white state of purity. (Jordan 1994: 197–8; all quotations from letters are transcribed *sic* from MS)

The ideological dodginess of the rape scene in *Heroes and Villains* resides in the fact that the rape might be read as the fulfilment of Marianne's repressed desire. On this question, Elaine Jordan, picking up on Carter's observation that Marianne's desire 'finds its embodiment as a stranger', notes first a distinction between actual rape and women's – *not* men's – rape fantasies, before going on to observe the way in which Carter's overall account of the relationship between Marianne and Jewel actually turns the tables on male objectification of the female by – as we have seen, for example, in the description of Jewel as an 'attractive stone ... an object' – having Marianne objectify Jewel:

> This suggests that Marianne's rape by Jewel can be read as an allegory of her fantasies (let me reiterate, regrettable as it is to have to be so cautious: the facts about rapes have nothing to do with *women's* rape fantasies, except in so far as representations of rape are culturally available at all levels; everything that is culturally available is Carter's territory). It is only their estrangement which Marianne and Jewel have in common: 'He was as complete a stranger as she could have wished to meet and her only companion' ... They are both symbolic or allegorical figures, not 'realistic characters'; and in this story it is she who is the subject, he the object of her fantastic desire, the young chief and sacrificial 'Unfortunate Lover' of the book's epigraph. (Jordan 1994: 198)

Marianne's turning of the gender tables in relation not only to Jewel and his world but also in relation to the Professors' world is, as I shall show later, the essence of Carter's allegory in this novel.

But to continue with the issue of repression: to the extent that it is endemic in the Professors' reality it is something that severely qualifies the achievement of that reality. While the Professors' world may see itself as superior to the Barbarian condition, it is nevertheless a world that bears marks of weakness, marks of woe. The Professors, failing to recognise their own repressions, have sought to hound that which is not gentle and ordered outside themselves. They have committed the crime of finding external scapegoats for realities within their own hearts and minds that they find problematical. At one point, Marianne's father, considering the warfare between the Professors and the Barbarians, perceptively observes: 'if the Barbarians are destroyed, who will we then be able to blame for the bad things?' (*HV* 11). While the Professors in general may see what they exclude as bad, *Heroes and Villains* emphasises that repression and exclusion are themselves bad.

The Professors' world is riven with disturbing phenomena. 'Everyone' in their community may be 'clean and proper' (*HV* 4), but that community has a notably high suicide rate. Again, while the soldiers who police the Professors' community at one level maintain a practically useful discipline, at another level they enforce a kind of fascistic, totalitarian order that oppresses anyone who does not conform. We hear that the soldiers 'dealt inscrutably with the deformed' (*HV* 9). In one Barbarian attack Marianne sees a Professor 'rush suddenly from the tower where the Professors lived and throw himself purposefully under the hooves of a horse, which trampled him' (*HV* 16). Marianne's uncle, 'the Colonel of the Soldiers' (*HV* 15), without imagination, interprets suicide only as a culpable failure to conform: 'Look at that fool Professor of Psychology ... kicked to death. Serve him right, maladjusted' (*HV* 17). Totalitarian discipline cooperates with a feudal power structure in the Professors' community. Feudal *and* patriarchal. When her father asks her if there is any young man in the community she would like to marry, Marianne

> considered the cadets one by one. Every Professor's eldest son became a cadet among the Soldiers, that was the tradition. Then she considered the Professors' younger sons, nascent Professors themselves since it was a hereditary caste. They were all hereditary castes. She even ran her mind's eye over the Workers. After all this consideration, Marianne

acknowledged it was impossible for her to consider marriage with any of the young men in the community.

'I don't want to marry,' she said. 'I don't see the point. I could maybe marry a stranger, someone from outside, but nobody here. Everybody here is so terribly boring, Father.' (*HV* 10–11)

Committed only to abstraction the Professors have evolved a society that is based upon an extreme and distasteful rationalism. When she is out in the Barbarian lands Marianne remembers the Professors' community 'when she was a child, encapsulated in a safe, white tower with unreason at bay outside, beyond the barbed wire, a community so rational that when her white rabbit died they cut it open to find out why' (*HV* 77). If the repressions and exclusions of this rationalism return in the form of suicides, then it is equally clear that unreason inhabits the community in the superstitious denigration of the 'other' amongst the workers of the community. Marianne's nurse tells her that the Barbarians 'slit the bellies of the women after they've raped them and sew up cats inside' (*HV* 10). In Marianne's case, the professorial rationalism that seeks to deny the power of the id sets up in her a longing – which she does not initially comprehend – to get in touch with the id. It sets up in her a longing to engage with the Barbarian strangeness that is physically outside her community but which resides in her own being.

When Marianne does make contact with the Barbarians she may indeed be able to recognise and relate to the desire in herself that had been negated in the antiseptic world of the Professors. She may indeed, after her marriage to Jewel, find something of herself in being drawn to and sleeping with a naked, beautiful stranger:

> She was filled with astonishment that the room contained the world or the world had become only the room; she put her arms around him and caressed him ... She pulled the nightdress over her head and threw it away, so she could be still closer to him or, rather, to the magic source of attraction constituted by his brown flesh ... There was no pain this time. The mysterious glide of planes of flesh within her bore no relation to anything she had heard, read or experienced. (*HV* 83)

But there is a good deal else in Barbarian life that appals her and arouses her respect for aspects, at least, of the Professors' world. On an early, secret excursion from her Professors' community she had glimpsed a troupe of Barbarians and had been struck by the extent of their material dispossession, a dispossession which rendered their faces 'sick, sad and worn' (*HV* 14). That impression does not fade once she is living amongst them. Marianne's father, a Professor of History, had been researching Rousseau's ideas on the innocence and contentment of humankind in a 'state of nature'. In a real situation Marianne discovers the misconceptions of Rousseau's idealisations. Carter said that *Heroes and Villains* involves 'a discussion of the theories of Jean-Jacques Rousseau, and ... it finds them wanting' (Haffenden 1985: 95):

> The children suffered promiscuously from ringworm, skin diseases and weeping eye. Also rickets. She considered the possibility of deficiency diseases such as pellagra and beri-beri. When she thought of the noble savage in her father's researches, her distaste was mixed with grief. (*HV* 45)

Nor is it just such things as the disease-inviting filth and excrement of the Barbarian living quarters which alienate Marianne. There is also a superstition about Marianne as a Professorial 'other' which at least matches the superstition of Marianne's nurse about the Barbarians:

> A woman came from the shadows at the back of the hall, raised her heavy skirt, squatted and urinated.
> 'Where has Jewel gone?' asked Marianne.
> The woman wobbled in the middle of the spreading puddle, made a sign against the evil eye and wailed.
> 'Oh, don't be stupid,' said Marianne angrily. 'I'm flesh and blood and I want to find Jewel.' (*HV* 36)

Marianne has not been living long with the Barbarians when we hear that 'whatever romantic attractions the idea of the Barbarians might have held for her as she sat by herself in the white tower ... had entirely evaporated' (*HV* 52). Nevertheless, the dispelling of romantic illusion does not qualify her discovery of her own deeper, motivating desire in her relationship with Jewel. It must be emphasised, however, that it is her own desire she finds and which is, fundamentally, much more important than Jewel himself. In itself, Marianne's relationship with Jewel is by no means simply liberating. For, within Barbarian society, that sexual relationship is as much circumscribed by patriarchal attitudes as the relations between the sexes had been patriarchally ordered in the Professors' community. Jewel's initial rape of Marianne is an expression of the dominating masculinism of his view of the world. And that view is significantly conditioned by Donally. It was Donally who tattooed on Jewel's back an image from one of the great patriarchal myths of all time:

> He wore the figure of a man on the right side, a woman on the left and, tattooed the length of his spine, a tree with a snake curled round and round the trunk. This elaborate design was executed in blue, red, black and green. The woman offered the man a red apple and more red apples grew among green leaves at the top of the tree, spreading across his shoulders, and the black roots of the tree twisted and ended at the top of his buttocks. The figures were both stiff and lifelike; Eve wore a perfidious smile. (*HV* 85)

Donally tries to give Jewel's Barbarian tribe a myth to live by. But his myth is coopted from the ancients and preserves an ancient denigration of women as deceitful violators of faith or trust. In respect of their views of the relative standing of each of the sexes, the Professors' world, with its patrilineal law of inheritance, and the Barbarian world, with its mythopoeic blame of women, are mirror images of each other. They are not to be contrasted: they are to be equated.

Marianne refuses the dead, patriarchal discipline of the Professors' rationalism. But she also comes to resist the irrational, patriarchal oppressiveness of the Barbarians. Most important, she grasps that, for all the apparent contrast between reason and un-reason, the Professors and the Barbarians should not be divided into absolute opposites. They imply each other. The foreigner lives within each of them. This mutual implication is suggested early in the novel when Marianne has a dream about her brother, who was killed by Jewel in an attack on the Professors' community many years before the one in which Jewel was wounded:

> She recalled with visionary clarity the face of the murdering boy with his necklaces, rings and knife, although the memory of her brother's face was totally blurred. Sometimes she dreamed of his death; one day, waking from this dream, she realised the two faces had super-imposed themselves entirely on each other and all she saw was the boy killing himself or his double. (*HV* 10)

The lack of difference between the Professors and the Barbarians is suggested also by other things. Not only do members of both societies superstitiously demonise the other; they share a common masking of themselves. The soldiers who defend the Professors' community wear 'glass visors' (*HV* 21), just as the barbarian warriors wear face-paint. Towards the end of the novel, when Jewel is about to attempt to rescue Donally from the Professors' soldiers, he prepares to put on face-paint. As he invites Marianne to watch him 'turn' himself into the Professors' 'nightmare', he comments that the Professors' soldiers are his nightmare. Marianne observes that the nightmare of the other has nothing to do with truth:

> 'Paint my face. Fetch my jars of paint, watch me turn into the nightmare.'
>
> Johnny signalled to the others and they were gone as suddenly as they had come. The boy went, also, to root about in their possessions until he found the paints.
>
> 'When the Soldiers see you coming, they will think you are the devil incarnate, riding a black horse.'
>
> 'They are the devils, with their glass faces. One cannot escape the consequences of one's appearance.'
>
> 'It is the true appearance of neither of you.' (*HV* 145)

For Marianne the 'true appearance' of either side is something that would suspend each side's categorisation of the other as 'other'. In their true appearance there is not the absolute divide that each side insists upon. Marianne, the Professor's child who has lived with the Barbarians, finds each side within herself. The foreigner, the stranger, is not outside herself. The novel offers Marianne as a model of a condition which slips the Professors' and the Barbarians' insistence on binary opposition and antagonism. Lorna Sage notes that *Heroes and Villains* offers readers the 'exhilarating sensation of recognising that the binary oppositions (inside/outside, culture/nature, masculine/feminine) are themselves being called into question' (Sage 1994a: 19). Above all, that questioning is conceived in gendered terms. The insistence on opposition and exclusion which characterises both the Professors and the Barbarians is seen in the novel as an effect of the prevailing masculinism of both societies. Marianne, as a woman, epitomises a feminine model that is not oppositional and antagonistic but reconciling and synthesising. At the very end of *Heroes and Villains*, when both Jewel and Donally have failed to return,

Marianne declares that she will be 'the tiger lady' and 'rule' the Barbarians 'with a rod of iron' (*HV* 150).

The idea of Marianne the 'tiger lady' associates her symbolically with the instinctual force of the Barbarians. But it is the 'lady' which is important and which distinguishes her from the Barbarian reality as it has been until her arrival. In the final sequences of the book Marianne is pregnant with Jewel's child. Donally, who promises to turn Jewel into the 'Tiger Man' (*HV* 146), says to Jewel: 'Give me your son and I'll turn him into the Tiger Boy' (*HV* 125). Donally wishes to further his aim of mythopoeically constituting the Barbarian world through conditioning Jewel's child, which he presumes will be a boy. He would continue the patriarchal mythification that is emblematised in the tattoo on Jewel's back. He would perpetuate the unequal contrast between male and female intrinsic to patriarchal myth. Somewhat earlier in the book we learn that Donally wishes to raise the Barbarians out of their 'indecent' (*HV* 63) state, but not to bring them to the condition of the Professors nor to find any synthesis between Barbarian and Professorial conditions. He wants to keep Jewel 'beautifully savage' (*HV* 62) and to push the Barbarians towards what he terms a state of 'the honest savage' (*HV* 63). In other words, Donally's patriarchal programme involves the maintenance not just of the unequal antagonism between male and female but of the opposition between 'civilised' and 'uncivilised', between reason and unreason, that Marianne in her own experience is busy dismantling. Although she refuses them, Marianne herself at one point directly feels that Donally is offering her all 'manner of potentialities' – on one condition, that she abandon reason and capitulate to its supposed opposite:

> that consciousness of reason in which her own had ripened was now withering away and she might soon be prepared to accept … whatever malign structure of the world with which the shaman who rode the donkey should one day choose to present her … the Doctor continued to watch her. The cracked mirrors of his dark glasses revealed all manner of potentialities for Marianne, modes of being to which she might aspire just as soon as she threw away her reason as of no further use to her. (*HV* 106–7)

As I have said, the maintenance of the sharp opposition between civilised and uncivilised, reason and unreason, man and woman, is presented in the novel as a symptom of patriarchal power. Marianne, refusing that power, refuses the divisions upon which it is structured. In the first chapter of the novel, Marianne as a girl intimates that she will not take part in a masculine game:

> The children played Soldiers and Barbarians ...
> 'The Soldiers are heroes but the Barbarians are villains,' said the son of the Professor of Mathematics aggressively, 'I'm a hero. I'll shoot you.'
> 'Oh, no, you won't,' said Marianne and grimaced frightfully. 'I'm not playing.' (*HV* 2)

Throughout, Marianne refuses to play within the mutually reflecting, patriarchal power-structures of the Professors and the Barbarians. At the end she will be the 'tiger lady': according to the terms of the book a tiger *man* would have fulfilled Donally's intention and maintained 'savagery' in principled opposition to civilisation. But while, as 'tiger lady', she is going to draw on primordial Barbarian energy, Marianne, it must be noted, does not give up her purchase on reason. It is this emphasis on maintaining reason that separates her from the Donally-inspired Barbarian cult of the irrational. At the same time as Marianne stops being a stranger to her own id during her sojourn amongst the Barbarians, reason emerges as a cardinal feature of her discovery of herself. Her patriarchally ordered marriage to Jewel is symbolised by the ancient wedding-dress, stored in a metal chest dating from pre-holocaust days, which she has to wear and which turns her into a 'mute, furious doll' (*HV* 69). This wedding-dress, symbolising the infection of ancient male dominance, is contrasted with the Reason that had once been valued, for a short time, during the French Enlightenment:

> As the room grew dark, the dress took on a moon-like glimmer and seemed to send out more and more filaments of tulle, like a growth of pale fungus shooting out airy spores, a palpable white infection; viruses of plagues named after the labels on the test-tubes in which they had been bred might survive for years under the briars of a dead city, nesting invisibly in the contents of just such a Pandora's box as this metal chest, starred with singed stickers of foreign places dating from those times when foreign places had more than an imaginative existence, for where was Paris any more, where they had briefly worshipped the goddess Reason. (*HV* 68)

Again, there is a moment after their marriage when Jewel, having sex with Marianne, growls 'Conceive, you bitch, conceive.' Shocked into 'the most lucid wakefulness', Marianne asks him 'Why?' (*HV* 90). Jewel finally explains that perpetrating his savage clones upon her would give him self-respect. She sees the masculineness of his imagination as irrational and grotesque. She alludes to Goya's etching 'The sleep of reason produces monsters':

> 'Why?'
> He was silent so long she began to wonder if she had actually spoken aloud.
> 'Dynastically', he said at last. 'It's a patriarchal system. I need a son.' ...
> 'Give me another reason.' ...
> 'Revenge,' he explained. 'Shoving a little me up you, a little me all furred, plaited and bristling with knives. Then I should have status in relation to myself.'
> 'By submitting me to the most irretrievable humiliation. By making me give birth to monsters?'
> 'What, like the sleep of reason?'
> 'You're very sophisticated,' she complained. (*HV* 90)

The sleep of reason amongst the Barbarians is a dimension of their reality that Marianne cannot, will not, come to terms with. Near the end of the novel, on the southern coastline, she fantasises about leaving the Barbarians and living alone with Jewel. She fantasises about bringing up a new breed of human being whose rationality would expunge the male sexism that now relegates women to secondary status. In her fantasy she enlists reason in her resistance to an identification of the female as the negative term in a binary opposition, in her insistence on the right of women to claim autonomy and self-determination, on the right of women to reclaim, as it were, the night so that they might walk home alone in safety:

> at best, they might begin a new subspecies of man ...
> This fearless and rational breed would eschew such mysteries as the one now forcing her to walk behind the figure on the shore [the father of the child], dark as the negative of a photograph, and preventing her from returning home alone. (*HV* 137)

Though this fantasy is never realised, Marianne's commitment to reason, stemming from the Professorial side of her mind, is never relinquished, for all that she has discovered about herself in the Barbarian world. Marianne's high valuation of reason is emphasised once more shortly after her fantasy about raising a new subspecies of human being:

> upon the cliff, a white tower glistened like a luminous finger pointing to heaven. It was a lighthouse ... To Marianne, it looked the twin of the white tower in which she had been born ... Thus this tower glimpsed in darkness symbolised and clarified her resolution; abhor shipwreck, said the lighthouse, go in fear of unreason. (*HV* 139)

For all that she has established a relationship with her 'own desire' (Jordan 1994: 198) through her relationship with Jewel, Marianne's attachment to reason at last overcomes the pure attraction that the savage had held for her:

> quite dissolved was the marvellous, defiant construction of textures and colours she first glimpsed marauding her tranquil village; it had vanished as if an illusion which could not sustain itself in the white beams of the lighthouse. (*HV* 147)

So Marianne refuses the extremes of either the Professors or the Barbarians. Her commitment to reason is not the same as the Professors' repressive and sterile rationalism. She goes out and engages with desire. Finding that desire, however, she does not enter into Barbarian unreason. The model she represents is one in which reason and desire do not stand in polar opposition. In Marianne's case reason may order, like an iron rod, the inchoate energies of the id, while the energies of the id – the energies of the 'tiger lady' – may enrich reason. This synthetic model is identified as specifically feminine, in contrast with the masculine insistence on self-definition through opposition to an other. The feminine aspect of the model is dramatised in details close to the novel's conclusion. First of all, there is the collapse of the anti-rational, arch-patriarch Donally. When Jewel and Donally fall out, he momentarily appears as a kind of God the Father towering over Jewel and Marianne as an Adam and Eve:

> 'I do believe we've come to the parting of the ways, at last.'
> 'Do you?' said Donally. He stood up and stretched. He appeared to reach to the top of the sky and the young man and woman cowered at his feet but this impression lasted only for a moment. (*HV* 126–7)

A little later, Donally has toppled:

> While Mrs Green was examining Marianne, Jewel went down to the
> stream and threw the boy's chain into the water. When he returned to
> the camp, the Doctor sought him out and attempted to shoot him with
> a pearl-handled revolver but he missed. Jewel knocked him down. When
> Mrs Green and Marianne came out of the barn, they found Donally
> lying on his back in the grass beside the apple tree ... Jewel stood
> beside him, running his thumb down the edge of his knife and the
> entire tribe had gathered in a wide, wonder-struck and apprehensive
> circle round the fallen figure of the shaman.
>   'I've not killed him yet,' said Jewel to Marianne. (*HV* 129)

After this fall, Jewel declares that he will burn Donally's snake,
emblem of the phallic authority that Donally had tried to reaffirm
to the Barbarians. Jewel and Marianne might now set off to fulfil
her fantasy about raising a new 'fearless and rational' breed of
human being. But Donally is not killed, only ejected from the
tribe. And Jewel finds the pull of his old shamanistic tutor so great
that he goes out to rescue him. In the end, then, Jewel backslides
into re-identification with the masculine cult that Donally had
offered him. At the very end of the novel, Donally's son relates
how Jewel died:

> 'He was writhing around ... and I held him, to keep him still, I suppose
> ... I held him and I felt him go ... there was nothing no more.'
>   He seemed purely and strangely surprised at the swiftness and ease
> with which Jewel had departed from life ...
>   'No more,' he said and relapsed into silence. (*HV* 150–1)

That last 'No more', in the last line of the novel, literally describes
Jewel's departing and, at the same time, signifies symbolically the
end of the dominating masculinism for which he, in the end, like
Donally, had stood.

With Jewel's death Marianne is free to set up as ruler of the
Barbarians, whom she will direct according to her model not of
antagonism and opposition but of combination. Jewel had once
said to Marianne: 'Pretend you're Eve at the end of the world'
(*HV* 124). At the conclusion of *Heroes and Villains* Marianne is an
Eve not at the end of the world as such, but at the end of the
patriarchal world. The original patriarchal myth of Eden, alluded
to throughout the novel, is revised at the close of *Heroes and*

Villains as it had been at the end of *The Magic Toyshop*. Marianne as a new Eve can build from a new Eden, one which has been shorn of baleful father figures and the old male sexist mythology. The analysis in *Heroes and Villains*, with its futuristic setting, of masculine power and the divisions it rests upon obviously pertains directly to the contemporary world. The novel takes to a new level of sophistication many of the points Carter had begun to explore in her first three books. But what is strikingly new in the novel is the identification of reason as a necessary, paramount element in the conceptualisation of an order beyond the patriarchal. It is the idea of reason as the ground of her feminist cause that is the crucial feature of the conceptual frame of reference that Carter will use after *Heroes and Villains*. In her succeeding works Carter was, time and again, both explicitly and implicitly, to complicate, deepen and extend her understanding of reason.

In the novel that followed *Heroes and Villains*, *Love*, written in 1969 though not published until 1971, Carter commended reason by emphasising the dangers of unreason. In this novel she explores a traditional pattern of understanding the nature of gender identity and the relations between the sexes, which is characterised in terms of unreason.

Love, which is structured not by chapters but by two long parts separated by a shorter middle section, deals with a triangle of three people living in late 1960s provincial bohemia. First, there is Annabel – middle-class, an art-school student – who is described by Carter in the 1987 'Afterword' she wrote to *Love* as 'the mad girl' (*L* 113). Annabel persistently fails to engage with the real and composes herself and her world through a mixture of fantasy and hallucination:

> she had the capacity for changing the appearance of the real world ... All she apprehended through her senses she took only as objects for interpretation in the expressionistic style and she saw, in everyday things, a world of mythic, fearful shapes of whose existence she was convinced. (*L* 3–4)

At the very end of the novel Annabel commits suicide, having already tried twice unsuccessfully. The second member of the triangle is Lee, a university student who becomes a schoolteacher.

Lee, an orphan, is from a working-class background and carries with him a 'chronic slum-child infection' of the eyes (*L* 12) which often causes him to weep tears that are merely physical rather than emotional in origin. Lee encounters Annabel, who two months before had tried to commit suicide by taking an overdose of sleeping tablets, at a party. The two start living together. In the early days of their relationship Lee is also 'sleeping with the wife of his philosophy tutor' (*L* 17). Annabel's parents one day arrive unexpectedly and discover that their daughter is living with Lee. They remove Annabel and insist that if she and Lee wish to see each other again, they must marry. After the marriage, Lee has an affair with another woman, Carolyn, who at one point goes to a party at Lee and Annabel's flat. Carolyn and Lee have sex at the party and he walks her home, where she invites him in: 'he was sufficiently sentimental or else, perhaps, vain enough to go upstairs with her' (*L* 47–8). Meanwhile Annabel, jealous of Lee and Carolyn, has slashed her wrists in the bathroom of their flat. Discovering this when he returns home the same night, Lee leaves the hospital to which Annabel is taken and spends the rest of the night with Carolyn. This brings us to the middle section of the book, where a psychiatrist at the psychiatric hospital in which Annabel is interned tells Lee that Annabel is unbalanced, and that it would be unhealthy for her to continue living with Lee *and* with the third member of the triangle, Buzz, Lee's half-brother, who shares the flat with Lee and Annabel.

Buzz is a drop-out with psychotic tendencies; a voyeuristic photographer who parallels Annabel in his inability to engage with the real: 'Buzz used the camera as if to see with ... in the end he saw everything at second hand, without depths' (*L* 25). Their comparable, though not identical, disengagement from reality is the basis of the interest which Annabel develops in Buzz before her suicide attempt. The psychiatrist tells Lee: 'There is a condition of shared or, rather, mutually stimulated psychotic disorder known as "folie à deux". Your brother and your wife would appear excellent candidates for it' (*L* 60). Though in many ways they are close, having been thrown together as orphans, there is troubling competition between Buzz and Lee, and Buzz draws Annabel to himself in the spirit of this competition. In the third section of the novel, Lee persuades Buzz to move out of the flat before Annabel comes back from hospital. When Buzz later returns, he and Annabel go off for a night of sex which Annabel finds surprisingly unsatisfactory:

> connoisseurs of unreality as they were, they could not bear the crude weight, the rank smell and the ripe taste of real flesh. It is always a dangerous experiment to act out a fantasy; they had undertaken the experiment rashly and had failed but Annabel suffered the worst for she had been trying to convince herself she was alive. (*L* 95)

Annabel's suffering, her failure to convince herself that she is alive, is such that after she has returned to Lee she privately plans what will be her final attempt at suicide. Having, one day, been driven by Annabel out of their flat, Lee goes to a café where he meets a pupil from his school, Joanne. While he is spending the night having sex with Joanne, Annabel is killing herself: 'now she was a painted doll, bluish at the extremities' (*L* 112). There the novel ended in 1969, probably the only entirely bleak conclusion in Carter's *oeuvre*.

In the 'Afterword' to *Love*, Carter continues the stories of the novel's surviving characters up to the mid-1980s. We are told that Buzz had been 'still waiting for his historic moment', a moment which came when punk happened in the 1970s and he became 'rich and famous' (*L* 116). He modified his name to Buzzz and 'now lives a life of paranoid seclusion in a midtown penthouse' in New York (*L* 117). In the mid-1980s Lee is still a schoolteacher, remarried to a woman named Rosie. Lee has recounted to Rosie his relationship with Annabel and has also told her how he had beaten her. At first Rosie 'did not want to blame' (*L* 118) Lee, but 'as she encountered and absorbed the women's movement' which had taken off during the 1970s 'she found she had no option but to do so, blaming him for sins of omission and commission, and, especially, for raising his hand to Annabel' (*L* 118). Annabel cannot, of course, be resurrected in this 'Afterword': 'even the women's movement would have been no help to her', Carter observes (*L* 113). The 'Afterword' places special emphasis on the women's movement. The wife of the philosophy tutor, for example, 'became a radical feminist in the early seventies' (*L* 114). In the mid-1980s she 'lives on a remote farm in Wales with three other women ... and ... thinks of her life as a heterosexual as a bad

dream from which she is now awake' (*L* 114). Even Joanne – who
had become a stripper and 'a model in the early days of soft porn
magazines in the seventies' – was 'radicalised', and by the mid-
1980s had become a 'social worker for the London borough of
Lambeth' (*L* 115). The manner in which the 'Afterword' stresses
the transformative power of the women's movement refocuses
attention on the gender issues at stake in the novel. In the
'Afterword' Carter informs us that she 'got the idea for *Love*, from
Benjamin Constant's early-nineteenth century novel of sensibility,
Adolphe [1816]; I was seized with the desire to write a kind of
modern-day, demotic version of *Adolphe*' (*L* 113). It is in relation
to the matter of 'sensibility' that *Love* explores a traditional pattern
of understanding the nature of gender identity and interrelation.

As a term, 'sensibility' refers to a literary and philosophical
phenomenon dominant in the mid-eighteenth century but which
continued to manifest itself right through to the early nineteenth
century. The term is usually thought of as sharing many features
in common with 'sentiment', and literary historians – although
making some important distinctions between the two terms – frequently speak of eighteenth-century novels of sensibility and of
sentimental novels as if they were more or less the same thing.
Janet Todd has given the following account of 'sensibility', which
she describes as the key term of the period:

> 'Sensibility', an innate sensitiveness or susceptibility revealing itself in
> a variety of spontaneous activities such as crying, swooning and kneel-
> ing, is defined in 1797 by the *Encyclopaedia Britannica* (3rd edn) as 'a
> nice and delicate perception of pleasure or pain, beauty or deformity' ...
>   The cult of sensibility that jangled the nerves of Europe in the mid-
> eighteenth century is the cultural movement devoted to tear-demanding
> exhibitions of pathos and unqualified virtue ...
>   Although it had its heyday from the 1740s to the late 1770s, the
> literature of sensibility is not discrete. Sentimental elements increase
> in importance through Restoration tragedy and early-eighteenth cen-
> tury comedy, and after the 1770s they also inhabit Gothic fiction and
> Romantic poetry. (Todd 1986: 7–9)

Sensibility came to be associated especially with women and the
feminine. In the eighteenth century the association was used to
deny women the faculty of reason. Alan Richardson has observed
that 'devaluation of the feminine' was 'particularly vehement in

the English Augustan period; women, considered sensible but not reasonable, were all but denied status as human, that is, rational beings' (Richardson 1988: 14). He goes on to note that the 'gendered division of reason and passion, with the degradation of women it entails', came to serve 'as a target for Mary Wollstone-craft throughout the second *Vindication*; women were granted primacy in the "culture of the heart", she held, only to have their "scanty ... portion of rationality" begrudged or withheld' (Richardson 1988: 14). With the Romantic movement of the late eighteenth and early nineteenth centuries, however, and all its emphasis on imagination and feeling as primary human faculties, there was, on the part of male writers, an appropriation of what Richardson calls the 'conventionally feminine domain of sensibility' (Richardson 1988: 13). This did not involve a redefinition of the male and the masculine in terms which would have enabled an equalisation of identity and power between men and women. It was an annexation of 'feminine' characteristics on behalf of a patriarchy which did not relinquish its dominance; an annexation which confirmed traditional masculine denial of the autonomy of the feminine. Richardson notes the existence in Romantic writing by men of images of the androgynous male, but goes on to say that 'when androgyny functions as another manifestation of the male poet's urge to absorb feminine characteristics, his (or his protagonist's) female counterpart stands to risk obliteration ... The Romantic tradition did not simply objectify women. It also subjected them, in a dual sense, portraying women as subject in order to appropriate the feminine for male subjectivity' (Richardson 1988: 19, 22).

Benjamin Constant's *Adolphe* presents a man of sensibility, and Carter, in writing *Love*, is reacting against the manner in which men of sensibility, whether early-nineteenth-century men or men in the second half of the twentieth century, notwithstanding their capacity for feeling and sympathy, may be perpetuating a masculinism which still works viciously against the female. Lee is repeatedly described in terms of his capacity for sentiment. Early on we learn that 'Lee was sentimental while Buzz was malign' (*L* 11). The eighteenth-century connection between sentiment and a capacity for virtue is sketched in when we hear that, when he was thirteen, Lee had 'persuaded his brother to run away with him to Cuba to fight for Castro ... The act was principally the expression of a sentimentality so pure it became his greatest virtue, in one sense, since his sentimentality often, when he grew up, made him act against his desires' (*L* 14). But Lee's sentimentalism, for all that it is conceived in a traditional, eighteenth-century mode, is not a consistent or reliable moral touchstone. For it is associated also with a questionable construction of reality, and with failures of moral nerve. When Lee is with Joanne on the night Annabel commits suicide we learn that Joanne 'was the artificial creation of his habitually romantic imagination' (*L* 110). Lee's sentimental romanticism is just as frequently connected with mere selfishness and culpable weakness as with virtue. Lee is no less of a 'bastard' to Annabel (*L* 119) because of his sentimentalism. Carter's ironic portrait of a man of sensibility is typified in her treatment of the principal symptom of such a man in eighteenth- and nineteenth-century writing: tears. Lee's ubiquitous tears, with their origin in a physical ailment, are not to be trusted. When he returns to sleep with Carolyn after discovering that Annabel has been hospitalised following her suicide attempt, we are told that Carolyn 'was crying a little' and that she thought that 'Lee must also be crying when it was only the scalding of his hypocritical eyes' (*L* 50).

Yet if Lee possesses a sensibility that does not compromise his male chauvinism, so Annabel is presented as a type of the female who has been brought up to a life of sensibility that profoundly disables her. Annabel's state of mind is described in terms which align its disturbance with her highly developed 'sensibility', and with the related phenomena of Gothicism and romanticism. As she is preparing for her suicide she is afflicted by a sensory hyper-sensitivity that borders on hallucination:

> She was troubled by an over-acuteness of the senses and wondered why they shouted so loudly upstairs or the cars outside made, today, such tigerish roarings. She was irritated rather than disturbed to sense occasionally the almost inarticulate breathings and the infinitely subtle movements of the figures on the walls and her sudden excess of sensibility made the paper between her fingers coarser than sandpaper. (*L* 103)

Annabel's 'excess of sensibility' at the novel's conclusion is anticipated at the outset of the book, where there is a description of an eighteenth-century landscaped park which she has to cross on her journeys home. The park is laid out on a hill, and its south side is executed in classical style. Annabel's highly strung sympathies, however, are with the Gothicism that is the motif of the park on the northern side of the hill:

> There was a stable built on the lines of a miniature Parthenon ... a focal point in the green composition on the south side of the hill where Annabel rarely ventured for serenity bored her and the Mediterranean aspect of this part of the park held no excitements for her. She preferred the Gothic north, where an ivy-covered tower with leaded ogive windows skulked among the trees. (*L* 1–2)

Annabel's sensibility and her taste for the Gothic are compounded in Carter's description of the romanticism of her means of incorporating Lee into her imaginative life:

> As for Annabel, she was like a child who reconstructs the world according to its whims and so she chose to populate her home with imaginary animals because she preferred them to the drab fauna of reality. She quickly incorporated [Lee] into her mythology but if, at first, he was a herbivorous lion, later he became a unicorn devouring raw meat and she never saw him the same twice, nor did these pictures have any continuity except for the constant romanticism of the imagery. She had no control over them, once they existed. And, as she drew him, so she saw him; he existed for her only intermittently. (*L* 34–5)

Nor are 'sensibility', the 'Gothic' or the 'romantic' the only terms which are aligned with Annabel's disturbance. The passage above also hints at further aesthetic-philosophical phenomena which are aligned with Annabel's disturbance: Dada and surrealism. The lack of continuity between Annabel's images and her lack of conscious control over them remind us of the Dadaist anarchist refusal of sense and order, and of the comparable, though not identical, surrealist principle of subverting rational and logical thought by allowing the unconscious to express itself – strategies which manifested themselves in artistic practices such as collage. Annabel's 'favourite painter', we are told, 'was Max Ernst' (*L* 30–1), the Dadaist and later surrealist who specialised in collage. The problem is that it is the surrealist quality of Annabel's sensibility which lies at the root of her alienation from the continuities and linearities of ordinary life. With dissociation at the root of her imagination she is permanently unable to centre and possess herself and hence she is unable to engage with the real. 'The surrealists were not good with women' Carter wrote in 1978 (*SL* 512) and Annabel is an exemplum of the point. She apprehends herself in the manner of the dissociated female bodies that litter surrealist art:

> she had never learned to think of herself as a living actor ... She did not even think of herself as a body but more as a pair of disembodied eyes – when she thought about herself at all, that is. She was eighteen, secretive and withdrawn, since childhood. Her favourite painter was Max Ernst. (*L* 30–1)

Sue Roe has read Annabel's specifically female disablement as the product of her conditioning. Annabel is

> a heroine held captive by the expectations of an earlier generation, of which we catch barely more than a glimpse ... Annabel is the victim of everything that has produced her and thereby outlawed her from herself ... she is, simply, marooned in an unnameable position outside the self ... The *real* criminality of her making is (almost) invisible, and has resulted in a kind of autism: the anorexia of the real. (Roe 1994: 61–4)

Roe connects this thematic point with the surreal formal elements of *Love* when she comments on Annabel's parents' invasion of her life with Lee:

> Annabel's parents make their intrusion on the scene ... This section of the novel is layered up in a series of images which seem to have no clear causal or temporal connection ... 'she quickly interpreted [Lee] into her mythology but if, at first, he was a herbivorous lion, later he became a unicorn' ... Waking in the night, she sometimes sees white birds – for the Surrealists, the ubiquitous symbol of repressed desire. So it goes, one image being stuck up against another, with no process, no development, no flow ...
> Like Freud's hysterics, Annabel has been rendered nearly inarticulate; like Ernst, she collects scraps of her untold story and puts them together to create not images, but contexts. She is in an impossible position: girl and woman; subdued and exposed; painter and model; artist and subject; she sees, but signifies nothing. (Roe: 1994: 75–6)

And she ends up as literally nothing. It is a nothing which Carter diagnoses – through her identification of Annabel with an older tradition of sensibility and with a newer tradition of surrealism – as produced by her inability to engage with reason and a rational definition of herself as a coherent, autonomous being.

When Lee visits Annabel after her suicide attempt in the bathroom he is 'intimidated' by the 'harmonious Palladian mansion' which houses the psychiatric hospital (*L* 68). As he approaches the building he encounters a boy who contrasts the ideals of the age in which the mansion was built with the use to which it is now put:

> A young boy in a long dressing gown and several mufflers who lurked on the porch glared mutinously at Lee as he ascended the wide, gleaming, marble steps to the front door.
>   'This house was built in the Age of Reason but now it has become a Fool's Tower', said the boy. 'Are you familiar with the tarot pack?' (*L* 68)

Lee comes across this boy again later in the story when, the day before the night on which Annabel gasses herself to death, he is in the eighteenth-century landscaped park:

> He collapsed on a bench in the white shadow of the Gothic tower and buried his head in his hands ... Lee ... saw a young boy with wild eyes and floating hair, clearly another mad person who might have been the crazed inhabitant of the Gothic pinnacle which, appropriately enough, served as the backdrop for their balked encounter ...
>   'I see you fled the Fool's Tower, then,' said Lee. (*L* 99–100)

But neither Lee nor Buzz nor, most importantly, Annabel have fled the Fool's Tower. The boy serves as a focal point in the allegory of the dangers of unreason which Carter has been drawing in her presentation of the triangle of Annabel, Lee and Buzz:

> In the sequence of events which now drew the two brothers and the girl down ... to the empty place at the centre of the labyrinth they had built between them, this nameless boy performed the function of the fool in the Elizabethan drama, a reference point outside events but inside another kind of logic, the remorseless logic of unreason where all vision is deranged, all action uncoordinated and all responses beyond prediction. Such logic now dominated Annabel. (*L* 101)

The unreason of the surreal sensibility to which Annabel has been conditioned, which was confirmed and stimulated by the unreason of Lee's sentimentalism and Buzz's manic disconnection from reality, conspires to erase her from reality altogether. In her 'Afterword' to *Love* Carter, as I have noted, says that 'even the women's movement' could not have helped Annabel, so profoundly disabled was she in her lack of a rational conception of herself and of the world. But the women's movement *was* able to help several of the women who had been touched by Lee's chauvinist sentimentalism. And through Rosie, the women's movement has touched even Lee:

> it takes a lot to make a man admit he has been a bastard, even a man so prone to masochistic self-abnegation as Lee. And, at the period of his very worst behaviour, he had no idea of how big a bastard he was being. Nowadays he can hardly bear to think his daughters might meet young men like him; he does not know that one of them already has ... Lee and Rosie ... quarrel a good deal, but he is always grateful to her, in spite of what he says, for bringing him out of his private chamber of horrors, even if sometimes he resents it; Buzzz has made a small fortune out of the very same chamber of horrors, after all. (*L* 119)

The transformative power of the women's movement is thus defined in the 'Afterword' to *Love* by its capacity to bring both women and men out of an irrational chamber of horrors. The high valuation of reason implicit in this definition is something that Carter was to endorse more explicitly in her next novel, *The Infernal Desire Machines of Doctor Hoffman*.

THREE

The Infernal Desire Machines of Doctor Hoffman and The Sadeian Woman

Referring to *The Infernal Desire Machines of Doctor Hoffman* (1972) in a letter to Lorna Sage, Angela Carter spoke of the book's 'dialectic between reason and passion, which it resolves in favour of reason' (Sage 1994a: 34). *Dr Hoffman* has also been described by Susan Rubin Suleiman as 'a postmodernist novel in its preoccupation with possible worlds or ontologies' (Suleiman 1994: 102). What I want to do in the following discussion is to examine the feminism of the book in relation to the issues of both reason and post-modernism.

The narrator and protagonist of *Dr Hoffman* is Desiderio, a name based on the active form of the Italian for 'desire', who tells the story of his life retrospectively. At the outset of the novel, Desiderio, now an old man, tells of when he was a young man in a city that lay under siege. The city is unnamed – Carter spoke of it as 'an inventory of imaginary cities' (Sage 1977: 56) – but it is broadly identifiable as Latin American. The terms of the siege are that the city, whose defence is led by the Minister of Determination, stands for the values of reason and empiricism, while the assaulting powers, commanded by Dr Hoffman, stand for the opposite of these things – what Carter called 'passion'; what sometimes in the book is called 'imagination' and which generally can be described as an active absence of reason. Desiderio tells us:

> I lived in the city when our adversary, the diabolical Dr Hoffman, filled it with mirages in order to drive us all mad. Nothing in the city was what it seemed – nothing at all! Because Dr Hoffman, you see, was waging a massive campaign against human reason itself. (*DH* 11)

The conceit is that Hoffman has built 'gigantic generators' which 'sent out a series of seismic vibrations' to disrupt the conventional 'time and space equation' (*DH* 17) upon which the rational world had been built. The result is that all the empirical, common-sense definitions of the grounds of reality no longer make sense. Desiderio relates how:

> A kind of orgiastic panic seized the city. Those bluff, complaisant avenues and piazzas were suddenly as fertile in metamorphoses as a magic forest. Whether the apparitions were shades of the dead, synthetic reconstructions of the living or in no way replicas of anything we knew, they inhabited the same dimension as the living for Dr Hoffman had enormously extended the limits of this dimension. The very stones were mouths that spoke ...
>
> Cloud palaces erected themselves then silently toppled to reveal for a moment the familiar warehouse beneath them ...
>
> By the end of the first year there was no longer any way of guessing what one would see when one opened one's eyes in the morning. (*DH* 17–19)

The problem was that these apparitions were not insubstantial. They were not mere visual hallucinations but had apparently the substance of reality. It was a 'time', as Desiderio tells us, of 'actualized desire' (*DH* 11). The result of all these modifications of what was conventionally held to be reality was a kind of apocalyptic breakdown of order:

> It seemed each one of us was trapped in some downward-drooping convoluted spiral of unreality from which we could never escape. Many committed suicide.
>
> Trade was at an end ... There was always the smell of dissolution in the air for the public services were utterly disorganized. Typhoid took a heavy toll and there were grim murmurs of cholera or worse. The only form of transport the Minister permitted in the city was the bicycle, since it can only be ridden by that constant effort of will which precludes the imagination ...
>
> Statistics for burglary, arson, robbery with violence and rape rose to astronomical heights. (*DH* 20–21)

Desiderio's boss, the Minister of Determination, was 'quite immune to ... the Hoffman effect' (*DH* 13). He did not suffer from the paradoxically substantial mirages that blighted everyone else's lives. He believed in the existence of objective reality and that this reality could be directly accessed. It wasn't a matter of human beings representing this reality in their minds: they could access it pure. Reality for the Minister was finite and quantifiable, so he sought to make a list of everything in objective reality in order that the apparitions generated by Dr Hoffman, however apparently substantial, could be distinguished and destroyed.

> The Minister had never in all his life felt the slightest quiver of empirical uncertainty ... He believed the criterion of reality was that a thing was determinate and the identity of a thing lay only in the extent to which it resembled itself. He was the most ascetic of logicians but, if he had a fatal flaw, it was his touch of scholasticism. He believed that the city – which he took as a microcosm of the universe – contained a finite set of objects and a finite set of their combinations and therefore a list could be made of all possible distinct forms which were logically viable. These could be counted, organized into a conceptual framework and so form a kind of check list for the verification of all phenomena. (*DH* 22–4)

In his resolute empiricism the Minister sees the human imagination as an undisciplined and even dangerous faculty. And it is the human imagination that Dr Hoffman has unleashed, so that it floats free of empirical anchorage. Diagnosing what Hoffman is doing, the Minister says that 'The Doctor has invented a virus which causes a cancer of the mind, so that the cells of the imagination run wild' (*DH* 22). When he meets the Minister, Dr Hoffman's Ambassador says:

> You murder the imagination in the womb, Minister.
> *Minister:* Somebody must impose restraint. If I am an abortionist, your master is a forger. He has passed off upon us an entire currency of counterfeit phenomena. (*DH* 37)

The distinction between the authentic and the counterfeit is not a distinction recognised by Dr Hoffman. At the end of the first chapter of the novel, the Minister asks Desiderio to go in search of and to assassinate Hoffman. There follow six chapters in which Desiderio relates – in a picaresque type of narrative – his adventures in search of Hoffman. The eighth and final chapter, in which Desiderio succeeds in his mission, is set first in Hoffman's castle and, at last, back in the now normalised city of Desiderio's old age. Desiderio's adventures in search of Hoffman extend and clarify, to Desiderio and to the reader, the nature of and issues of principle raised by Hoffman's subversion of empirical reason.

Hoffman's world-view is one which exemplifies many features
of the postmodern. The idea of the postmodern is a notoriously
slippery thing to define. For Jean-François Lyotard the 'modern'
part of the word refers to the early modern ideas of the eighteenth-
century European Enlightenment. Patricia Waugh sketches
Enlightenment ideology when she speaks of 'Enlightened modernity and its models of reason, justice and autonomous subjectivity
as universal categories' (Waugh 1992: 189). It is the universalising
claim made by the Enlightenment model of reason that Lyotard
criticises. He speaks of the Enlightenment's grand narrative or
metanarrative of reason, and celebrates postmodernism as an
'incredulity toward metanarratives' (Lyotard 1984: xxiv), as a
twentieth-century outlook in which people no longer subscribe to
total and totalising explanations of reality. There are numerous
readings of the term postmodernism which, while they might differ to a greater or lesser degree from Lyotard's definition, tend in
the main to share the assumption that the 'modern' which postmodernism succeeds is the rational–empirical modernity which was
instituted by the Enlightenment and which has shaped and is still
shaping the ideology and institutions of the Western world. Hans
Bertens, summarising varying views of the postmodern, makes the
further point that: 'If there is a common denominator to all these
postmodernisms, it is that of a crisis in representation: a deeply
felt loss of faith in our ability to represent the real, in the widest
sense' (Bertens 1995: 11). The issue of representation and reality
is central to Carter's *Dr Hoffman*. In order to illustrate the ways in
which Hoffman himself stands as something like an arch-
postmodernist, I want first to look at a novel, published just a few
years before *Dr Hoffman*, which lays out a number of key postmodern attitudes to reality and representation.

John Fowles's *The French Lieutenant's Woman* was first published
in 1969. As a work of fiction it seems generically a far cry from *Dr
Hoffman* and its science fiction or magical realist tones. Marguerite
Alexander has observed of *The French Lieutenant's Woman* that:

> Most of the characters are frankly derivative from nineteenth century
> fiction. The hero, Charles Smithson – an upright and honourable man,
> sensitive to conflicts of principle, an archetypal Victorian hero – is a
> gentleman naturalist who has recently become engaged to Ernestina
> Freeman, heiress to a trade fortune; while her social aspirations, iron

will and playful manipulativeness conform to the type of Rosamund Vincy in George Eliot's *Middlemarch*. Charles' feelings are then torn by the rival attractions of Sarah Woodruff, the French lieutenant's woman of the title, an object of both scandal and charitable patronage in Lyme, who recalls the 'forbidden woman' of a number of Victorian novels ... Dialogue, plot development, authorial omniscience ... the manipulation of a large group of characters are all familiar to readers of Victorian fiction. (Alexander 1990: 128)

As well as invoking the manners and conventions of classic Victorian realist fiction *The French Lieutenant's Woman*, a work of the 1960s, also invokes the manners and conventions of historical romance. What gives the book its postmodern aspect is that both these novelistic genres are invoked in order that they may be called in question. Patricia Waugh says that *The French Lieutenant's Woman* is 'metafictional' in that it employs parody self-consciously. She notes that it takes as its '"object" languages the structures of nineteenth century realism and of historical romance', but she goes on to observe that the 'parody of these "languages" functions to defamiliarise such structures by setting up various counter-techniques to undermine the authority of the omniscient author, of the closure of the "final" ending, of the definitive interpretation' (Waugh 1984: 13).

The undermining of the idea of the omniscient author so central to Victorian realist fiction (as, indeed, to conventional historical romance) goes to the heart of *The French Lieutenant's Woman*'s postmodernism. It is in chapter thirteen of *The French Lieutenant's Woman* that Fowles commits his most notorious debunking of the idea of the all-seeing, all-knowing, transcendent author. Chapter twelve has ended with the novelist narrator saying: 'Who is Sarah? Out of what shadows does she come?' (Fowles 1987: 84). Chapter thirteen opens with the novelist confessing bluntly:

I do not know. This story I am telling is all imagination. These characters I create never existed outside my own mind. If I have pretended until now to know my characters' minds and innermost thoughts, it is because I am writing in ... a convention universally accepted at the time of my story: that the novelist stands next to God. But I live in the age of Alain Robbe-Grillet and Roland Barthes. (Fowles 1987: 85)

This interposition on the part of the author in his own story is talked about by commentators on Fowles as a frame-breaking device. It breaks the convention or illusion of realism that the novel has so far been working with. It breaks the illusion that the author is a detached, impartial eye compiling an inventory of things that happened, and substitutes an image of the author as a partial and imperfect maker or manufacturer of the things that are recorded as having happened. As such, Fowles goes on to point out, the novelist is involved in an organic, creative process, the growths and outgrowths of which he or she is not in complete control from the outset. The fiction, in short, takes on a life of its own which qualifies the command that the novelist has over it.

But we are not to think of the actual novelist as someone unproblematically 'real' who can be distinguished from the fiction that is running away with him or her. The principle of fiction-making, of constructedness, affects not only the literal fiction but infects the so-called 'real' self who is making the fiction. This is, moreover, a point that embraces the reader, indeed the whole of humanity, as well as the author of literal fictions. 'I have disgracefully broken the illusion?' Fowles asks rhetorically of his frame-break. His answer is 'No':

> No. My characters still exist, and in a reality no less, or no more, real than the one I have just broken. Fiction is woven into all ... I would have you share my own sense that I do not fully control these creatures of my mind, any more than you control ... your children, colleagues, friends or even yourself.
> But this is preposterous? A character is either 'real' or 'imagined'? If you think that ... I can only smile. You do not even think of your own past as quite real; you dress it up, you gild it or blacken it, censor it, tinker with it ... fictionalize it, in a word, and put it away on a shelf – your book, your romanced autobiography. (Fowles 1987: 86–7)

Fowles's critical intrusion into his story breaks the authority of the God-like author and the convention of the story being real history, replacing these with the authority of the author as merely imagining the story on the same principle as he or she imaginatively adjusts the story of his or her own life. But that new authority, as Brian McHale has observed, has a different ontological status from the old authority of the omniscient author (McHale 1994), because the collapsing of our neat distinction between the 'real' and the imagined or fictional has the effect of relativising reality. Or, to put in another way, it displaces the idea of an objective and transparently accessible reality and replaces it with the idea that all we have are versions of reality – different constructions of reality, different fictions. We have no stable hold on ourselves and no stable hold on a reality outside ourselves. It is not that there is no reality outside us, but that we can never access it pure. We are always interpreting it, just as we interpret ourselves, and in that act of interpretation we partly invent the thing we are representing to ourselves. Interpretations of reality differ from individual to individual and from culture to culture. And no *one* of these interpretations, versions or fictions, can claim priority over the others: they stand relative to each other.

In *Dr Hoffman* the Minister may want to refuse what is, in effect, a relativising of reality that occurs during Hoffman's attacks on the city. But the enemy is not simply outside the city. The imaginative power of the human mind exists inside the minds of the inhabitants of the city: 'if the city was in a state of siege, the enemy was inside the barricades, and lived in the minds of each of us' (*DH* 12). Hoffman lets loose anarchy upon the world of the city by releasing the imaginations, the constitutive powers of mind, of its inhabitants. The repression that let only one version or interpretation of reality dominate is lifted. So that there is no longer a common agreement upon what is real and what is not, just a multiplicity of individual representations of reality which differ according to different frames of reference, different values, different fantasies, anxieties and desires.

In *The French Lieutenant's Woman*, as in much postmodernist writing, the author cannot be relied upon to give a true account of events because the author is as engaged upon contributing to the nature of reality, as involved in manufacturing reality as is the reader or, indeed, any member of the human race. The authority of the author in this postmodern perspective is considerably diminished, compared with that assumed by and traditionally attributed to the authors of classic realist fiction.

To underline this point, Fowles famously offers three different endings to *The French Lieutenant's Woman*. The first occurs about three-quarters of the way through the novel, when Fowles has Charles and his fiancée Ernestina getting it together and looking forward to being married. Sarah, the 'forbidden woman', drops out of the picture. Fowles himself then intrudes to say that this

ending is 'thoroughly traditional' (Fowles 1987: 295); it would be
a conventional one within the terms of Victorian realist fiction.
But Fowles as postmodern author takes the liberty of continuing
the narrative along a different line. The other two endings occur
at the conclusion of the book. In the first, Charles has broken with
Ernestina and union with Sarah is fulfilled. In the second, Charles
has likewise broken with Ernestina but he and Sarah do not end
up together. Fowles is not as 'postmodernist' as some novelists. He
doesn't refuse an ending to his story altogether. He maintains
linearity in the development of his narrative, as the conventions of
realist fiction which he has been following would demand. But the
different endings ironise or parody the linearity they are concluding. Fowles then tries to fend off the possibility that the last ending
of the sequence might seem to be the 'real' ending by intruding,
in chapter fifty-five, to say that he is aware that such is the un-
avoidable tyranny of our linear, sequential way of thinking: the
only way of qualifying that tyranny is to show that he is self-
consciously aware of it. With this in mind we should, in theory,
not take the ending that is the last given as having precedence
over the others. It is just one of three fictional devices.

The recognition that, as Fowles puts it, fiction is woven into
all, dismisses the old idea of the absolute, objective, omniscient
author. And that dismissal parallels the disappearance of God in
much twentieth-century and particularly postmodernist thought.
Fowles takes up the matter of God through, for example, the epigraph to his final chapter, which is from Martin Gardiner's *The
Ambidextrous Universe* (1967) in which we hear that 'Evolution is
simply the process by which chance ... co-operates with natural
law to create living forms better and better adapted to survive'
(Fowles 1987: 394). This view that a directing principle behind
evolution is merely chance, the view that there is no directing
power such as God, contrasts with, say, Tennyson's reading of
evolutionary process in the middle of the nineteenth century. In *In
Memoriam*, first published in 1850, Tennyson showed himself
severely discomforted by the evolutionary perspectives which a
number of people were advancing at the time and which were
preparing the ground for Charles Darwin's great 1859 work *On
the Origin of Species by Means of Natural Selection*. Section 55 of
the poem, for instance, which Fowles uses as an epigraph to

chapter twenty of *The French Lieutenant's Woman*, has Tennyson questioning the nature of a 'Nature' that seems to care not for the individual but only for the species:

> Are God and Nature then at strife,
> That Nature Lends such evil dreams?
> So careful of the type [species] she seems,
> So careless of the single life.
>
> (LV.5–8; Day 1991: 165)

Tennyson moves on in the next section of the poem from this perception that the individual is unimportant to the realisation – born of an understanding of what fossil records can tell us about past life on earth – that Nature eradicates entire species. This realisation is part of Tennyson's appalled confrontation in *In Memoriam* not only with the idea that humankind has evolved out of the animal world but also with the idea that as a species humankind may be subject to exactly the same laws of extinction as have governed the fates of other species:

> 'So careful of the type?' but no.
> From scarpèd cliff and quarried stone
> She [Nature] cries, 'A thousand types are gone:
> I care for nothing, all shall go.'
>
> (LVI.1–4; Day 1991: 165)

Tennyson saves the day not by giving up belief in the idea of evolution but by developing a notion of evolution as something directed by and forming part of God's overall providential plan for the universe: 'all, as in some piece of art,/ Is toil cooperant to an end' (CXXVIII.23–4; Day 1991: 218). In contrast with this teleological conception of evolution, the dominant notion of evolution in the second half of the twentieth century dispenses with God altogether; evolution is seen, as a reviewer for the *Times Higher Education Supplement* of 22 March 1996 put it, as 'simply a genetic lottery – a purely random walk through the realm of all possibilities, devoid of any trend or directionality' (p. 30). This last is the same kind of observation as that made by Martin Gardiner when he speaks of chance as a motivating principle of evolution. Towards the end of his last chapter, Fowles himself makes a direct connection between such a way of thinking about evolution and postmodernist fictional practice. He comments on the third ending to his story, which he has just given, and compares it with the two endings he had given previously. He says to the reader: 'what you must not think is that this is a less plausible ending to their story' (Fowles 1987: 398). Not less plausible, not more plausible. Just plausible. As are the other endings. And so could be a large number of other endings which Fowles does not give (presumably on the principle that once you've exploded the idea of the single authoritative ending, it really doesn't matter whether you have three endings or thirty-three). Fowles's point is that the author does not have a God-like status any more than God can be said to hold ultimate authority over evolutionary process. Just as evolution and the emergence of different species are subject to a principle of accident and chance – just as some branches of the organism grow and then die out, some continue and mutate, and some never, as it were, even get started – so the versions of reality that human beings come up with are randomly and accidentally directed, and no single version can claim to be the summit or crowning achievement of human versions of reality. There are multiple possibilities in evolution and these parallel the multiple possibilities of fiction making: a point which Fowles's postmodern strategies in *The French Lieutenant's Woman* emphasise. Having just made his comment on the equal plausibility of the finally given ending to his story Fowles goes on to say, explicitly invoking his chapter epigraph on evolution from Martin Gardiner,

> I have returned ... to my original principle: that there is no intervening god beyond whatever can be seen, in that way, in the first epigraph to this chapter; thus only life as we have, within our hazard-given abilities, made it ourselves. (Fowles 1987: 398)

Fowles has his protagonist Charles accepting a kind of postmodern plurality of selves and worlds (or construction of selves and worlds) in the closing passage of the book:

> he has at last found an atom of faith in himself, a true uniqueness, on which to build; has already begun ... to realize that life, however advantageously Sarah may in some ways seem to fit the role of Sphinx, is not a symbol, is not one riddle and one failure to guess it, is not to inhabit one face alone or to be given up after one losing throw of the dice. (Fowles 1987: 399)

Charles here is understood to have internalised lessons taught him by Sarah. Sarah explicitly fictionalised her own life. She presented herself as a fallen woman when, in fact, she wasn't. This may seem odd, but it can be seen as a kind of protest against the repressive moral conditions of her age. It sets her apart from her age. At the end of the novel she is seen in the company of what the book sees as the proto-twentieth-century circle that gathered around Dante Gabriel Rossetti, an avant-garde circle which, the book implies, set no conventional store by the classification 'fallen woman'. The scene is a dramatisation of the way the world changed from the Victorian era to the twentieth century. It also illustrates how the values of the two are not essential but constructions. Sarah constructs herself as a proto-twentieth-century person and stands at the threshold of an age when her version of reality will be no longer the property of a minority but the norm of the majority.

John Fowles offers his world of relativised truths as preferable to an interpretation of the world which insists on the existence of absolute Truth. For he sees in a realm of truths the possibility of an existential freedom for individual human beings. Human beings can *choose* to live in different worlds, different value-systems. Change is possible because any one interpretation of reality is not essential or founded in the Absolute but has been *made* by human beings who can then choose to change. This, for Fowles, is true existential freedom. And since there is no one Truth, no single divine impulse behind human fictions, literary or larger, the choices are potentially infinite: any number of worlds can, in theory, be made. Erasing God, like erasing the omniscient author, sets people free to be self-determining, responsible and genuinely creative. Fowles writes on these matters in a way that operates simultaneously at the level of metaphysics, aesthetic theory and biology:

> We know a world is an organism, not a machine. We also know that a genuinely created world must be independent of its creator; a planned world (a world that fully reveals its planning) is a dead world. It is only when our characters and events begin to disobey us that they begin to live ... There is only one good definition of God: the freedom that allows other freedoms to exist. And I must conform to that definition ...
>
> The novelist is still a god, since he creates ... what has changed is that we are no longer the gods of the Victorian image, omniscient and decreeing; but in the new theological image, with freedom our first

principle, not authority … Fiction is woven into all, as a Greek observed some two and a half thousand years ago. I find this new reality (or unreality) more valid. (Fowles 1987: 86–7)

In *Dr Hoffman* it is unreality that Desiderio describes as overwhelming the inhabitants of the city once Hoffman starts his siege; an unreality that the Minister tries to distinguish from reality but which Hoffman refuses to allow to be so distinguished. Desiderio learns many of the details of Hoffman's view of the world from the proprietor of a peep-show whom he encounters in his travels in search of the Doctor. The proprietor is an old tutor of Hoffman's and he still acts as a mouthpiece for Hoffman's ideas. He keeps changing the pictures that he exhibits in his show. The principle underlying the changes he makes is random: the peep-show proprietor is himself blind and has never seen the pictures. The peep-show and the travelling fair that, in chapter four, it is displayed in, are metaphors for the world once Hoffman has started the war. It is a world, paralleling that endorsed by Fowles in *The French Lieutenant's Woman*, which is governed by no single, transcendent authority and which does not proceed in a progressive line. In fact, it is not a world, but a series of worlds. Desiderio describes the metaphoric fair and recounts the peep-show proprietor's metaphoric reflections as follows:

> I often watched the roundabouts circulate upon their static journeys. 'Nothing,' said the peep-show proprietor, 'is ever completed; it only changes.' As he pleased, he altered the displays he had never seen, murmuring: 'No hidden unity.' … The fairground was a moving toyshop, an ambulant raree-show coming to life in convulsive fits and starts whenever the procession stopped, regulated only by the implicit awareness of a lack of rules. (*DH* 99)

The lack of rules in peep-show and fair means that they run according to a dynamic that stands contrary to the Minister's belief in rules for distinguishing reality from unreality. The distinction is not meaningful to Hoffman, because the human imagination is so involved in constituting reality that it is invalid to separate the authentically real from the constructed. In Hoffman's world-view we are inside the postmodern 'awareness', as Hans Bertens puts it, 'that representations create rather than reflect reality' (Bertens 1995: 11). Through the peep-show proprietor, Desiderio learns of the ideas of another of Hoffman's teachers, Mendoza. The peep-show proprietor reports that:

> Mendoza ... claimed that if a thing were sufficiently artificial, it became absolutely equivalent to the genuine ... Hoffman refined Mendoza's initially crude hypotheses of fissile time and synthetic authenticity and wove them together to form another mode of consciousness altogether. (*DH* 102–3)

This dissolving of boundaries between the synthetic and the authentic aligns Hoffman's world-view with postmodern ideas about representation and reality. For one of his main principles, as summarised by Desiderio in the fourth chapter, is that 'everything it is possible to imagine can also exist' (*DH* 97). The principle is elaborated by Hoffman himself in the last chapter of the book, when he says to Desiderio: 'I can make you perceive ideas with your senses because I do not acknowledge any essential difference in the phenomenological bases of the two modes of thought' (*DH* 206). Hoffman's vision of the possibility of actualising any of the imagination's imaginings threatens Desiderio's city, where empirical reality is usurped by the manifold, unstable and ever-changing concretisations of fantasy. And, just as in the peep-show and travelling fair, there is no single authority directing these manifestations in the city along a single line. Hoffman lets the peep-show proprietor keep a set of 'magic samples' (*DH* 105): these are something like paradigms of everything that may exist in the universe, everything mental or corporeal, except that in Hoffman's universe, of course, the 'or' has no meaning since all mental things can be actualised. Desiderio says that he 'came to the conclusion' that the samples, which included peep-show slides together with wax models and photographs (*DH* 107), 'did indeed represent everything it was possible to believe' (*DH* 108). In the peep-show proprietor's words, the samples he keeps in his sack are the

> symbolic constituents of representations of the basic constituents of the universe ...
> The symbols serve as patterns and templates from which physical objects and real events may be evolved by the process he calls 'effective evolving'. I go about the world like Santa with a sack and nobody knows it is filled up with changes. (*DH* 95–6)

The samples are the source of energy which enables the manifold and changing substantial mirages, the concretisations of fantasies, to appear in the city. And the absence of any coherence in the appearance of those substantial mirages is captured when Desiderio describes the peep-show proprietor turning up a 'handful of magic samples in the air' and letting them fall randomly. The proprietor believes that

> the haphazard patterns they made as they fell at the blind dictation of chance were echoed in the flesh in the beleaguered city which, he informed me with irritation, was still managing to hold out. (*DH* 105)

The world according to the peep-show proprietor is – not unlike the world of chance rather than of single, authoritative direction in *The French Lieutenant's Woman* – subject only to the principles of infinity, randomness and change. Desiderio notes the peep-show proprietor's observations that '"Things cannot be exhausted"; or "In the imagination, nothing is past, nothing can be forgotten". Or: "Change is the only valid response to phenomena"' (*DH* 104). Fowles, as I have noted, sees the idea of the endlessness and openness of creativity, natural or human, as a liberating idea. In a comparable vein, Hoffman and his aide the peep-show proprietor see what has been unleashed on the city as a stage in the liberation of humanity. The proprietor looks forward to when the Doctor will bring about a state of 'Nebulous Time', which will be 'a period of absolute mutability' (*DH* 99). As he describes this stage to Desiderio, the proprietor sounds like a postmodernist theorist going on about the depthlessness of the signs, the depthlessness of the representations that constitute the world and which make untenable any idea of autonomous, objective reality:

> you must never forget that the Doctor's philosophy is not so much transcendental as incidental. It utilizes all the incidents that ripple the depthless surfaces of, you understand, the sensual world ... we will live on as many layers of consciousness as we can, all at the same time. After the Doctor liberates us, that is. (*DH* 99–100)

The penultimate chapter of *Dr Hoffman* represents the achieved state of 'Nebulous Time'; I will have more to say on this a little later. For the moment, I need to sketch in some further details on Desiderio's place in the antagonism between the Minister and

Hoffman. Desiderio is not an unreliable narrating protagonist. Carter is in sympathy with him, and he represents and articulates a position which is close to, though perhaps not exactly identical with, Carter's own. First of all, unlike the Minister, Desiderio does suffer from the Hoffman effect. Yet at the same time he retains a rational sense of things:

> if the city was in a state of siege, the enemy was inside the barricades, and lived in the minds of each of us.
> But I survived it because I knew that some things were necessarily impossible. I did not believe it when I saw the ghost of my dead mother clutching her rosary and whimpering into the folds of the winding sheet issued her by the convent where she died attempting to atone for her sins. (*DH* 12)

Nor were Desiderio and the Minister entirely alone in their resistance to the Hoffman effect, although the resisters continually felt the magnetic power of that effect:

> we – that is, those of us who retained some notion of what was real and what was not – felt the vertigo of those teetering on the edge of a magic precipice. (*DH* 21)

Desiderio's empirical scepticism does not leave him. It is apparent again in a simultaneously trivial and important observation that he makes in the final chapter of the book, while at supper with Hoffman in Hoffman's castle: 'ironically enough, one could not judge the Prospero effect in his own castle for he could not alter the constituents of the aromatic coffee which we sipped by so much as an iota' (*DH* 200). Desiderio's empiricism is the basis for his allegiance to the Minister, even though he is aware of the Minister's reductionism and his 'touch of scholasticism' (*DH* 23–4). For Desiderio, the Minister's extreme scepticism and empiricism meant that his work 'consisted essentially in setting a limit to thought' (*DH* 22). If such setting of limits seems limited to Desiderio, then he is equally suspicious of the fascistic form of social control that seems to go along with limit-setting. Of the Minister's police, for example, Desiderio says:

> I was suspicious of the Determination Police for their ankle-length, truculently belted coats of black leather, their low-crowned, wide-brimmed fedoras and their altogether too highly polished boots woke

in me an uncomfortable progression of associations. They looked as if they had been recruited wholesale from a Jewish nightmare. (*DH* 22)

It is partly because of his own susceptibility to the Hoffman effect that Desiderio is aware of the limitations in the Minister's view of reality; the inadequacy of his view of the human imagination. This susceptibility is explored in the novel through the adventures Desiderio undertakes in his search for Hoffman, and simultaneously through Desiderio's obsession with Albertina, Hoffman's daughter. In the first chapter of the novel, while he was still living in the city under siege, Desiderio was visited by a manifestation which he could not dismiss as he dismissed that of his mother:

> I would be visited by a young woman in a négligé made of a fabric the colour and texture of the petals of poppies which clung about her but did not conceal her quite transparent flesh, so that the exquisite filigree of her skeleton was revealed quite clearly. Where her heart should have been there flickered a knot of flames like ribbons and she shimmered a little ...
> She stayed beside me until I slept, waveringly, brilliantly, hooded in diaphanous scarlet, and occasionally she left an imperative written in lipstick on my dusty windowpane. BE AMOROUS! she exhorted one night. (*DH* 25–6)

This manifestation is succeeded by other mysterious appearances – in a dream of a black swan and in the person of Hoffman's ambassador – of a figure associated with the name Albertina. Desiderio becomes convinced that an actual woman of that name lies behind his premonitions of her. This, of course, turns out to be the case, even though Albertina appears to him in several more guises – as the manservant of the Sadeian Count in chapter six, or as the Madame of a brothel which Desiderio and the Count visit in the same chapter – before at last appearing to him as she actually is. Albertina is a type of the male fantasy of an ideal female 'other': mysterious and alluring. When she speaks to Desiderio in her real self in the final chapter she points out that 'all the time you have known me, I've been maintained in my various appearances only by the power of your desire' (*DH* 204). In chapter six, after Albertina as the brothel Madame has suddenly dissolved into the air, Desiderio himself observes that it was 'As if, all the time she kissed me, she had been only a ghost born of nothing but my longing – the first ghost who had deceived me in all those years of ghostly visitants!' (*DH* 140). For all his conviction that 'some things were necessarily impossible' (*DH* 12), Desiderio's imagination helped generate, under the Hoffman effect, a variety of manifestations of his deepest or unconscious desires. In the same way, many of the happenings in the chaotic worlds he wanders through after having left the city were generated by his own imaginative reveries or unconscious longings; longings which, under the Hoffman effect, were able to actualise themselves. In the penultimate chapter of the book, 'Lost in nebulous time', Desiderio and Albertina find themselves in the midst of a society of centaurs. The male centaurs rape Albertina and Desiderio becomes glimmeringly aware of his own responsibility for this event:

> At the back of my mind flickered a teasing image, that of a young girl trampled by horses. I could not remember when or where I had seen it, such a horrible thing; but it was the most graphic and haunting of memories and a voice in my mind, the cracked, hoarse, drunken voice of the dead peep-show proprietor, told me that I was somehow, all unknowing, the instigator of this horror. (*DH* 179–80)

The point is underlined a little later by Albertina herself:

> she was convinced that even though every male in the village had obtained carnal knowledge of her, the beasts were still only emanations of her own desires, dredged up and objectively reified from the dark abysses of the unconscious. And she told me that, according to her father's theory, all the subjects and objects we had encountered in the loose grammar of Nebulous Time were derived from a similar source – my desires; or hers. (*DH* 186)

In the end, however, Desiderio doesn't go along with the idea that releasing the unconscious, enabling the imagination to actualise its longings and fantasies, is really some kind of liberation, a 'day of independence' which is to be celebrated. He goes against Hoffman and his daughter. To understand why is to touch the feminist position Carter is coming from in her portrayal of the conflict between reason, on one hand, and unreason, on the other. Time and again, in the chaos that has been let loose by Hoffman and his principle of actualised desire, there is not only promiscuous criminality, grotesquerie and violence, but specifically there is uncontrolled violence, spiritual and physical, against the female.

Rape statistics increase in the city once Hoffman has started his siege. The peep-show proprietor's images – randomly chosen because he is blind – keep turning up spectacles of abused women. We hear that the women of the River People in chapter three wore thick face-paint and were taught to move in a manner that dehumanised them: 'I found that all the women moved in this same, stereotyped way, like benign automata, so what with that and their musical box speech, it was quite possible to feel they were not fully human' (*DH* 73). Chapter five, 'The erotic traveller', introduces us to the Count, who is a vampiric, sadistic exploiter and murderer. His perverse sexuality is directed particularly against women. He has passed beyond ideas of good and evil: 'since there is no God, well, there is no damnation, either' (*DH* 124). He takes his pleasure in a brothel where the objects of his masculine desire have been transfigured by that desire. Desiderio relates that:

> There were, perhaps, a dozen girls in the cages in the reception room … Each was as circumscribed as a figure in rhetoric and you could not imagine they had names, for they had been reduced by the rigorous discipline of their vocation to the undifferentiated essence of the idea of the female. This ideational femaleness took amazingly different shapes though its nature was not that of Woman; when I examined them more closely, I saw that none of them were any longer, or might never have been, woman. All, without exception, passed beyond or did not enter the realm of simple humanity. They were sinister, abominable, inverted mutations, part clockwork, part vegetable and part brute. (*DH* 132)

As if to underline the point that oppression of women is not merely a white European perversion, the women of the African people that Desiderio meets in the sixth chapter all bear the marks of physical mutilation. The male chief of the tribe proudly points out that 'I and my surgeons take the precaution of brutally excising the clitoris of every girl child born to the tribe as soon as she reaches puberty … So our women folk are entirely cold and respond only to cruelty and abuse' (*DH* 160–1). The female centaurs of the penultimate chapter are part of a culture whose mythology and beliefs – in Carter's parody of Christianity – demean and degrade the female gender.

What Carter is dramatising in the various episodes of *Dr Hoffman* is the idea that the imagination, operating outside the pale and the restraint of reason, is capable of imagining unspeakable things. Ricarda Schmidt, using a specifically psychoanalytic frame of reference, has commented on this dimension of the novel. She reads the 'war between the Minister and Dr Hoffman' as 'the war between super-ego and id' (Schmidt 1990: 56–7) and observes that Hoffman's liberation of the unconscious 'would not simply entail freedom and happiness for everybody. Nor is desublimation synonymous with moral goodness. Unrepressed desire may just as well be destructive, cruel, repressive for others' (Schmidt 1990: 58). If everything that the imagination conjured were actualised, some of the results would be appalling. To see the world as a postmodernist – to see everything as a matter of representation and simultaneously to celebrate the legitimacy of all representations or imaginings – is to see the world as Hoffman sees it. And that world may be thrilling but more importantly it may also be a terrifying place to live. There may be an ominously troubling dimension to postmodern perspectives on the world. Seeing human interpretations or constructions of reality as having no essential nature, no objective ground – seeing them as *merely* interpretations or constructions, none having a special authority – can lead to a relativist nightmare, in which the meaninglessness of everything, even the most local act of love or comradeship, of charity or social aid, is revealed. M. H. Abrams has written that:

> An undertaking in some postmodernist writings is to subvert the foundations of our accepted modes of thought and experience so as to reveal the 'meaninglessness' of existence and the underlying 'abyss', or 'void', or 'nothingness' on which any supposed security is conceived to be precariously suspended. (Abrams 1993: 120)

Now it would certainly be possible to see this as a summary of postmodern trends by an old traditionalist. But one doesn't have to be an old traditionalist to be disconcerted by some extreme postmodernist positions. It would, for example, be disconcerting to think that the arguments of a racist have as much authority as those of an anti-racist. One might as well say that the Nazis were as 'right' as their opponents: in the end the only difference was in their material resources, or whatever. One doesn't have to be an old traditionalist to be disconcerted at the thought of having to think such things. In the end, the problem posed by postmodern relativism, as numerous commentators have pointed out, is a political one. It is disconcerting, for instance, to read the relativist views of the postmodern philosopher of science Paul Feyerabend. In the following passage from his 1987 book *Farewell to Reason*, Feyerabend is talking about good and evil:

> With this remark I come to a point which has enraged many readers and disappointed many friends – my refusal to condemn even an extreme fascism and my suggestion that it should be allowed to survive. Now one thing should have been clear: fascism is not my cup of tea ... *That* is not the problem. The problem is the *relevance* of my attitude: is it an inclination which I follow and welcome in others; or has it an 'objective core' that would enable me to combat fascism not just because *it does not please me*, but because *it is inherently evil*? And my answer is: we have an inclination – nothing more. The inclination, like every other inclination, is surrounded by lots of hot air and entire philosophical systems have been built on it. Some of these systems speak of objective qualities and of objective duties to maintain them. But my question is not how we speak but what content can be given to our verbiage. And all I can find when trying to identify some content are different systems asserting different sets of values with nothing but our inclination to decide between them ... Now if inclination opposes inclination then in the end the stronger inclination wins. (Feyerabend 1987: 309)

One has to ask here, first of all, whether it's even an imaginable bathos to say 'fascism is not my cup of tea'. One wants something better grounded than an idea of different inclinations on which to base one's ideas of different political systems. The abyss of mere inclination and mere strength seems to lie that way, measured not in metaphysical but in humanitarian terms.

Let me take a few examples of writers who have commented on the problems of postmodernism. In 1989 Sabina Lovibond made a number of points about the relationship between Enlightenment values, postmodernism and, specifically, feminism. She observed that postmodernism's dismissal of enlightened modernity's ideals of reason, emancipation and equality conspires to deprive feminism of some of its fundamental principles. Identifying Nietzsche as the precursor of much postmodern thought, she spoke of a postmodernism which 'is informed by an irrationalism whose historical origin lies in reactionary distaste for modernist social movements' (Lovibond 1989: 19):

'Feminism' ... occurs in Nietzsche's writing not only as the name of a contemporary political movement ... but also as a shorthand term for the mental impotence implicit (or so he believes) in the bondage of thought to regulative ideals such as truth, reality and goodness ... I wish to suggest that we take seriously Nietzsche's own understanding of his work as a contribution to the overcoming of 'feminism'; and that we maintain, as feminists, a suitably critical attitude to the reappearance in contemporary philosophy of one of Nietzsche's central themes – that of the supersession of 'modernity' by a *harder*, less wimpish form of subjectivity ... [M]y suggestion is that in reading postmodernist theory we should be on the watch for signs of indulgence in a certain collective *fantasy* of masculine agency or identity. Turning upon the Nietzscheans their own preferred genealogical method, we might ask: *who* thinks it is so humiliating to be caught out in an attitude of ... longing for a world of human subjects sufficiently 'centred' to speak to and understand one another? (Lovibond 1989: 18–19)

Lovibond regards the postmodern view that 'justification ... is always local and context-relative' (Lovibond 1989: 8) as inherently masculinist and reactionary *and* as capable of engendering a 'terrible pessimism' (Lovibond 1989: 28). It is inimical, she says, to the feminist enterprise in general:

I suggest ... that feminists should continue to think of their efforts as directed not simply towards various local political programmes, but ultimately towards a global one – the abolition of the sex class system ... This programme is 'global' not just in the sense that it addresses itself to every corner of the planet, but also in the sense that its aims eventually converge with those of all other egalitarian or liberationist movements. (It would be arbitrary to work for *sexual* equality unless one believed that human society was disfigured by inequality *as such*.)

If this is a convincing overall characterisation of feminism, it follows that the movement should persist in seeing itself as a component or offshoot of Enlightenment modernism, rather than as one more 'exciting' feature (or cluster of features) in a postmodern social landscape. (Lovibond 1989: 28)

Lovibond's political opposition to postmodernism is paralleled by Terry Eagleton, who questions postmodernism's dissolving of the distinction between reality and representation:

The productivist aesthetics of the early twentieth century avant garde spurned the notion of artistic 'representation' for an art which would be less 'reflection' than material intervention and organizing forces. The aesthetics of postmodernism is a dark parody of such anti-representationalism: if art no longer reflects it is not because it seeks to change the world rather than mimic it, but because there is in truth nothing there to be reflected, no reality which is not itself already image, spectacle, simulacrum, gratuitous fiction. (Eagleton 1985: 62)

Eagleton's questioning turns into mocking attack as he summarises the complicity between postmodern (poststructuralist) relativism and late-twentieth-century capitalism:

In his *The Postmodern Condition*, Lyotard calls attention to capitalism's 'massive subordination of cognitive statements to the finality of the best possible performance'. 'The games of scientific language', he writes, 'become the games of the rich, in which whoever is wealthiest has the best chance of being right'. It is not difficult, then, to see a relationship between the philosophy of J. L. Austin and IBM, or between the various neo-Nietzscheanisms of a post-structuralist epoch and Standard Oil. It is not surprising that classical models of truth and cognition are increasingly out of favour in a society where what matters is whether you deliver the commercial or rhetorical goods. Whether among discourse theorists or the Institute of Directors, the goal is no longer truth but performativity, not reason but power. The Confederation of British Industry are in this sense spontaneous post-structuralists to a man, utterly disenchanted (did they but know it) with epistemological realism and the correspondence theory of truth. (Eagleton 1985: 62–3)

A critic such as Patricia Waugh again takes a politically alert line in her resistance to an extreme postmodernism. Waugh sees, first of all, how useful postmodern questioning of repressive patriarchal discourse has been. That discourse is not, of course, God-given or objectively founded. It is a human – specifically masculine – construction. As such it can be subverted. But the feminist theory that wants so to subvert patriarchal discourse itself stands liable to subversion if its grounds are as precarious as the discourse it is subverting. If it is a matter merely of different inclinations, then there is nothing to choose at the level of content between sexism and non-sexism. Waugh argues for an Enlightenment, rationalist ground to feminist thinking that can't readily be subverted. In making this argument she has to refuse going the whole way with postmodernism:

at this point in my argument, I will have to declare my own situatedness and argue that if feminism can learn from Postmodernism it has finally to resist the logic of its arguments or at least to attempt to combine them with a modified adherence to an epistemological anchorage in the discourses of Enlightened modernity. Even if feminists have come to recognize in their own articulations some of the radical perspectivism and thoroughgoing epistemological doubt of the postmodern, feminism cannot sustain itself as an emancipatory movement unless it acknowledges its foundation in the discourses of modernity. It seems possible to me, to draw on the aesthetics of Postmodernism as strategies for narrative disruption of traditional stories and construction of new identity scripts, without embracing its more extreme nihilistic or pragmatist implications. (Waugh 1992: 189–90)

It is the political and hence the human implications of the view that truth is just a matter of interpretive consensus – local to a particular interpretive community, without any larger ground of justification – that distresses these commentators. It is not humiliating to long for an egalitarian world of human subjects sufficiently 'centred' to speak to and understand one another. It is not humiliating to oppose 'performativity' as the sole criterion of success. The *human* implications of an extreme pluralist or relativist way of thinking emphasise the negative possibilities of an extreme postmodernist outlook. And it is the human implication of Hoffman's postmodern chaos of multiple worlds – the River People, the Africans, the Count, the centaurs and so on – that causes Carter and her protagonist Desiderio to turn against the liberation that Hoffman apparently offers.

It is humanity that Desiderio thinks of when he finally kills both Hoffman *and* his daughter Albertina. Elisabeth Bronfen takes one kind of feminist line when she argues that Desiderio kills Albertina at the end because she has finally appeared as she authentically is and that as such she fails to measure up to his specifically masculine fantasies of her:

The only solution for Desiderio ... who prefers the woman fashioned as an image of his desire to any actuality which may cause the strife of disappointment or contradiction, is then to actualise her imaginary existence by making her irrevocably absent. (Bronfen 1992: 423)

But without denying that Desiderio has fantasy images of Albertina which are contradicted by her actual presence, it remains possible to say that he kills her for other, less politically incorrect, reasons. One can say, first of all, that Desiderio kills Albertina quite simply because, in her authentic self, she is on her father's side: a side that Desiderio concludes is too fraught with disturbing excess to be contemplated. The excess is not only a matter of licensed mutilation and destruction. Albertina endorses, for example, her father's postmodern disregard for facts of any order. Desiderio is puzzled by certain pictures in Hoffman's castle:

> When I read the titles engraved on metal plaques at the bottom of each frame, I saw they depicted such scenes as 'Leon Trotsky Composing the Eroica Symphony' ... Van Gogh was shown writing 'Wuthering Heights' in the parlour of Haworth Parsonage, with bandaged ear, all complete. I was especially struck by a gigantic canvas of Milton blindly executing divine frescos upon the walls of the Sistine Chapel. Seeing my bewilderment, Albertina said smiling: 'When my father rewrites the history books, these are some of the things that everyone will suddenly perceive to have always been true.' (*DH* 198)

Albertina would also have included the Count in her father's war against reason: 'I would have taken him to my father's castle if I could, to enlist him in our campaign for he was a man of great power though he was sometimes a little ludicrous because the real world fell so far short of his desires' (*DH* 167). But for all her and her father's talk of the liberation of humanity, the Count was the ultimate anti-social agent, an utter egoist whose sole aim was to chain and bind others to the desires by which he was himself entrapped. 'It was impossible to converse with him', Desiderio relates,

> for he had no interest in anyone but himself and he offered his companion only a series of monologues of varying lengths, which ... always ... remained true to his infernal egoism. I never heard another man use the word 'I', so often. (*DH* 124)

In their own ways, Hoffman and Albertina are extreme egoists, and what they expect of Desiderio, in asking him to join them, is a comparable egoism, a comparable desire to make the world in his own image. Postmodernism, because of its emphasis on the cultural construction of identity, is not normally seen as a movement which endorses an ideology of individualism. Nor can it be said – to the extent that Hoffman and Albertina display postmodern traits – that *Doctor Hoffman* as a whole identifies postmodernism with individualism. What the novel does do is to see that the relativisation of human values and codes may sanction an egoism by which any one person's position – since it, like a culture in general, stands merely relative to the positions of others – may be developed beyond what is socially constructive, because there are no onto-logical checks on self-interest. Hoffman and Albertina both mani-fest characteristics of unrestrained selfishness. Desiderio tells us that he reacted against Albertina's blind presumption that he, too, would want to join her in her proprietorial egoism:

> So the princess was taking it for granted that I was interested in her patrimonial apple blossom, was she? What presumption! Perhaps she should not have told me so plainly, in her ownership tone of voice, that all this was hers, the castle, the orchards, the mountains, the earth, the sky, all that lay between them. I don't know. All I know is, I could not transcend myself sufficiently to inherit the universe. (*DH* 197)

But that was precisely what Hoffman wished to inherit. He had wanted to control and direct the anarchy he had unleashed on the city. But the 'magic samples' that he entrusted into the care of the peep-show proprietor, those paradigms of everything that may exist in the universe, were lost in a landslide that is described at the end of the fourth chapter. It was after the loss of the samples that true chaos descended. As Albertina tells Desiderio in the 'Nebulous time' chapter:

> 'Because all this country exists only in Nebulous Time, I haven't the least idea what might happen,' she said, 'Now ... his sets of samples are gone, my father cannot structure anything until he makes new models. And desires must take whatever form they please, for the time being.' (*DH* 169)

The infinity of imagined or desired worlds, the true postmodern nightmare, was let loose by Hoffman even though behind that nightmare lay his original monomaniacal drive to control and direct fantasy. It is because of this paradoxical drive to direct the un-leashed imagination that Desiderio calls Hoffman 'a hypocrite' (*DH* 208). Hoffman sought to cage and manipulate the energies of de-sire, not really to liberate them. In this respect his motives seem indistinguishable from the Minister and his Determination Police. Hoffman was a totalitarian whose ambitions produced a nightmare born of a freedom that his totalitarianism had not originally en-visaged. Lorna Sage very effectively sums up Hoffman's nature when she writes that 'he is the great patriarchal Forbidder turned Permitter' (Sage 1994a: 34).

So Desiderio kills him and his accomplice child Albertina: 'I might not want the Minister's world but I did not want the Doctor's world either' (*DH* 207). In destroying Hoffman Desiderio acted against egoism and relativism. He acted, as he himself puts it, 'for the common good' (*DH* 207): the common good being defined by a rational refusal selfishly to abandon the self to the imagination's whims, since the imagination contains potencies that can be utterly destructive of other human beings. And, as Carter points out throughout the novel, in the state of universal abandon it is most frequently the female that suffers the severest depredations. Her protagonist, Desiderio, chooses reason: 'Reason was stamped into me as if it were a chromosome, even if I loved the high priestess of passion' (*DH* 195). He doesn't accept the Minister's reductionism. He knows that desires and the imagination's longings will not, can not, be stopped. But he knows that they need restraining. Through Desiderio's scepticism about the Hoffman effect – his knowledge, for example, that it *isn't* his mother that he sees – the novel illustrates the fact that desire or the imagination can exceed what is possible, can exceed what is objectifiable. Yet while that much may be true, the novel simultaneously explores – in its illustrative episodes of exploitation and violence – the fact that desire or the imagination *can* be objectified in many ways that are individually and socially dangerous and unacceptable. So the novel concerns itself with the need for the rational restraint of desire, with the need to draw limits on what people objectify of their fantasies or desires. In that it is about that, it is about doing the right thing. But it also registers the way that doing the right thing does not, can not, exorcise desire, and it presents the desire that has been limited as continuing to haunt and frustrate the mind because though it has been banned, it cannot be exorcised. Hence Desiderio remains, in his old age, teased and frustrated by his mind's image of Albertina. The last line of the novel is 'Unbidden, she comes' (*DH* 221).

Susan Rubin Suleiman, who provides a valuable commentary on Carter's allusions in *Dr Hoffman* to various examples of surrealist art, finds the ending of the novel 'hopelessly compromised by [Desiderio's] regret at killing the Doctor's daughter' (Suleiman 1994: 107). But it is not necessary to see the ending like this. Such a view seems, to a degree, still caught in the romantic idea that restraint of the imagination can only ever be a bad thing. As if the imagination were simply a positive term. But if it is seen as something which may bear negative potencies, then its partial restraint, at least, can itself emerge as a positive term. Rational control may be something which has not merely to be tolerated but which may be celebrated. The criteria for such celebration may be communal rather than egoistical, but they remain criteria for celebration. Such celebration of course precludes the possibility of a single tone to the ending of *Dr Hoffman*. Albertina will continue to haunt Desiderio, on the one hand, but he did the right thing, on the other, and that is cause to see the ending of *Dr Hoffman* as including a strong note of affirmation.

Several of the themes of *Dr Hoffman* reappear, in a different form, in Carter's non-fictional work of the late 1970s, *The Sadeian Woman. An Exercise in Cultural History* , and it is that book which I want to discuss in the remainder of this chapter.

If *Dr Hoffman* seems to endorse reason in the name of 'the common good', then we need to be precise about the kind of reason we are talking about. As I noted in my Introduction, Elaine Jordan has said that Carter is good at 'rethinking the fables of Enlightened modernity' (Jordan 1994: 196). It is the rethinking that is important here. Because the problem with the Enlightenment and its 'universal categories' (Waugh 1992: 189) is that it can be seen as having universalised a partial position. Enlightenment notions of reason derived in significant part from the theory of mind advanced by Descartes in the first half of the seventeenth century. The Cartesian split between subject and object was radical. It presupposed a subject, a reflective mind, which was a non-physical entity, which was not rooted in material and historical circumstance and which stood autonomous and self-sufficient: 'I ... concluded that I was a substance whose whole essence or nature consists only in thinking, and which, that it may exist, has need of no place, nor is dependent on any material thing; so that "I", that is to say, the mind by which I am what I am, is wholly distinct from the body' (Descartes 1965: 27). The Cartesian emphasis on the transcendent individuality of the subject or self meant that selfhood or personal identity in Enlightenment thought was always defined in sharp opposition to an 'other'. Thomas McCarthy has commented on the way in which

Enlightenment thought was trapped within the dualistic frame of reference established by Descartes:

> The Cartesian paradigm of the solitary thinker – *solus ipse* – as the proper, even unavoidable, framework for radical reflection on knowledge and morality dominated philosophical thought in the early modern period. The methodological solipsism it entailed marked the approach of Kant at the end of the eighteenth century no less than that of his empiricist and rationalist predecessors in the two preceding centuries. This monological approach pre-ordained certain ways of posing the basic problems of thought and action: subject versus object, reason versus sense, reason versus desire, mind versus body, self versus other, and so on. (Habermas 1984: vii)

Whatever the object or 'other' was, it was conceived of as passively open to manipulation by the primary agency of the reflective subject or self. And that subject or self was characteristically assumed to be white, European and male. Enlightenment reason defined itself against unreason, certainly. But, as has often been pointed out, it was specifically white, masculine reason. The ideology of white, masculine reason conspired to dismiss, for example, the non-white and the feminine to the realm of the non-rational 'other' against which it defined itself, thereby vitiating its claim to universality. The reason of the Enlightenment, the reason of the modernity that was instituted by the Enlightenment, now appears complicit in the power politics and the will to domination of imperialism and male sexism.

First of all, imperialism. Here, I must note that Enlightenment reason cannot be separated from Enlightenment conceptions of history. Paul Hamilton has commented on Kant's view of history, for example, as exemplifying an important aspect of the Enlightenment ideal of universal rational truth:

> In his *Idea for a Universal History with a Cosmopolitan Purpose* [1784] Kant proposes the writing of a history which will ... be ... the interpretation of world events as conforming to certain rational ends ... In the case of mankind, nature's unifying purpose is to develop our distinctive rationality. Such an achievement exceeds the scope of any single individual, and so nature in this purposive, teleological aspect describes a striving for enlightenment characterising the human species from generation to generation. Historical interpretation, then, detects this progressive fulfilment of rationality which connects the present with the past. (Hamilton 1996: 42–3)

Equally, Enlightenment conceptions of history cannot be separated from the matter of European imperialism. Robert Young has spoken of Marxism as the 'fullest political development' of liberating Enlightenment ideals (Young 1990: 7). Yet even Marxism manifests an exclusive and oppressive Eurocentrism. At the end of the following quotation, Young refers to the feminist theorist Hélène Cixous. Cixous grew up as an Algerian French Jew at the time of the Algerian War of Independence, and she has written on the situation of those – non-Europeans and women – who are posited as the 'other' against which and upon which European history is founded:

> Marxism's universalising narrative of the unfolding of a rational system of world history is simply a negative form of the history of European imperialism: it was Hegel, after all, who declared that 'Africa has no history', and it was Marx who, though critical of British imperialism, concluded that the British colonisation of India was ultimately for the best because it brought India into the evolutionary narrative of Western history, thus creating the conditions for future class struggle there. Such an arrogant and arrogating narrative means that the story of 'world history' not only involves what Fredric Jameson describes as the wresting of freedom from the realm of necessity but always also the creation, subjection and final appropriation of Europe's 'others'. This is why 'History', which for Marxism promises liberation, for Cixous also entails another forgotten story of oppression. (Young 1990: 2)

Second, the relations between Enlightenment reason and male sexism. Genevieve Lloyd has written on the masculineness of Western conceptions of reason, from Ancient Greece to the Enlightenment, and on the way in which women and the feminine have been denied participation in the discourse of reason. She writes: 'To suggest that the celebrated objectivity and universality of our canons of rational belief might not in fact transcend even sexual difference seems to go beyond even the more outrageous versions of cultural relativism' (Lloyd 1993: xvii). But her book discriminatingly argues that universal reason is not universal. It is, rather, part and parcel of a gendered discourse that denigrates the feminine:

> The pursuit of rational knowledge has been a major strand in western culture's definitions of itself as opposed to Nature. It is for us in many ways equatable with Culture's transforming or transcending of Nature. Rational knowledge has been construed as a transcending, transformation

or control of rational forces; and the feminine has been associated with what rational knowledge transcends, dominates or simply leaves behind. (Lloyd 1993: 2)

The attack from several directions in the twentieth century on the partiality of the Enlightenment's supposed universals has been summarised by Thomas McCarthy. In some twentieth-century systems of thought, he notes, the individual subject is no longer seen as unrooted and transcendent but rather as profoundly implicated in history and the material world. Such revisions of Enlightenment perspectives have, McCarthy notes, more than merely philosophical implications. They are, as the critiques of Enlightenment racism and sexism would suggest, part of a widespread reevaluation of the egoistical and oppressive side of European bourgeois individualism and humanism in general:

> we are said to be living in a 'post-Heideggerian', 'post-Wittgensteinian', 'poststructuralist' age ... Subjectivity has been shown to be 'infiltrated with the world' in such a way that 'otherness is carried to the very heart of selfhood'. This 'twilight of subjectivity' is not merely an intraphilosophic affair ... The critique of 'rootless rationalism' goes hand in hand with an unmasking of the anthropocentric, egoistic, possessive, and domineering aspects of Western individualism; together they frequently serve as a prologue to the rejection of central concepts of European humanism. (Habermas 1984: viii)

Anthropocentric, egoistic, possessive and domineering are words that define the object of Carter's feminist critique in much of her writing. The Count in *Dr Hoffman* is all these things, and the criticism that Carter makes of him is repeated in more abstract terms, with specific connections being made between such egoism and aspects of Enlightenment thought, in *The Sadeian Woman*. In a nice, if unusual, conjunction, Carter pictures an unacceptable egoism at work in Enlightenment thought *and* in the type of postmodernist outlook that is conventionally understood to subvert Enlightenment perspectives.

In *Dr Hoffman* the Count is a kind of *reductio ad absurdum* of the Cartesian model of personal identity – the *solus ipse*, 'himself alone' paradigm – with its emphasis on individual, subjective transcendence. In his 'infernal egoism' (*DH* 124) the Count seeks to expand his subjectivity to fill the universe: 'I am entirely alone. I and my shadow fill the universe' (*DH* 148). The problem is the shadow. Caught in the subject–object paradigm of identity the Count defines himself in relation to and in contrast with an 'other', an object which, in order that he may define his subjectivity to himself, he views as devoid of subjectivity, lifeless. This is how he views the human objects of his sexual lusts. They are not subjects: merely meat upon which his subjectivity operates. In order fully to realise his egoistic subjectivity, in order to become an absolute self, he must suspend the subject–object dualism and unite with the other. But the other – that *different* thing, that thing against which he defines his imperious subjectivity – is lifeless. So to join with the other is to find annihilation. The Count's 'shadow' is his own annihilation and it is only in union with his shadow that he can overcome the subject–object split and achieve the void fulfilment that he compulsively seeks. His 'shadow' is dramatised in the novel as the black pimp of a prostitute he once murdered. This pimp chases the Count, looking for revenge, and in the pursuit reverses the subject-object relation and turns the Count from a subject into an object: 'I became the object of the vengeance of her enraged pimp, a black of more than superhuman inhumanity, in whom I sense a twin' (*DH* 127). The Count flees the pimp, but in so doing he is only evading the death-wish that fuels his conception of his own absolute subjectivity. Only when the pimp finally catches him and boils him alive does the self-obliteration which his self-aggrandisement has latently been pursuing show itself as the 'fulfilment' of his desire: 'using the very last of his strength, he rose up out of the cauldron in an upward surging leap, as of a fully liberated man' (*DH* 163). The Count and his shadow fuse and the distinction between subject and object dissolves in a consummation that is a negation. The Count himself had articulated the nullity of his own subjectivity when he had earlier chanted: 'I am my own antithesis./ My loins rave. I unleash negation./ The burning arrows of negation' (*DH* 135).

In her portrayal of the Count and his shadow Carter unravels the Cartesian dualism of transcendent subject and inert object, self and other, to show that selfhood so defined can only ever seek fulfilment according to a logic of self-annihilation. The problem is that this logic incorporates and destroys others – things or people – as it is being followed through. Again, the Count is clear about the self-defeating nature of his attempts to ground himself in the domination and violation of others:

> 'I fear my lost shadow who lurks in every shadow. I, who perpetrated atrocities to render to the world incontrovertible proof that my glorious misanthropy overruled it, I – now I exist only as an atrocity about to be perpetrated on myself.' (*DH* 147)

Carter was to provide a variation on this theme of the self-cancelling logic of extreme individualism in the tale 'Master', which she published in her 1974 collection *Fireworks: Nine Profane Pieces*. This tale tells of an Englishman who travelled in Africa and Latin America obsessively shooting wild beasts: 'he became the white hunter ... to kill became the only means that remained to him to confirm he himself was still alive' (*BB* 75–6). In Latin America he bought a 'pubescent girl ... taught her to say "Master" and then let her know that was to be his name' (*BB* 77). With this girl he moved deeper into the unpopulated rain forest, endlessly slaughtering the wild beasts: 'He wanted to destroy them all, so that he would feel less lonely, and, in order to penetrate this absence with his annihilating presence' (*BB* 78). He regarded the girl as no more than an inexpensive 'piece of curious flesh' (*BB* 77) and treated her with the same obliterating selfishness as he meted out to the animals:

> he would first abuse her with the butt of his rifle about the shoulders and, after that, with his sex ... he mounted her in a frenzy, forcing apart her genital lips so roughly the crimson skin on the inside bruised and festered ... Her screams were a universal language; even the monkeys understood she suffered when the Master took his pleasure, yet he did not. (BB 78–9)

But she learns to shoot and, like her 'master', to enjoy shooting the wild animals. Under the influence of his attitude she becomes his negative image and as such she literalises the self-negating impulse of his destructiveness. 'As she grew more like him', we are told, 'so she began to resent him' (*BB* 79) and in the end she annihilates him: 'His prey had shot the hunter' (*BB* 80). In his death the man met the logical end of his egocentric compulsions. But the point of the tale is that such compulsions may engender only similar compulsions in their victims, so that a world defined only in these terms would be a world which endlessly repeats destruction, a world of pure negativity.

The Count in *Dr Hoffman* is an amalgam of archetypal Western figures, from Nosferatu to the Marquis de Sade. In *The Sadeian Woman* Carter speaks of the Marquis de Sade as 'the last, bleak, disillusioned voice of the Enlightenment' (*SW* 34). What Sade's work reveals, for Carter, is the dead-end of a concept of reason that is founded on the egocentricity of the Cartesian paradigm of personal identity. Sade's work, Carter comments, is effectively 'a rewriting of the Cartesian cogito: "*I fuck therefore I am*"' (*SW* 26). Noting that Sade's library included the complete works of Enlightenment thinkers such as Rousseau and Voltaire, Carter observes that

> It is of this world of reason that Sade produces a critique in the guise of a pornographic vision; his heroine, the terrible Juliette, can say, as a hero of Voltaire might: 'I have no light to guide me but my reason.' Yet rationality without humanism founders on itself. (*SW* 35)

In Sade's story of *Juliette* (1796) the heroine is 'rationality personified' and by 'the use of her reason', says Carter, she 'rids herself of some of the more crippling aspects' of the 'femininity' constructed by traditional patriarchal culture (*SW* 79). But Juliette's reason is the masculinist, egoistic reason which defines itself only in opposition to an other that is construed as inert object. In so adopting a conventional Enlightenment reason Juliette forgoes the interests of common humanity. In Sade's story, Juliette at one point murders her own child:

> When she hurls her daughter into the fire ... she is, at last, absolutely free from any lingering traces of the human responses that can only be learned through the society of others who are not accomplices, who are not aspects of the self that confirm the omnipotence of the self. She has indeed attained the lonely freedom of the libertine, which is the freedom of the outlaw, a tautological condition that exists only for itself and is without any meaning in the general context of human life. (*SW* 99)

Sade draws this egocentric individualism time and again in a pornography which, as Carter says, allegorises the Enlightenment's assumption of a Cartesian dualism of self and other. And Sade is the last 'bleak' voice of the Enlightenment because, as in the case

of the Count in *Dr Hoffman*, that antagonistic dualism of self and
other can fulfil itself only in various modes of negation. In the
story of Juliette's sister, *Justine* (1791), the monk Don Clement
'outlines an economic theory of the nature of sexual pleasure':

> Clement argues that there is not enough pleasure to go round and he
> must have it all ... Pleasure may never be shared, or it will be dimin-
> ished. A shared pleasure is a betrayal of the self, a seeping away of
> some of the subject's precious egotism ... The nature of Clement's
> pleasure is by no means a sensual one; his pleasure is a cerebral one,
> even an intellectual one – that of the enhancement of the ego. When
> pleasure is violently denied the partner, the self's pleasure is enhanced
> in direct relation to the visible unpleasure of the victim. And so the
> self knows it exists.
>   Sexual pleasure, therefore, consists primarily in the submission of
> the partner; but that is not enough. The annihilation of the partner is
> the only sufficient proof of the triumph of the ego. (*SW* 142–3)

If Clement offers an instance of and a theory of the self's domination over the other, then Justine herself, the victim of so much
male domination, contributes in her own way to the loop of egocentricity that characterises the existential and metaphysical dualism of active subject and inert object. The reader of *Justine* is
repeatedly put in the position of wanting Justine to *act* in order
that she may escape the perverts and murderers who assail her,
even if such action is itself the act of murder. But Justine's virtue
is such that she will not so act, even though failing to take action
commits her to further abuse. As their 'other' she therefore confirms the dominating selves of her abusers in their practice of
domination. She is the condition of their existence just as they are
of hers. The self and the other in Sade are, for Carter, mutually
confirming opposites. Both sides, locked into a framework of rigid
dualisms – reason and unreason, aggressor and victim, annihilator
and annihilated – confirm egoism and a lack of humanity and
communality. Carter writes that

> Justine's organ of perception is the heart that forbids her to engage in
> certain activities she feels to be immoral and her autobiography illus-
> trates the moral limitations of a life conducted solely according to the
> virtuous promptings of the heart ... Through its own unreason, the
> heart finds itself in complicity with the morality of cruelty it abhors ...
> the unreason of the heart, the false logic of feeling, forbid her to exert
> mastery for even one moment ...

> Virtue has produced in Justine the same kind of apathy, of insensibility, that criminality has produced in Sade's libertines ... Her virtue is egocentric, like the vice of the libertines. (*SW* 51, 53–4)

The freedom that Juliette attains, in contrast with Justine, is seen by Carter as the essence of an oppressive Western ideology of the individual. Juliette learns this ideology from 'a man of power, the statesman Noirceuil' (*SW* 84), who

> teaches her how Nature made the weak to be the slaves of the strong. She learns her lesson at once; to escape slavery, she must embrace tyranny. All living creatures are born and die in isolation, says Noirceuil; in the cultivation and practice of egoism and self-interest alone may be found true happiness. Juliette is immediately drawn to this credo of bourgeois individualism. (*SW* 84)

It is important that Juliette learns her lesson from a man. For Carter, while Juliette uses her reason to escape some of her society's prescriptions for the female, she does not escape determination by the male and the masculine. She becomes, in fact, masculine in her egocentric definition of herself. She becomes the friend and accomplice of the 'beautiful and terrible Madame de Clairwil, who prides herself upon never having shed a tear' (*SW* 88). These two women both adopt a dominant masculinist ideology of dominance: 'Having acceded, as women, to the world of men, their mastery of that world reveals its monomaniac inhumanity to the full' (*SW* 89). Justine and Juliette are, for Carter, 'thesis' and 'antithesis' (*SW* 79) in a male-defined economy:

> Justine's only triumph is her refusal to treat herself as a thing, although everybody she meets does. Since this awareness of herself is not shared by anybody else, it remains a victory in a void. She is the bourgeois individualist in its tragic aspect; her sister, Juliette, offers its heroic side. Both are women whose identities have been defined exclusively by men. (*SW* 77)

Sade was, in fact, 'unusual in his period', argues Carter, 'in installing women' such as Juliette and Madame de Clairwil 'as beings of power in his imaginary worlds' (*SW* 36). But they remained in a world of power defined by the masculine and hence did not challenge the norms of their society as a whole:

> The Sadeian woman, then, subverts only her own socially conditioned role in the world of god, the king and the law. She does not subvert her

society, except incidentally, as a storm trooper of the individual consciousness. She remains in the area of privilege created by her class, just as Sade remains in the philosophic framework of his time. (*SW* 133)

This philosophic framework involved Cartesian assumptions about the rational self which were, as Thomas McCarthy says, 'anthropocentric, egoistic, possessive, and domineering' (Habermas 1984: viii). Juliette adopts such reason. But if Carter is opposed to the 'terrible' Juliette's 'rationality without humanism' (*SW* 35), then she is equally opposed to Justine's 'unreason of the heart' and 'false logic of feeling' (*SW* 53). It is a model different to the Sadeian Enlightenment one of reason/unreason, self/other, thesis/antithesis which Carter endorses in *The Sadeian Woman*. That reason remains a valued term in Carter's vision is indicated by her outraged protest in *The Sadeian Woman* at the way in which pornography and myth together conspire to deprive women of rationality:

> Pornography involves an abstraction of human intercourse in which the self is reduced to its formal elements. In its most basic form, these elements are represented by the probe and the fringed hole, the twin signs of male and female in graffiti ...
>
> In the stylisation of graffiti, the prick ... always ... points upwards, it asserts. The hole is open, an inert space ... The male is positive ... Woman is negative. Between her legs lies nothing but zero, the sign for nothing, that only becomes something when the male principle fills it with meaning ... graffiti directs me back to my mythic generation as a woman and, as a woman, my symbolic value is primarily that of a myth of patience and receptivity, a dumb mouth from which the teeth have been pulled.
>
> Sometimes ... a more archaic mouth is allowed to exert an atavistic dominance. Then ... my nether mouth may be acknowledged as one capable of speech – were there not, of old, divinatory priestesses, female oracles and so forth? ... Since that female, oracular mouth is located so near the beastly backside, my vagina might indeed be patronisingly regarded as a speaking mouth, but never one that issues the voice of reason. In this most insulting mythic redefinition of myself, that of occult priestess, I am indeed allowed to speak but only of things that male society does not take seriously. I can hint at dreams, I can even personify imagination; but that is only because I am not rational enough to cope with reality. (*SW* 4–5)

Carter wants it recognised that women have as much purchase on reason as men but it has to be a recognition based on a different premise from the masculine definition of reason which Juliette adopts. Carter wants a reason defined outside the binary antagonisms of masculine and feminine, reason and unreason, thought and feeling. She wants a model in which reason and thought are not defined against unreason and feeling. She wants a model for the relationship between people that is based on the principle of reciprocity rather than of self-definition by exclusion. 'Justine is the thesis, Juliette the antithesis', writes Carter,

> both are without hope and neither pays any heed to a future in which might lie the possibility of a synthesis of their modes of being, neither submissive nor aggressive, capable of both thought and feeling. (*SW* 79)

The Sadeian subject never confronts an object that – or who – is at once a subject:

> the libertine chooses to surround himself, not with lovers or partners, but with accomplices ...
> The presence of his accomplices preserves his ego from the singular confrontation with the object of a reciprocal desire which is, in itself, both passive object and active subject. Such a partner acts on us as we act on it. (*SW* 146)

The model of reciprocity, of mutuality or communication, in which human beings interact each as both subject and object, individually both thesis and antithesis, is one which defines the humane. It is the model which sustains humanism and which prevents rationality from foundering on itself. Juliette's adoption of egocentric, masculinist rationality grounds her capacity to murder her own daughter and to exorcise 'the human responses that can only be learned through the society of others who are not accomplices, who are not aspects of the self that confirm the omnipotence of the self' (*SW* 99). She attains the freedom of the libertine, the freedom of the outlaw, that litigates against what Desiderio in *Dr Hoffman* called 'the common good' (*DH* 207), a freedom that is 'without any meaning in the general context of human life' (*SW* 99). Carter's model of reciprocity seeks to preserve reason not as the property of the transcendent subject but as a function of the 'common good'. In any case, reason as the prerogative of the transcendent subject is bound into a logic of negation and founders on itself. Sade's use of sexuality as a means

by which to explore Enlightenment ideology exposes the in-
sufficiency of that ideology as a means of supporting human life in
general:

> Sexuality, in this estranged form, becomes a denial of a basis of mutu-
> ality, of the acknowledgement of equal rights to exist in the world,
> from which any durable form of human intercourse can spring. (*SW*
> 141)

Having spoken throughout her book in a discourse that leans
on philosophical language, Carter ends her work by defining her
model of reciprocity and mutuality using the more emotive term
'love'. The egocentricity, isolation and alienation which she sees
Sade's work characterising and exploring are contrasted with the
reciprocity of thought and feeling properly implied by the word
love:

> In his diabolic solitude, only the possibility of love could awake the
> libertine to perfect, immaculate terror. It is in this holy terror of love
> that we find, in both men and women themselves, the source of all
> opposition to the emancipation of women. (*SW* 150)

Carter's feminism is essentially comedic in nature. She speaks
equally to both women and men *as* equals, seeking to avoid tragedy
by imagining means of resolving antagonism. The postscript to
The Sadeian Woman is from Emma Goldman's 'The Tragedy of
Woman's Emancipation' (1910):

> The demand for equal rights in every vocation of life is just and fair;
> but, after all, the most vital right is the right to love and be loved.
> Indeed, if partial emancipation is to become a complete and true eman-
> cipation of woman, it will have to do away with the ridiculous notion
> that to be loved, to be sweetheart and mother, is synonymous with
> being slave or subordinate. It will have to do away with the absurd
> notion of the dualism of the sexes, or that man and woman represent
> two antagonistic worlds ... A true conception of the relation of the
> sexes will not admit of conqueror and conquered. (*SW* 151)

In the light of *The Sadeian Woman*, Desiderio's attachment
simultaneously to reason and to the value of the common good
emerges as an anti-Cartesian, anti-Enlightenment view of the
nature and value of reason. Or, rather, it is not simply anti-
Enlightenment. It is a view – like Carter's own directly expressed

view in *The Sadeian Woman* – which significantly modifies the Enlightenment structuring of rationality. The model of reason defined in terms of reciprocity rather than exclusion – rationality *with* humanism – which underlies *The Sadeian Woman* has certain parallels in contemporary philosophical work. Jürgen Habermas, for example, in considering our inheritance of Enlightenment values, strives not to throw the baby of reason, truth and justice out with the bathwater of things like sexism and racism. Habermas wants to have it both ways. He agrees up to a point with the postmodern deconstruction of Enlightenment universals; he agrees with the idea that concepts of reason and justice are historically and socially embedded; he agrees likewise with the idea that the subject is not autonomous but historically and socially situated. He shares the view that human identities and ideas have no absolute ground or foundation. But he does not go along with an extreme postmodern relativism. 'Habermas' problem', writes Hans Bertens, 'is to define and to argue for the plausibility of a rationality that distinguishes itself from' the autonomous, subject-centred rationality attacked by postmodern theorists and which 'is not transcendent in the sense that it is foundationalist', but which 'yet transcends the limitations of time and place. Such a rationality, although inevitably subject to change over time, must have a "unifying power" that will enable a workable consensus. Without such a rationality, emancipatory, that is, leftist politics become an illusion' (Bertens 1995: 115). Habermas sees the original Enlightenment project as one in which the specialised knowledges of science, philosophy and ethics, and art were to be integrated with ordinary life in a way that would guarantee, as he puts it 'the justice of institutions and even the happiness of human beings' (Habermas 1985: 9). But Habermas sees that such integration has not taken place, that the ideal of 'the rational organisation of everyday social life' has not been realised (Habermas 1985: 9). And this because of the inherently solipsistic, exclusive and excluding character of detached subject-centred reason which, as it were, usurped the original Enlightenment project. However, rather than rejecting, like Jean-François Lyotard, the whole of Enlightenment ideology as an oppressive failure, Habermas prefers to see enlightened modernity as a project which is as yet uncompleted. Rather than rejecting, he chooses to *develop* the concept of reason, refusing the old centring of rationality on the individual consciousness or ego and arguing instead for a 'change of paradigm from subject-centred to communicative reason' (Habermas 1987: 301); a paradigm shift which defines reason in intersubjective terms. The 'construal of reason in terms of a noncoercive intersubjectivity of mutual understanding and reciprocal recognition', as Thomas McCarthy puts it (Habermas 1987: xvi), stands contrary to the transcendent, non-situated character of subject-centred reason. It re-embeds reason in social practice and history while retaining the claim that reason and rational ideals of truth and justice transcend – though not in an absolute sense – local social and historical circumstance.

Language is the primary medium of social interaction and it is language – the ordinary language of everyday social communication – that Habermas concentrates on in his definition of intersubjective reason. Thomas McCarthy summarises Habermas's view of the relationship between social communication, reason and language when he writes that there is

> an internal relation of communicative practice to reason, for language use is oriented to validity claims, and validity claims can in the end be redeemed only through intersubjective recognition brought about by the unforced force of reason. The internal relation of meaning to validity means that communication is not only always 'immanent' – that is, situated, conditioned – but also always 'transcendent' – that is, geared to validity claims that are meant to hold beyond any local context and thus can be indefinitely criticized, defended, revised. (Habermas 1987: xvi–xvii)

Habermas himself describes validity claims as having 'a Janus face':

> As claims, they transcend any local context; at the same time, they have to be raised here and now and be de facto recognized if they are going to bear the agreement of interaction participants that is needed for effective cooperation. The transcendent moment of *universal* validity bursts every provinciality asunder; the obligatory moment of accepted validity claims renders them carriers of a *context-bound* everyday practice. Inasmuch as communicative agents reciprocally raise validity claims with their speech acts, they are relying on the potential of assailable grounds. Hence, a moment of *unconditionality* is built into *factual* processes of mutual understanding – the validity laid claim to is distinguished from the social currency of a de facto established practice and yet serves it as the foundation of an existing consensus. (Habermas 1987: 322–3)

Through his view of the inherent rationality of human language, his notion that 'the structure of language itself' has a 'procedural rationality' (Bertens 1995: 116), Habermas argues, then, for an order of rationality that transcends individual or cultural difference but which is still rooted in local, everyday social praxis. Hans Bertens notes that Habermas 'like his opponents rejects intuition and metaphysics in defining what is reasonable' but that, unlike his opponents, he argues that 'a universal rationality that is latently present in the procedures that structure argumentative discourse can be brought to light "through the analysis of the *already* operative potential for rationality contained in the everyday practices of communication"' (Bertens 1995: 116). Such a local but simultaneously 'universal' rationality is, indeed, the condition of any one culture ever being able to understand anything of another. The philosopher Donald Davidson makes a comparable point against the kind of relativism that it is possible to find in an extreme postmodernism when he writes that:

> The dominant metaphor of conceptual relativism, that of differing points of view, seems to betray an underlying paradox. Different points of view make sense, but only if there is a common co-ordinate system on which to plot them; yet the existence of a common system belies the claim of dramatic incomparability. (Davidson 1984: 184)

At the same time, of course, in Habermas, 'universal' rationality is not, as I have observed, given some kind of absolute metaphysical foundation, so that it stands unchangingly outside of human social experience. Reason as defined by Habermas is neither absolute nor absolutely relative. It is something that is able to revise itself, to correct things it has got wrong in the past, such as excluding the feminine from the field of rationality, to seek to move towards a more inclusively enlightened condition. In this way, Habermas holds that the solution to the deficiencies of the Enlightenment are to be found not in cancelling all Enlightenment values but only in further enlightenment. The ability of rationality to criticise the exclusive reason of the Enlightenment remains itself part of the inheritance of the Enlightenment. Habermas's rethinking of the Enlightenment idea of reason is not a jettisoning but an attempt, as Thomas McCarthy writes, to 'recast … our received humanistic ideals' (Habermas 1987: x).

The social and political implications of Habermas's resistance to postmodern relativism and his attempt to keep alive the humanist values of the Enlightenment are what attract a feminist critic like Patricia Waugh. She observes that '[t]he feminist cry' has 'situated its politics firmly within what Lyotard wishes to denounce and Habermas to affirm in modified form as the "project of modernity"' (Waugh 1992: 189). She argues, as we have seen, that while feminism can indeed learn from postmodernism, it nevertheless has finally to resist the relativist logic of postmodernism's arguments, for fear that postmodernism's deconstructive processes may empty feminism of content as readily as they are able to empty patriarchy of its essentialist claims. Feminism must, she argues, adopt a 'modified adherence to an epistemological anchorage in the discourses of Enlightened modernity' (Waugh 1992: 190):

> Feminism needs coherent subjects and has found a variety of ways of articulating them which avoid the fetishization of Pure Reason as the locus of subjecthood and the irrationalism born out of the perceived failure of this ideal. (Waugh 1992: 194)

Waugh cites Habermas's attempt to recast and hence revivify the humanist ideals of the Enlightenment, observing the parallels he himself does not acknowledge between his work and much recent feminist thought:

> Jürgen Habermas has ... suggested that modernity is not exhausted, simply unfinished ... Like so many theorists within the postmodern debate, however, he seems singularly unaware of many of the developments in feminist thinking over the last twenty years. It seems to me that many feminists have been working for some time with models which are not fundamentally incompatible with Habermas's whether or not they have used them in specifically theoretical ways. (Waugh 1992: 201)

Angela Carter's fictional depiction in *Dr Hoffman* of Desiderio choosing 'reason' for 'the common good', and her attacks in *The Sadeian Woman* on 'rationality without humanism', fit into this notion of someone working with a model not incompatible with that developed by Habermas. It is a model that shadows Carter's investigation into the need for a rational appraisal of heterosexual identity in the novel that followed *Dr Hoffman*, *The Passion of New Eve*. While *Dr Hoffman* takes up the issue of gender relations, *New Eve* focuses more centrally and directly on the matter.

FOUR

The Passion of New Eve

'[O]ur flesh arrives to us out of history' writes Carter in *The Sadeian Woman* (*SW* 9). *The Passion of New Eve* (1977) appeared a couple of years before *The Sadeian Woman*, but like the still earlier *Dr Hoffman* the novel includes ideas and themes that recur and are treated more abstractly in *The Sadeian Woman*. Above all, *The Passion of New Eve* is a fictional exploration of the anti-essentialist notion that 'our flesh arrives to us out of history', the notion that the categories and characteristics of the masculine and the feminine are not absolutely founded: 'We may believe we fuck stripped of social artifice; in bed, we even feel we touch the bedrock of human nature itself. But we are deceived. Flesh is not an irreducible human universal' (*SW* 9).

At the outset of *The Passion of New Eve* we meet Evelyn, an Englishman on his last night in a fantasy 1970s London before he sets out for New York. We also meet Evelyn's erotic dream, an actress named Tristessa, one of the pantheon of glamorous female film stars of the 1930s and 1940s. In her films, Tristessa, as her name implies, made a speciality of sadness and suffering. On his last night in London Evelyn goes to see one of Tristessa's films, and remembers the connection that had been induced in him as a boy between sexual arousal and the image of Tristessa's suffering: 'the twitch in my budding groin the spectacle of Tristessa's suffering always aroused in me' (*PNE* 8). Later in the book, once he is in America, Evelyn will meet Tristessa in person.

The New York that Evelyn arrives at is a city of 'lurid, Gothic darkness' (*PNE* 10), a city on the edge of terminal breakdown.

107

Disorder and violence are rife. Rats the size of babies attack dogs in the street. The sewerage system breaks down. A militant women's movement has sharpshooters who aim at men staring at blue movie posters. A militant black movement builds a wall around Harlem and drives tanks down Park Avenue. The university where Evelyn is supposed to teach is occupied and then blown up.

Evelyn meets Baroslav, an old Czech soldier who lives in the same block of flats. Baroslav, Evelyn tells us, 'was, God help us all, an alchemist and distilled a demented logic in his attic' (*PNE* 13). Baroslav gave Evelyn an ingot of gold made in his alchemist's crucible:

> He made me some gold, following the same method as James Price, Fellow of the Royal Society, but I do not know if he was a charlatan, like Price, who introduced his gold into the crucible through a hollow stirring rod. (*PNE* 14)

The metaphor of alchemy and its associated figure of the hermaphrodite are to be central to the allegory of *The Passion of New Eve*. Evelyn records that Baroslav possessed 'a seventeenth century print ... of a hermaphrodite ... that exercised a curious fascination upon me, the dual form with its breasts and its cock ... (Coming events?)' (*PNE* 13). Popularly known as the art of transmuting base metals into gold, medieval and seventeenth-century alchemy encompassed a range of magical and pseudo-philosophical and spiritual dimensions. A standard definition in the *Encyclopaedia Britannica* notes that 'Philosophical sanction and explanation' of the belief in the possibility of making gold from substances which were not gold was found by bringing the belief 'into relation with the theory of the *prima materia*, which was identical in all bodies but received its actual form by the adjunction of qualities expressed by the Aristotelian elements – earth, air, fire and water' (*Encyclopaedia Britannica* 1910–11: I, 519). The *Britannica* describes the work of transmutation, by which the alchemist could arrive at prime matter and then reconstitute gold through the addition of particular qualities, as follows:

> Regarding all substances as being composed of one primitive matter – the *prima materia*, and as owing their specific differences to the presence of different qualities imposed upon it, the alchemist hoped, by taking away these qualities, to obtain the *prima materia* itself, and then to get

from it the particular substance he desired by the addition of the appropriate qualities. The *prima materia* was early identified with mercury, not ordinary mercury, but the 'mercury of the philosophers', which was the essence or soul of mercury, freed from the four Aristotelian elements – earth, air, fire and water – or rather from the qualities which they represent. (*Encyclopaedia Britannica* 1910–11: I, 521)

In alchemical thought mercury was personified as a hermaphrodite, and it was through such an image of a union of opposites that alchemy made its pseudo-philosophical or spiritual claims. Ad de Vries writes that the alchemical Mercury was represented 'as a two-headed figure':

> the ultimate transmutation leads to a substance in which the male and female are completely united (as in God); it is represented in recipes as a hermaphrodite, a two-faced head, a man and woman in coition, or the marriage of a king and queen. (Vries 1984: 249)

This idea of a primary oneness in which all differences are resolved is associated by Baroslav himself with the disintegration of form in the New York in which he lives. It is a disintegration that, for Baroslav, holds possibilities of creativity:

> The police car wailed in the street below; a loud hailer advised a number of unknown persons in an adjacent ruin to come out, since they were all surrounded. Then the sound of guns.
> 'Chaos, the primordial substance,' said Baroslav. 'Chaos, the earliest state of disorganised creation, blindly impelled towards the creation of a new order of phenomena of hidden meanings. The fructifying chaos of anteriority, the state before the beginning of the beginning.' ...
> 'Chaos', said the Czech alchemist with grim relish, 'embraces all opposing forms in a state of undifferentiated dissolution'. (*PNE* 13–14)

Baroslav also observes that what this dissolution defines is that '[t]he age of reason is over' (*PNE* 13). The rest of the story of *The Passion of New Eve* will take place in a world unstructured by reason. New York, '[b]uilt on a grid ... planned ... in strict accord with the dictates of a doctrine of reason ... A city of visible reason', has become, as Evelyn puts it, 'an alchemical city. It was chaos, dissolution, nigredo, night' (*PNE* 16). In this alchemical city, Evelyn meets Leilah, a girl to whom he gives Baroslav's ingot of alchemical gold. Leilah is a symptom of the alchemical city: 'a girl all softly black in colour – nigredo, the stage of darkness' (*PNE*

14). And while Baroslav may celebrate the condition of chaos in the city, Evelyn's treatment of Leilah highlights the negative aspects of the chaos in which they both find themselves.

Leilah is an incarnation of one type of male sexual fantasy. Evelyn first sees her wearing what a little later he calls her 'public face' (*PNE* 30):

> Her tense and resilient legs attracted my attention first for they seemed to quiver with the energy repressed in their repose ... but the black mesh stockings she wore designated their length and slenderness as specifically erotic, she would not use them to run away with ...
> She had on a pair of black, patent leather shoes with straps around the ankles, fetishistic heels six inches high and ... an immense coat of red fox was slung around her shoulders ... This coat revealed only the hem of a dark blue, white coin-dotted dress that hardly covered her. Her hair was a furze-bush, à la Africain, and she had bright purple lipstick on her mouth. She loitered among the confession magazines, chewing a stick of candy. (*PNE* 19)

This public guise is something Leilah consciously constructs using a mirror and as she is constructing it she becomes it:

> I used to adore watching her dressing herself in the evenings, before she went out to the clubs ... She became absorbed in the contemplation of the figure in the mirror but she did not seem to me to apprehend the person in the mirror as, in any degree, herself. The reflected Leilah had a concrete form and ... we all knew, all three of us in the room, it was another Leilah. Leilah invoked this formal other with a gravity and ritual that recalled witchcraft; she brought into being a Leilah who lived only in the not-world of the mirror and then became her own reflection. (*PNE* 28)

Above all, of course, this 'not-self' is designed to suit masculine taste. In 1972 John Berger characterised the masculine gaze in terms which, though not identical, were comparable to Carter's picture of the way in which Leilah constructs herself as a reflection of a masculine view of what makes her erotically desirable. Berger further comments on various Renaissance and other paintings where the spectator of the painting 'is presumed to be a man' (Berger 1972: 54) and in which a nude woman is figured looking at herself in a mirror:

> To be born a woman has been to be born, within an allotted and confined space, into the keeping of men. The social presence of women has

developed as a result of their ingenuity in living under such tutelage within such a limited space. But this has been at the cost of a woman's self being split into two. A woman must continually watch herself. She is almost continually accompanied by her own image of herself ...

And so she comes to consider the *surveyor* and the *surveyed* within her as the two constituent yet always distinct elements of her identity as a woman ...

Men survey women before treating them. Consequently how a woman appears to a man can determine how she will be treated ...

One might simplify this by saying: *men act* and *women appear*. Men look at women. Women watch themselves being looked at. This determines not only most relations between men and women but also the relation of women to themselves. The surveyor of woman in herself is male: the surveyed female. Thus she turns herself into an object – and most particularly an object of vision: a sight ...

The ... function of the mirror was.... to make the woman connive in treating herself as, first and foremost, a sight. (Berger 1972: 46–7, 51)

Carter, however, goes further than Berger in analysing the nature of the gaze. In Berger the woman who turns herself into an object that stands in relation to a male subject is presumed to forfeit her own autonomous subjectivity in the act. The man's subjectivity and its gaze seem to be assumed to have an ontological status. In Carter, however, the masculine subject is itself implicated in the emptiness of a subjectivity defined in terms of representation or reflection. The male subject and his erotic dream of the woman may deprive her of autonomous subjectivity, but he, too, in that act of gazing, becomes a function of the mirror, an agent not of being but of representation. It may be a self-confirming self-representation, dependent on constructing the woman as an other, an object, but that male self, constituted in representation, is as empty as the woman who abandons herself to the masculine construction of what she is:

she ... seemed to abandon her self in the mirror, to abandon her self to the mirror, and allowed herself to function only as a fiction of the erotic dream into which the mirror cast me.

So, together, we entered the same reverie, the self-created, self-perpetuating, solipsistic world of the woman watching herself being watched in a mirror. (*PNE* 30)

The power relations do not, of course, change in Carter's subtilisation of the point made by Berger. The masculine gaze still defines the woman and turns her, as Evelyn comments of her, into a 'victim' (*PNE* 28). Being the object of the masculine gaze turns her into 'dressed meat' (*PNE* 31). But what Carter does point out is the extent to which the masculine subject doing the watching is itself deprived of ontological substance as it is cast in the role of gazer. Evelyn comments on this in terms which anticipate *The Sadeian Woman* when he writes that what is missing in this representational game of masculine viewer and feminine viewed, where both are empty, is love:

> She was a perfect woman; like the moon, she only gave reflected light. She had mimicked me, she had become the thing I wanted of her, so that she could make me love her and yet she had mimicked me so well she had also mimicked the fatal lack in me that meant I was not able to love her because I myself was so unlovable. (*PNE* 34)

The pay-off to this relationship is predictable. Evelyn grows tired of Leilah but she gets pregnant. Evelyn insists she has an abortion. Her womb becomes infected and she has a hysterectomy. Evelyn blames Leilah for everything that has gone wrong ('why did you seduce me, in the first place ...?', *PNE* 36) and he decides to leave for the western deserts of the States: 'I would go to the desert ... there ... I thought I might find that most elusive of chimeras, myself' (*PNE* 38). In retrospect Evelyn writes of Leilah: 'I gave her nothing but an ingot of alchemical gold, and a baby, and mutilation, and sterility' (*PNE* 31). Like the figure of Tristessa, Evelyn will meet Leilah again later in the story.

Sterility is once more the motif in the ensuing episode of Evelyn's wanderings: 'I reached the desert, the abode of enforced sterility, the dehydrated sea of infertility' (*PNE* 40). The sterility Evelyn gave to Leilah he now thinks of as a part of himself: 'I have found a landscape that matches the landscape of my heart' (*PNE* 41). In the desert Evelyn is captured by a wing of the women's movement he had first come across in New York. The emblem of this desert women's movement is a broken phallus and the women themselves live in an underground city whose architecture is modelled on the womb. The head of the matriarchy of this city is 'Mother', the 'woman who calls herself the Great Parricide' (*PNE* 49). Mother perpetuates a cult of the female as the essential beginning and end and ruler of all things in the

universe. The matriarchy, while at once appealing to mythic prec-
edent, is technologically highly sophisticated. Mother has turned
herself artificially, by a kind of super plastic surgery, into a version
of the Greek 'goddess of fertility' the 'many-breasted Artemis'
(*PNE* 77): 'she was breasted like a sow – she possessed two tiers
of nipples, the result ... of a strenuous programme of grafting ...
she had made herself!' (*PNE* 60). Mother rapes Evelyn and ejects
him 'just as' his 'seed pumped helplessly out' (*PNE* 65). Evelyn
learns from another of the city's inhabitants that Mother is

> going to castrate you, Evelyn, and then excavate what we call the
> 'fructifying female space' inside you and make you a perfect specimen
> of womanhood. Then, as soon as you're ready, she's going to impregnate
> you with your own sperm, which I collected from you after you copu-
> lated with her. (*PNE* 68)

After Evelyn has been turned into a woman (he is never actually
impregnated with his own sperm), he learns the garbled, mis-
anthropic mythological and apocalyptic vision through which
Mother justifies the deed:

> 'now, first of beings in the world, you can seed yourself and fruit
> yourself ...
>   That is why you have become New Eve, and your child will rejuve-
> nate the world!' ... Then she spoke in rolling iambic pentameters of
> eternity ... and the halting of the phallocentric thrust so that the world
> could ripen in female space without the mortal interventions of male
> time. (*PNE* 76–7)

Mother's eulogy of space and eternity as against time and death
is derived from William Blake's observation in 'A Vision of the
Last Judgement' that 'Time is a Man, Space is a Woman, & her
Masculine Portion is Death' (Keynes 1966: 614). This is modified
in the matriarchal city to three propositions:

> 'Proposition one: time is a man, space is a woman.
> Proposition two: time is a killer.
> Proposition three: kill time and live forever.' (*PNE* 53)

The name of the matriarchal city, 'Beulah' (*PNE* 46), is also
derived primarily from Blake's writings. In Blake's private mythology Beulah is the title of one of four states of being. The allusion to Blake in the name of the matriarchal city alerts us to what

Carter sees as its questionable aspects. For, as Harold Bloom has pointed out, Blake's Beulah is an ambivalent state:

> Of Blake's four states of being – innocence, or Beulah; experience, or Generation; organized higher innocence, or Eden; and the Hell of rational self-absorption or Ulro – it is the lower, unorganised innocence or Beulah, about which he has most to say. For Beulah is the most ambiguous state. Its innocence dwells dangerously near to ignorance, its creativity is allied to destructiveness, its beauty to terror. (Bloom 1963: 17)

In Blake, Beulah is 'the world', as Northrop Frye summarises, 'of the consolations of religion ... the world of wonder and romance, of fairy tales and dreams' (Frye 1974: 230); it is the world in which these possibilities may inspire but where they may also delude. Beulah is also, in Blake, a characteristically feminine state. As such, it stands secondary and inferior to Eden in specifically gendered terms:

> Beulah is female, Eden male ...
>   Beulah, according to Blake, is the emanation of Eden – that is, its outer and feminine or created form. Beulah is therefore temporal and illusory ... Its emotions are all of the forgiving variety, emphasizing feminine self-sacrifice ... Beulah is possible only because the Daughters of Beulah (who are Blake's Muses) are willing to sacrifice the Female Will. (Bloom 1963: 21–2, 24)

It may seem odd that the matriarchy of Carter's underground city should invoke a feminine space that is associated with romance, dreams, religious consolation and also with transience and female self-abnegation. But that is because the myth of the great female principle which the Mother of the city asserts is seen by Carter as being less an escape than a confirmation of patriarchy. In *The Sadeian Woman* Carter was to write:

> If women allow themselves to be consoled for their culturally determined lack of access to the modes of intellectual debate by the invocation of hypothetical great goddesses, they are simply flattering themselves into submission (a technique often used on them by men). All the mythic versions of women, from the myth of the redeeming purity of the virgin to that of the healing, reconciling mother, are consolatory nonsenses; and consolatory nonsense seems to me a fair definition of myth, anyway. Mother goddesses are just as silly a notion as father gods. If a revival of the myths of these cults gives women

emotional satisfaction, it does so at the price of obscuring the real conditions of life. This is why they were invented in the first place.

Myth deals in false universals, to dull the pain of particular circumstances. In no area is this more true than in that of relations between the sexes. (*SW* 5–6)

For Carter, then, women simply should not be consoled for their literal, historical oppression by myths of the eternal female. Lorna Sage has observed that, for Carter, '[c]onsolatory fictions must be exposed, and reasoned (and jeered) out of countenance' (Sage 1994a: 39). The reasoning away of myth in *The Passion of New Eve* lies just beneath the jeering that Carter indulges in. Ricarda Schmidt notes that 'Mother's glorification of the womb, female space, biological essentialism (which stands for one position within the women's movement in the 1970s), is satirised in its involuntarily comic self-pronunciation' (Schmidt 1990: 63). Carter goes delightfully over the top in her mockery of an essentialist myth of the female, from the pretensions and absurd psalmodies of Mother's devotees –

> Ineradicable vent of being, oracular mouth
> absolute beginning without which negation is impossible ...
> Danae Alphito Demeter
> who reap with the sickle moon ...
> Our lady of the cannibals
> Carridwen/Cerridwen the white sow pigs it in the byre.
> White mare child guzzler
> the meaty one.
>
> (*PNE* 61–62)

– to the burlesque humour with which Evelyn himself describes Mother and the ceremonies surrounding her:

> Then she took me on her immense knee and pressed my reluctant head against her double tier of breasts. It was like being seated at the console of a gigantic cinema organ ...
>
> Again, the chorus took up the hiccuping yowl, Ma-ma-ma-ma, crashing in archaic waves over the clamour of the trumpets and the hosannaing. (*PNE* 65, 67)

So it is appropriate that this matriarchy should adopt a Blakeian name for its city, given that the matriarchy (and behind it, Blake's sexist private mythology itself) are being parodied and not endorsed. In Carter, Beulah's myth of the female does not connect with any essential, universal ground. Just as Mother is a construction, 'her own mythological artefact' (*PNE* 60), so is the ideology of her city: 'In Beulah, myth is a made thing, not a found thing' (*PNE* 56). The construction of Beulah and its consolatory myth is in the end a construction determined by the masculine. As such, it and its presiding Mother represent an unproductive condition of being, like the Greek virgin goddess of child-labour on whom Mother has modelled herself: 'What rage, what desperation could have forced her to mimic in her own body the refulgent form of many-breasted Artemis, another *sterile* goddess of fertility?' (*PNE* 77, my italics).

Whatever the rage and desperation, Mother reconstructs Evelyn as a woman in the same manner as she constructed herself: that is, effectively as a reflection of masculine images of the female. For all Mother's sympathies with the female, they are sympathies that Carter sees as inadvertently colluding with patriarchy and it is noticeable that Mother constructs Eve according to a masculine view of what the perfect woman should look like. In a 1975 article for *New Society* Carter wrote: '"The feminine character, and the idea of femininity on which it is modelled, are products of masculine society", says Theodor Adorno' (*SL* 110). So it is with Eve's appearance in *The Passion of New Eve*. Eve emerges as a variation upon what Leilah had been, an incarnation of male sexual fantasy, a 'not-self'. The new Eve records that:

> when I looked in the mirror, I saw Eve; I did not see myself. I saw a young woman who, though she was I, I could in no way acknowledge as myself, for this one was only a lyrical abstraction of femininity to me ... They had turned me into the *Playboy* centerfold. I was the object of all the unfocused desires that had ever existed in my own head. I had become my own masturbatory fantasy. (*PNE* 74–5)

It is not surprising that all this should be the case, since the appearance upon which Eve was modelled was derived from those media-images that merely confirm the dominance of the masculine gaze in the culture at large:

> In the evenings, cool Sophia ... showed me the plastic surgeries where a team of women had worked on my new shape according to a blue-print taken from a consensus agreement on the physical nature of an

ideal woman drawn up from a protracted study of the media and constructed here, in this well-equipped studio, where Mother approved it.
(*PNE* 78)

This new Eve, then, is not at all new: she simply reconfirms the
patriarchal bias of the old myth of Eve. She is still masculine, not
simply in the literal sense that the old Evelyn persists in her body,
but in the sense that her body is a construction of the masculine
gaze. As far as being a woman is concerned, she is as empty as the
void that had lain at the heart of Evelyn in his representation of
what woman as the object of his desire should be.

The new Eve escapes the sterility of the essentialist matriarchy
only to find herself caught by its twin: the essentialist masculinity of a man named Zero who – partly styled, perhaps, on the
1960s murderer of Sharon Tate, Charles Manson – lives in the
desert with a group of girls, his harem, whom he abuses in cari-
catured male fashion. Zero 'believed women were fashioned of a
different soul substance from men, a more primitive, animal stuff'
and thus did not need 'the paraphernalia of civilised society'
(*PNE* 87) such as soap, shoes or cutlery. He beat his women, did
not allow them to speak in words and demeaned them by cover-
ing them with pigs' and his own excrement. Needless to say, it is
Zero who is the pig. But his women love him nevertheless: 'they
gave in to him freely, as though they knew they must be wicked
and so deserved to be inflicted with such pain ... his myth
depended on their conviction ... his power depended on his
dependants' (*PNE* 95, 99, 102). We are, of course, once again, in
a Sadeian structure of relations here and the vacuity that Zero
projects on to his women and which they then internalise lies, in
fact, in himself. Carter points to this through his name, but also
through presenting him, for all that he loved guns, whips, Wagner
and Nietzsche, as deficient in the maleness he himself mytholo-
gises. He is one-eyed, one-legged and infertile. Eve, formerly
Evelyn, experiences him from two perspectives simultaneously.
She tells us that his rape of her: 'forced me to know myself as a
former violator at the moment of my own violation' (*PNE* 102).
Nevertheless, it is Zero's repeated rapes which succeed in fitting
Eve's/Evelyn's mind to her body: 'The mediation of Zero turned
me into a woman. More. His peremptory prick turned me into a
savage woman' (*PNE* 107–8).

Zero is obsessed, as it turns out, by Evelyn's old film icon, Tristessa, whom he believes caused his infertility by casting a spell on him from out of the silver screen. Zero claims she is a 'Witch' and a 'Dyke' (*PNE* 92) and spends much of his time searching the desert for the home to which she has retired so that he can ravish and murder her, and thus restore his fertility. When Zero and his harem, including Eve, do eventually find Tristessa they discover something about her that surprises them all. She is a man. This female idol of the silver screen was and is a man in drag. Tristessa is, in other words, nothing to do with an actual woman. She is a masculine projection of what a woman is. She is another incarnation of masculine sexual fantasy, another 'not-self', another piece of mythology:

> *That* was why he had been the perfect man's woman! He had made himself the shrine of his own desires, had made of himself the only woman he could have loved! ...
> Tristessa, the sensuous fabrication of the mythology of the flea-pits. How could a real woman ever have been so much a woman as you? ...
> Tristessa had no function in this world except as an idea of himself; no ontological status, only an iconographic one. (*PNE* 128–9)

This critique of the film star Tristessa is part of Carter's general critique of twentieth-century Western cultural images – particularly filmic images – of women. Tristessa is a version of Sade's Justine, a comparable product of the masculine imagination, and as Carter was to point out in *The Sadeian Woman*, Justine is a kind of model for many twentieth-century representations of women. It was her entrapment within a masculine image of what she should be that, suggests Carter, destroyed the film star Marilyn Monroe:

> Justine marks the start of a kind of self-regarding female masochism ...
> Justine's place in the aetiology of the female condition in the twentieth century is assured; she is the personification of the pornography of that condition.
> She is obscene to the extent to which she is beautiful. Her beauty, her submissiveness ... are what make her obscene ...
> In herself, this lovely ghost, this zombie, or woman who has never been completely born as a woman, only as a debased cultural idea of a woman, is appreciated only for her decorative value. Final condition of the imaginary prostitute: men would rather have slept with her than sleep with her. She is most arousing as a memory or as a masturbatory

fantasy. If she perceives herself as something else, the contradictions of her situation will destroy her. This is the Monroe syndrome ...

Justine is the model for the nineteenth and early twentieth-century denial of femininity as praxis, the denial of femininity as a positive mode of dealing with the world. Worst of all, a cultural conspiracy has deluded Justine and her sisters into a belief that their dear being is in itself sufficient contribution to the world; so they present the enigmatic image of irresistibility and powerlessness, forever trapped in impotence. (*SW* 57, 70–1)

Tristessa the man in drag is an agent of this masculine cultural conspiracy. It is a point underlined by his full name, Tristessa de St Ange. In Sade's *Philosophy in the Boudoir* (1795) Madame de Sant-Ange is the libertine who initiates the girl Eugenie into the practices of sadism. These two females become, like Juliette, co-opted by and agents of patriarchal power. The image of woman which Tristessa perpetuated in scores of film roles was a denial of history, an act of masculine mythologising and a definition of female impotence:

'Passivity,' he said, 'Inaction. That time should not act upon me, that I should not die. So I was seduced by the notion of a woman's being, which is negativity. Passivity, the absence of being. To be everything and nothing. To be a pane the sun strikes through.' (*PNE* 137)

Eve describes Tristessa in a manner that is traced with a memory of how the film star's victim role had turned her on when she was growing up as a boy: 'Tall, pale, attenuated enigma, your face an invitation to necrophilia, face of an angel upon a tombstone, a face that will haunt me forever, a face dominated by hooded eyes whose tears were distillations of the sorrows of the world' (*PNE* 121). Tristessa's image of woman defines a female masochism which is both produced by and sustains sadism. Tristessa the man projects an image of woman as object, devoid of subjectivity. As Carter was to write in *The Sadeian Woman*:

To be the *object* of desire is to be defined in the passive case.
To exist in the passive case is to die in the passive case – that is, to be killed.
This is the moral of the fairy tale about the perfect woman. (*SW* 76–7)

Above all, like the Count in *The Infernal Desire Machines of Dr Hoffman*, the masculine subject's desire to destroy the object of its desires is simultaneously a desire for self-annihilation. In Tristessa's case this syndrome is contained within the one figure of a man in drag. That figure finds an actual fulfilment – the same kind of void fulfilment as the Count found in *Dr Hoffman* – when Zero arrives to destroy her/him. The whole syndrome – its lack of relation to actual women and its encapsulation of a masculine death wish – is symbolised by the transparency and brittleness of Tristessa's house, which is built of glass:

> While Zero ingeniously tortured you in your gallery of glass, you must have been in absolute complicity with him. You must have thought Zero, with his guns and knives and whips and attendant chorus of cringing slaves, was a man worth the ironic gift of that female appearance which was your symbolic autobiography. I read it at a glance. You had turned yourself into an object as lucid as the objects you made from glass; and this object was, itself, an idea. (*PNE* 129)

But if Tristessa is like this, so is Eve. Eve has been constructed by Mother's matriarchy according to the same principles as Tristessa used to construct himself as woman; according to the predilections of the masculine gaze. In the programme of conditioning to which the matriarchy subjected her after Evelyn's physical transformation into a *Playboy* centrefold, the media image of Tristessa herself was of paramount importance: 'New Eve, whose sensibility had been impregnated with that of Tristessa during the insomniac nights of transmutation in the desert' (*PNE* 119). Eve recognises her kinship with the masculine fantasy that is Tristessa: 'The abyss on which her eyes open, ah! it is the abyss of myself, of emptiness, of inward void … We are beings without a history, we are mysteriously twinned by our synthetic life' (*PNE* 125). There is a sense in which Eve is as much in drag as Tristessa, not just because Eve was once Evelyn, but because Eve's physical appearance is concocted out of media-images of the female that were generated by the masculine gaze.

Tristessa's construction of himself as a woman – his construction of women in general – in terms of passivity is contradicted at the point when he is forced by Zero to have sex with Eve. Tristessa, stripped of his clothes, is made to lie on top of Eve and he mutters to her about 'woman's being' which he associates with 'Inaction' and 'Passivity' (*PNE* 137). Eve finds all this tiresome and takes the initiative: 'I was tired of waiting. I clasped my legs about him and drew him into me' (*PNE* 137–8). This activity on Eve's part contradicts the female passivity emblematised by Tristessa, who here is put into a passive role as a man. He even observes: 'I thought I was immune to rape' (*PNE* 137). The issue of activity and passivity in sexual roles is further elaborated when Carter describes Eve's and Tristessa's lovemaking once they have escaped the clutches of Zero and his mad harem. Here, Eve, on top, beats down mercilessly on Tristessa and – again in contradiction to the image of female passivity – smashes the image of the passive woman he had constructed himself as. This activity on Eve's part is returned by the man who then overwhelms *her*:

> We sucked at the water bottle of each other's mouth for there was nothing else to drink. Turn and turn about, now docile, now virile – when you lay below me all that white hair shifted from side to side … your hair dragged your head impetuously with it, this way and that way; I beat down upon you mercilessly, with atavistic relish, but the glass woman I saw beneath me smashed under my passion and the splinters scattered and recomposed themselves into a man who over-whelmed me. (*PNE* 149)

I disagree with Ricarda Schmidt's reading of this passage as one which simply equates 'the male role with active pursuit and the female one with being overwhelmed' (Schmidt 1990: 64). It is not simply that Eve actively smashes Tristessa as a construction representing female passivity. It is, more, that the scene refuses to represent either partner as singly active or passive. Each is, in turn, both. The account describes a reciprocity in lovemaking which anticipates the passage in *The Sadeian Woman* in which Carter speaks of 'the object of a reciprocal desire which is, in itself, both passive object and active subject. Such a partner acts on us as we act on it' (*SW* 146). 'Turn and turn about, now docile, now virile' is the more poetic way the idea is put in the *New Eve* passage.

The reciprocity of sexual roles in the passage is anticipated a little earlier when Eve describes her relations with Tristessa in terms of hermaphroditism:

> Alone, quite alone, in the heart of that gigantic metaphor for sterility … we peopled this immemorial loneliness with all we had been, or might be, or had dreamed of being, or had thought we were – every

modulation of the selves we now projected upon each other's flesh, selves – aspects of being, ideas – that seemed, during our embraces, to be the very essence of our selves; the concentrated essence of being, as if, out of these fathomless kisses and our interpenetrating, undifferentiated sex, we had made the great Platonic hermaphrodite together. (*PNE* 148)

This passage recalls the alchemical myth of hermaphroditic unity and might be thought to key in with the alchemical theme introduced towards the beginning of *New Eve*. It might, indeed, be thought to be an endorsement of the alchemical myth. This is apparently how Ricarda Schmidt takes the passage when she writes that it offers 'a model for a future symbol of femininity':

> The fact that this vision of a model for a future symbol of femininity implies the unification of what had been split into feminine and masculine in the course of evolution, i.e. the creation of symbolic hermaphroditism, documents the novel's origin in ideas of the 1970s. For Carolyn Heilbrun's book *Toward a Recognition of Androgyny* [1973] started off a lively discussion in the women's movement about the progressive value for women of the revival of this old Platonic concept. Those in favour of the concept of androgyny looked upon it as a helpful construction to overcome the present sex-role division and thus finally to reach a stage in which the term itself becomes meaningless. Others criticised it as a perpetuation of patriarchal norms because the term androgyny tended to assume femininity and masculinity as fixed entities that corresponded to the old stereotypes. This weakness of the concept of androgyny is also apparent in *Eve*. For, as I pointed out above, Eve's and Tristessa's playful role-change during their love-making still equates active pursuit with masculinity and docile submission with femininity. (Schmidt 1990: 65–6)

Among those '[o]thers' who, as Schmidt mentions, attacked the concept of androgyny was Daniel Harris, who observed in 1974 that

> For feminist men as well as for feminist women, the myth of androgyny has no positive value. As an ideal image of liberation from traditional sex-role stereotypes, it is false. We cannot discuss the myth, in psychological terms, without resorting to sexist polarisations for the definition of identity ('My intellect is my masculine self; my intuition, my feminine self') ... As Barbara Gelpi observes ... the myth of androgyny has been created by men, and its design is the co-option, incorporation, or subjugation of women: in seeking 'feminine' elements with which to complete himself, the man reduces woman to merely symbolic status,

plays parasite, and paradoxically demands from the creature he has mentally enslaved his own freedom. (Harris 1974: 171–2)

Returning to Carter, it is possible to read her passage on the 'great Platonic hermaphrodite' as other than a literal endorsement of the myth. The myth may be seen to presume, as Ricarda Schmidt points out, essentialist or archetypal characteristics – 'fixed entities' – of the female and the male. Now we know that Carter was sharply opposed to the idea of such mythic essences or archetypes. We have seen her saying, in *The Sadeian Woman*, that 'consolatory nonsense seems to me a fair definition of myth ... Mother goddesses are just as silly a notion as father gods ... Myth deals in false universals, to dull the pain of particular circumstances' (*SW* 5). She also says in *The Sadeian Woman* that 'All archetypes are spurious but some are more spurious than others' (*SW* 6). In *The Passion of New Eve* there is a verbal premonition of *The Sadeian Woman* when Carter has Eve say of herself and Tristessa when they are being forced into 'marriage' by Zero: 'the false universals of myth transformed us' (*PNE* 136). Eve as narrator observes that Mother's myth is a constructed not an essential or universal thing when she notes that: 'In Beulah, myth is a made thing not a found thing' (*PNE* 56). The negative critique of myth and mythologising is, as we have seen, carried to the point of parody in Carter's treatment of Mother and her matriarchy. The parody of Mother's cult includes also a parody of alchemy, for, in the burlesque litanies of the matriarchy there is an allusion to Mother as queen of the vessel used by alchemists to distil their gold:

> Maze-queen corn-queen barley-queen
> fructifier quickener pestilence-bringer
> queen of the crucible.
>
> (*PNE* 61)

A more subtle deconstruction of the alchemical hermaphroditic union between Eve and Tristessa occurs when Eve describes the night that followed their union. Eve first relates the end of the day on which the union occurred, before going on to the night that followed:

> The lateral beams of the setting sun melted the gold; it turned to alchemical gold ...

> So many stars! And such moonlight, enough moonlight to let a regi-
> ment of alchemists perform the ritual of the dissolution of the contents
> of the crucible, which, Baroslav, the Czech, had told me, may only be
> taken in polarised light, that is, light reflected from a mirror, or else by
> moonlight. (*PNE* 150)

What is important here is the fact that the alchemists' ultimate
ritual can only be observed by the light of the moon and that this
borrowed light is described in terms of light reflected from a *mirror*.
What this description of alchemical ritual in terms of a mirror
image does is to equate alchemy with the mirror images that have
been explored in respect of Leilah and her loss of herself in a
mirror image that is controlled by the masculine gaze ('a Leilah
who lived only in the not-world of the mirror', *PNE* 28). The
alchemical myth is here identified as a matter of representation
rather than as something rooted in essences. Like the gaze in the
mirror which constructs women, the myth is a construction rather
than a truth. Carter's passage on the 'great Platonic hermaphrodite' is daring because it goes right into mythic territory in order
to make a point which is anti-mythic. It is a description of a
sharing of bodies which is delighted by the sharing but which is
not itself *mythologising* that sharing. Like the description of the
setting sun turning 'to alchemical gold', the myth of the hermaphrodite here has at most a metaphoric status, quite different
from any claim that it is fundamentally true. We notice that the
various selves which each partner projects upon the other only
'seemed' to be 'the very essence of our selves' and that it is only
'as if' they had made the 'great Platonic hermaphrodite' together.
But more than that, we notice the lack of gender fixedness in the
modulation of selves that they project on each other. There is no
suggestion of an identification of, say, the intellect with the male
or of intuition with the female in the fixed, stereotypical manner
that Daniel Harris characterises as typical of the myth of androgyny. Carter's passage celebrates a reciprocity and interchangeableness – and hence a lack of rootedness – in identity and gender
roles. Carter was asked by Toril Moi in 1984: 'Is this book [*New
Eve*] a defence of androgyny?' 'Absolutely not', was Carter's reply.
'None of the two is an androgyne', she went on to say of Eve and
Tristessa (Moi 1984: 20). In fact, the figure of the 'great Platonic
hermaphrodite' is less a figure of androgyny than a figure of drag.

As I said earlier, there is a sense in which Eve may be seen to be as much in drag as Tristessa. And as Judith Butler has observed: '*In imitating gender, drag implicitly reveals the imitative structure of gender itself – as well as its contingency*' (Butler 1990: 137), a point which concurs with Carter's representation in the 'great Platonic hermaphrodite' passage of the contingency and interchangeability of identity and gender roles.

Carter's anti-mythic orientation in *The Passion of New Eve* is pursued in the episode which follows the scene of Eve's and Tristessa's lovemaking. The two are captured by a band of militant Christians who are travelling west to take part in the civil war that has broken out in California while Eve was in the desert. The striking thing about these Christians is that they are all children. Their leader, the Colonel, has had, in true evangelical fashion, a vision:

> Tossing fitfully in his bunk after watching the TV news ... the Colonel was visited by a vision. The Son of Man, who looked, to his unsurprise, very much like himself, dressed in the uniform of the Green Berets, pointed West.
>
> 'I come,' said the Colonel, 'to bring, not peace, but a sword.'
>
> His voice had hardly broken. It was the Children's Crusade. (*PNE* 159)

Carter's presentation of this band of little warmongers satirises the naivety, prejudice and violence of a certain kind of American right-wing Christian belief. The child soldiers, who have seen Eve and Tristessa making love, cannot stand what they call lechery, and while they tell Eve that Christ forgave the woman taken in adultery they also note that the Bible says nothing of 'the treatment of the man in the case' (*PNE* 155). Tristessa is shot after he kisses the startled Colonel. Once again, the peripatetic Eve manages to make her escape: this time into the final movement of the book.

It is a movement defined as a return to 'historicity' (*PNE* 166) following Eve's desert adventures in the land of myth, her desert adventures in the 'void of negation, that centre-piece of sterility' (*PNE* 161). For all that the desert and its myths may have been sterile, on the west coast of the United States history is raging in the form of the civil war. Tristessa now meets Leilah again. She is fighting as a partisan in the war. It turns out that Leilah is actually

Mother's daughter, and that her appearance in New York had been part of an elaborate plan to draw Evelyn to the desert and to Mother: 'what's become of the slut of Harlem ... She can never have objectively existed, all the time mostly a projection of the lusts and greed and self-loathing of a young man called Evelyn' (*PNE* 175). Leilah – who has now reassumed her real name, Lilith – holds no grudges against Eve for what Eve had been when she was Evelyn. What is important as far as the novel's overall rejection of myth is concerned, is that Leilah/Lilith repeatedly tells Eve that Mother has given up her mythic pretensions. In the period since Eve 'ran away from Beulah and set all her mother's plans awry' (*PNE* 173), Lilith relates,

> 'History overtook myth.' ... 'And rendered it obsolete.' ...
> 'Historicity rendered myth unnecessary,' said Leilah, 'The Priestesses of Cybele have left off simulating miraculous births ... and have turned into storm-troopers.' ...'Mother has voluntarily resigned from the god-head ... When she found she could not make time stand still, she suffered a kind of ... nervous breakdown. She has become quite gentle and introspective. She has retired to a cave by the sea for the duration of the hostilities.' ... 'the gods are all dead, there's a good deal of redundancy in the spirit world.' (*PNE* 172–5)

The very closing sequence of *New Eve* is a conclusive, sustained piece of demythologisation as Eve, taken by Lilith to a beach on the west coast, enters the cave by the sea to find Mother. Her reaching down into the cave is like a reaching into the 'earth's entrails' (*PNE* 180). It is a symbolically highly charged entry to the extent that she finds *no* symbols of any *necessary* ground or fundament to her identity. First of all, she finds a mirror which fails to offer an image of herself: 'the glass was broken, cracked right across many times so it reflected nothing, was a bewilderment of splinters and I could not see myself nor any portion of myself in it' (*PNE* 181). The world of representation in which women are constructed in a particular way does not exist down here in the cave. The earth's entrails are, as it were, blank as far as the *representation* of women and, for that matter, men, are concerned. Next, Eve finds a photograph of Tristessa; a glass flask, the like of which she had seen in the 'laboratory of Baroslav, the Czech alchemist' (*PNE* 182), containing a 'chunk of amber' (*PNE* 182) and the feather of a bird; and 'a mystery object wrapped up

in a scrap of paper' (*PNE* 182). Eve first tears up the photograph
of Tristessa, so *that* image of womanhood defined in masculine
terms is dispensed with. Then she holds the glass flask until the
amber becomes viscous and Eve experiences time running backwards, and she sees history and prehistory and the various stages
of evolution in reverse:

> The foal leaps back into its mother's womb; the gravid mare sniffs the
> air, which smells of entropy, and takes fright, trots briskly back down
> the sinuous by-ways of evolution ... through successive generations of
> her own ancestors; her hoof shrinks, now it's only the middle fingernail
> of the five toes of her paws. What stumpy little legs she has. She scamp-
> ers away into the Tertiary forests ... She herself becomes smaller and
> smaller until, in the alchemical vase, she becomes a solution of amino-
> acids and a tuft of hair, and then dissolves into the amniotic sea. (*PNE*
> 185–6)

As she witnesses the Eocene period, early in evolutionary time,
Eve notes that

> At that time, there was a bird called 'archaeopteryx' whose fossil will
> be found in the schist at Solenhofen; bird and lizard both at once, a
> being composed of the contradictory elements of air and earth. From
> its angelic aspect spring the whole family tree of feathered, flying things
> and from its reptilian or satanic side the saurians, creepy crawlers, crocs,
> the scaled leaper and the lovely little salamander. The archaeopteryx
> has feathers on its back but bones in its tail, as well; claws on the tips
> of its wings; and a fine set of teeth ...
> A miraculous, seminal, intermediate being whose nature I grasped
> in the desert. (*PNE* 185)

What, in effect, Eve is describing here – and it is something that
in principle she has grasped in her desert union with Tristessa –
is the absence in nature and evolutionary process of those differ-
entiated characteristics which human – specifically masculine –
convention and myth have attributed to men and women. In the
evolutionary origins of men and women there is nothing to ground
the differences that patriarchy has constructed to render women
inferior to men. Things in nature that now seem fixed – the
differences between species, say – are in evolutionary terms not so.
This vision is *not* of the oneness or wholeness of things. It is a
vision of the interchangeableness of things. In evolution there are
multiple possible combinations of things. What we see today in

nature has not always been so and will change again in the future. Just so, the differences between men and women constructed by culture have no essential, no natural ground. Men and women can be constructed differently from how they have been. And that is all – or everything – that Eve discovers in the cave of origins. She suddenly finds herself going back forwards through evolutionary time and being ejected from the depths of the cave. She never found Mother. Like a new-born child she cries for her mother, but the myth of origins that was Mother's myth has no foundation and there is no answer:

> I emitted, at last, a single, frail, inconsolable cry like that of a new-born child. But there was no answering sound at all in that vast, sonorous place where I found myself but the resonance of the sea and the small echo of my voice. I called for my mother but she did not answer me.
> 'Mama – mama – mama!'
> She never answered. (*PNE* 186)

Having failed to find a determining origin, Eve, returning to the beach, to Lilith and to history, now has a clean slate. Carter lastly captures the jettisoning of old myths by presenting two related details in the story. First, there is 'a mad old lady' (*PNE* 176) whom Lilith and Eve find living on the beach near the cave:

> The hair was dyed a brave canary yellow and piled in an elaboration of many tiers of curls, giving the general impression of a very expensive ice-cream sundae. All was decorated with peek-a-boo bows of pale pink silk ribbon and would have looked well under a glass dome on grandmother's mantlepiece. She was wearing a two-piece bathing costume in a red and white spotted fabric and, round her shoulders, a stole of glossy and extravagant blonde fur but her flesh was wrinkled and ravaged and sagged from her bones. Her face was very dirty but magnificently painted; a fresh coating of white powder and scarlet lipstick and maroon rouge must have been added that very morning. She was quite oblivious of our presence. She sat on her chair and sang of the lights of Broadway, of foggy days in London Town and how she'd learned her lesson but she wished she were in love again. Her swimming eyes had retreated deeply into her head down cavernous sockets frosted with glittering turquoise eye-grease. Her fingernails were fully six inches long and lacquered a glinting red, though badly chipped and scratched. She wore high-heeled silver sandals on her gnarled old feet and sat facing the ocean like the guardian of the shore; her fissured high soprano mingled with the slumbrous chords of the sea. (*PNE* 177)

At the opening of *New Eve*, Evelyn/Eve observed that:

> Our external symbols must always express the life within us with abso-
> lute precision; how could they do otherwise, since that life has gener-
> ated them? Therefore we must not blame our poor symbols if they take
> forms that seem trivial to us, or absurd, for the symbols themselves
> have no control over their own fleshly manifestations, however paltry
> they may be; the nature of our life alone has determined their forms.
> A critique of these symbols is a critique of our lives. (*PNE* 6)

In the decrepitude of the old lady on the beach may be read a
critique – at once derisory and pitying – of old symbols of womanhood. The old lady can also be read as, in part, a representation
of Mother, now demythologised, secularised and near extinction
(when Eve speaks the old lady nods her head 'as if she recognised
me at once', and her touch 'was as gentle as a surgeon's', *PNE*
189). The second related detail concerning the abandonment of
old myths is that Eve decides to take the old lady's boat, in return
giving her the 'mystery object wrapped up in a scrap of paper'
that she had found in the cave. This mystery object is the ingot of
alchemical gold that Baroslav had given to Eve when she was Evelyn. The relinquishing of this object to a figure embodying clichés
of the female signifies a relinquishing to the past of the alchemical
myth of the relations between the sexes, as well as a farewell to old
images of women.

At the outset of Evelyn's/Eve's journeying through the realms
of myth Baroslav the alchemist had said 'The age of reason is
over' (*PNE* 13). Now that myth has been exorcised, reason may
return. Eve is carrying a child conceived in her love-making in the
desert with Tristessa. Eve and her child may set out in the boat on
the ocean of life firmly oriented within the rational possibilities of
history rather than the irrational prejudices of myth. History, as
Lilith observed, has overtaken myth, 'rendered it obsolete' (*PNE*
172–3), and Eve's child will not be the child of mythic unreason.
Lilith returns to current historical battles – for all that they involve destruction, in *The Passion of New Eve* it is seen as more
worth fighting these than labouring under the dead weight of myth.
Eve and her child will comparably set out in history on a course
as yet unmapped but, at least, similarly undetermined by the dead
weight of myth.

In John Fowles's *The French Lieutenant's Woman*, evolution understood as a random process is taken as paradigm for a postmodernism which stresses the human and cultural contingency of interpretations of the world. This is not entirely unlike Carter's view in *The Passion of New Eve* of evolution as something which does not sanction mythic essentialism. But there is a very important difference. Carter's vision of the mutability and interchangeableness of things in evolution is not the same as an argument for the pure relativity of all human versions of reality. Carter uses the rational scientific conception of evolution in a rationalistic manner: to argue against those interpretations of gender – myths of Mother, Zero's myths of the male as against the female, Tristessa's 'irrational and absurd' (*PNE* 144) construction of womanhood – that make essentialist claims which contradict scientific, evolutionary evidence that there is nothing essential. The evidence that there is nothing essential is not taken, as in some extreme postmodernisms, to authorise versions of reality – specifically versions of gender – which claim that there *is* something essential. An author like Fowles may have made the point that no *one* interpretation of reality is essential or founded in the Absolute. But Carter introduces an additional manoeuvre into the anti-essentialist argument when she distinguishes between myth and irrationalism, on the one hand, and history and rationalism, on the other; when she comes out against mythic, irrational interpretations of reality that indeed claim absolute grounds. Carter's rational understanding that nothing is essential rules out of court any views, particularly of gender, which claim that certain things *are* essential. The rational understanding of non-essentialism does not lead here to relativism but to a ground from which judgement between views of the world can be made. The politics of gender are not relativised in *The Passion of New Eve* any more than Carter relativises herself as the author of her fictions. To this extent Carter resists postmodernism. Evelyn's or Zero's or Tristessa's or Mother's projections of what *is* are clearly seen as wrong. The book sustains a commitment to reason as the ground from which such wrongness may be discovered and as the ground upon which further debates and conflicts, but also the genuine possibility of growth, may be based. That things are *made* rather than *determined* is a rational perception that itself is not relativised by Carter.

The new Eve, constructed along the patriarchal lines which constructed the old Eve, has yet to become genuinely new. But that is what, now free of old myths, she can become. The last line of the novel, thus far spoken retrospectively by Eve, is spoken prospectively: 'Ocean, ocean, mother of mysteries, bear me to the place of birth' (*PNE* 191). No figure in *The Passion of New Eve* is a model either of femininity or of the ideal relation between the sexes. But the demythologising sympathies of the book are with the rational disquisitions and conflicts of history. Only on the basis of those disquisitions and conflicts can a new condition be imagined. It won't be until 1984 and *Nights at the Circus* that Carter offers a novel-length development and figuration of the anti-irrational position established in *New Eve*. *Nights at the Circus* is founded not just on the model of reason but on the model of rationality *with* humanism that Carter had argued for in *The Sadeian Woman*. It is also concerned, perhaps above all, with history. Just as we can detect in *Dr Hoffman* and *New Eve* a redefinition rather than a jettisoning of the Enlightenment ideal of reason, so in *Nights at the Circus* we do not find simply a wholesale rejection of the Enlightenment idea of history as an encyclopaedia of reasoned knowledge. What we find is an adjustment of the one-sidedness to be found in the history that has actually been written under an Enlightenment dispensation; that is, the exclusion of women's side of the story. But this extension in *Nights at the Circus* of the preoccupations of *Dr Hoffman* and *New Eve* into a preoccupation not only with reason but also with history will take place via a further critique of myth in the tales in the 1979 collection *The Bloody Chamber*.

FIVE

The Bloody Chamber
and Other Stories

Not 'myth', exactly. *The Bloody Chamber* (1979) is a collection of tales that are derived from fairy tales. In 1983 Carter noted: 'I wrote one anti-mythic novel in 1977, *The Passion of New Eve* ... and relaxed into folklore with a book of stories about fairy stories, *The Bloody Chamber*' (*SL* 38). The word 'about' is what is important here. The spirit of *The Bloody Chamber* tales is not escapist, but ironic and critical. Carter's conviction that 'in order to question the nature of reality one must move from a strongly grounded base in what constitutes material reality' (*SL* 38) remains the motivating principle of these tales which are based largely, though not exclusively, on Charles Perrault's 1697 collection of fairy tales, *Histoires et contes du temps passé*. Carter's interest in Perrault's rendering of fairy tales was precisely that, in his telling, Perrault remained grounded in material reality. In a piece written for *New Society* in 1976, a year before her own translation of *The Fairy Tales of Charles Perrault* was published, Carter expressed impatience with the adult escapism that lies at the heart of many retellings of fairy tales. She attacked 'the horns of elfland faintly blowing' school of thought about fairy tales and wrote that the 'free conventions of fairy tale, fantasy and imagination' are the 'perfect excuse' for demented adult indulgence in a 'domain of psychoanalytic privilege', *à la* Hans Christian Andersen, or for 'super-kitsch', in the manner of Oscar Wilde's 'over-upholstered fairy tales' (*SL* 454, 451–2). By contrast, Carter celebrated Perrault's worldliness, even though she may not have agreed with the morals he was pushing:

What an unexpected treat to find that in this great Ur-collection –
whence sprang the Sleeping Beauty, Puss in Boots, Little Red Riding
Hood, Cinderella, Tom Thumb, all the heroes of pantomime – all these
nursery tales are purposely dressed up as fables of the politics of
experience ...

Here all the stories are – sprightly and fresh, and so very worldly. It
is the succinct brutality of the folk tale modified by the first stirrings
of the Age of Reason. The wolf consumes Red Riding Hood; what else
do you expect if you talk to strange men, comments Perrault briskly ...

Archaic patterns of ritual initiation; forbidden thresholds; invitatory
incantations to pubertal rites ... all the elements that our more barba-
rous times rejoice in for their own sakes as part of the rarest show of
the unconscious, are subsumed by Perrault into a project for worldly
instruction ...

If there is something odd about a grown man who devotes most of
his time on the *qui vive* for the horns of elfland faintly blowing, I don't
think its too good for children, either. Rather let them learn enlightened
self-interest from Puss; resourcefulness from Tom Thumb; the advantages of patronage from Cinderella, and of long engagements from
the Sleeping Beauty ...

Ban Tolkien. Ban Andersen. Too much imaginative richness makes
Jack a dull boy; and no good at killing giants. (*SL* 452–4)

Carter's telling of fairy tales was designed to help kill giants in
the everyday, patriarchal world. Not that, in her telling, Carter is
in any sense blind to the psychoanalytic content of fairy tales. It
was simply that such content was just too obvious to be her
primary concern. In her 1985 interview with John Haffenden, she
resisted the idea that her tellings of fairy tales were to be understood in the light of the ideas of Bruno Bettelheim:

*Bruno Bettelheim, I think, takes the view that fairy tales use fantasy
materials to reflect inner experiences and processes ... Do you subscribe to
the arguments and interpretations he puts forward in 'The Uses of
Enchantment'?*

Not really, no. When I wrote my book of fairy tales, *The Bloody Chamber*,
I had read Bettelheim, and I was interested in the psychoanalytic content of the stories. Everyone knows that Bettelheim is terrific with
children, but I think he is sometimes wrong ... An historian named
Robert Darnton, in a very nice book called *The Great Cat Massacre*, has
a long essay about the oral tradition in seventeenth-century France
which really lams into the psychoanalytic school of interpretation of
fairy tales. He says you can hardly talk about the latent content of
stories which are explicitly about cannibalism, incest, bestiality and
infanticide, and of course he's right. (Haffenden 1985: 82–3)

Carter's fairy tales are, then, informed but not contained by psychoanalytic insight. They are better described as materialist, rationalist 'fables of the politics of experience'. Specifically, of course, it is the gender politics and the intimately related class politics of experience that they are preoccupied with. Carter's tales go deeper than Perrault's kind of moralising about experience: they look at the way in which experience is fundamentally structured in gendered terms. Carter's desire, in *The Bloody Chamber*, to impart a knowledge of this structuring of everyday experience means that the comments she made in the 'Afterword' to her collection of tales in *Fireworks* apply just as much to the tales she tells in *The Bloody Chamber*:

> though the play of surfaces never ceased to fascinate me, I was not so much exploring them as making abstractions from them, I was writing, therefore, tales ... Formally the tale differs from the short story in that it makes few pretences at the imitation of life. The tale does not log everyday experience, as the short story does; it interprets everyday experience through a system of imagery derived from subterranean areas behind everyday experience, and therefore the tale cannot betray its readers into a false knowledge of everyday experience. (*BB* 459)

Carter's further comment on one aspect of the Gothic mode in the 'Afterword' to *Fireworks* also highlights the peculiar realism that dictates the extravaganzas of *The Bloody Chamber*. The wildness of the tales is used to expose the things that lie behind ideological assertions about the nature of reality:

> The Gothic tradition in which Poe writes grandly ignores the value systems of our institutions ... Character and events are exaggerated beyond reality, to become symbols, ideas, passions. Its style will tend to be ornate, unnatural – and thus operate against the perennial human desire to believe the word as fact. (*BB* 459)

In *The Bloody Chamber* Carter is concerned not simply to point out what is wrong with conventional representations of gender; she is concerned at once to offer different representations, different models. These two concerns may be apparent simultaneously in a single tale. Sometimes the two concerns emerge most clearly in the counterpointing between two different tellings of the same tale. This is the case, for example, with Carter's two Beauty and the Beast tales, 'The Courtship of Mr Lyon' and 'The Tiger's Bride'.

'The Courtship of Mr Lyon' repeats, in basic outline, the plot of the traditional Beauty and the Beast fable, where Beauty, who loves her father, saves his life by agreeing to live with the Beast; the Beast is relieved of his enchantment by Beauty's love and turns into a handsome prince who marries her. At the outset of Carter's story, Beauty's father has just learned that he is financially ruined. Returning home to Beauty, he accidentally meets Mr Lyon, the leonine Beast of the tale, who, seeing a photograph of Beauty, invites father and daughter to dinner. At dinner Mr Lyon offers to help Beauty's father regain his fortune. This entails Beauty's father leaving for London 'to take up the legal cudgels again' (*BB* 148), while Beauty remains with Mr Lyon. News comes through that Beauty's father has won back his fortune. Beauty sets out to join him in London, but only after Mr Lyon has extracted from her a promise that she will return to him. After some months in London, Beauty forgets her promise but is eventually alerted, by Mr Lyon's pet spaniel dog, to the fact that something is wrong with the Beast and so she returns to him. When she meets him he tells her that he has been unable to eat since she left and is, therefore, dying. She takes pity on him: 'Don't die, Beast! If you'll have me, I'll never leave you' (*BB* 153). The Beast, accordingly, turns into a man and the tale ends with a note of their marriage.

In *The Uses of Enchantment* Bruno Bettelheim reads Beauty and the Beast as a tale imaging a healthy and positive transfer of a girl's affection for her father to a man who is to be her sexual partner. It is a transfer that describes the successful maturation of the girl into a woman:

> In this story all is gentleness and loving devotion to one another on the part of the three main characters: Beauty, her father, and the Beast ... No other well-known fairy tale makes it as obvious as 'Beauty and the Beast' that a child's oedipal attachment to a parent is natural, desirable, and has the most positive consequences for all, if during the process of maturation it is transferred and transformed as it becomes detached from the parent and concentrated on the lover. Our oedipal attachments, far from being only the source of our greatest emotional difficulties ... are the soil out of which permanent happiness grows if we experience the right evolution and resolution of these feelings. (Bettelheim 1977: 303, 307)

In her interview with John Haffenden Carter observed that 'some of the stories in *The Bloody Chamber* are the result of quarrelling furiously with Bettelheim' and she specified the fable of Beauty and the Beast as one where her reading disagreed markedly with Bettelheim's (Haffenden 1985: 83). Bettelheim might see the fable as an allegory of women's growth into adulthood but, in 'The Courtship of Mr Lyon', Carter sees the story as summarising a masculine conspiracy to deny women the chance of ever reaching autonomous, self-responsible adulthood. Carter makes the point not by altering the plot of the original, but through her emphases and observations in the telling of the plot.

First of all, Beauty's father is, quite simply, a patriarch. He thinks of Beauty as 'his girl-child, his pet' (*BB* 144). Carter points to the position of the female in patriarchy as an object in an economic system of exchange when she allows, in a sentence about the white rose that Beauty's father had promised to buy her, a momentary ambiguity about whether it is Beauty who is bought or the rose that she wanted to be bought for her. Later in the story it will become apparent that the white rose itself signifies Beauty's status as a commodity:

> Ruined, once; then ruined again, as he had learnt from his lawyers that very morning ... And not even enough money left over to buy his Beauty, his girl-child, his pet, the one white rose she said she wanted. (*BB* 144)

On his way home from his lawyers Beauty's father's car – a clichéd symbol of masculine potency that is used so blatantly here that it slips cliché – breaks down. He calls for help at what turns out to be the Beast's house. It is a house offering comforts of a caricaturedly masculine taste: 'a snug little leather-panelled study', 'a roaring log fire', a 'whisky decanter' and 'sandwiches of thick-cut roast beef, still bloody'; '[a]ll that remained to make Beauty's father entirely comfortable was to find, in a curtained recess, not only a telephone but the card of a garage that advertised a twenty-four-hour rescue service' (*BB* 145–6). There is no human to greet Beauty's father in this house. The only living thing he meets at first is the Beast's pet spaniel. The dog is female and actualises, in its relation to the Beast, the manner in which Beauty's father images Beauty as less than human, as his 'pet'. The entrapping, proprietorial aspect of this way of thinking is emphasised when, in the case of the dog, we hear that it gave Beauty's father 'comforting proof of his unseen host's wealth and eccentricity to see the dog wore, in place of a collar, a diamond necklace' (*BB* 145). Later, we will hear that on another day 'the spaniel wore a neat choker of turquoises' (*BB* 148), where the choker also carries the connotation of asphyxiation.

Having organised the repair of his car, Beauty's father, who has still not met the Beast, prepares to leave the Beast's house. On his way out he takes a white rose from the Beast's garden to give to his daughter in fulfilment of his promise to buy her one. Suddenly the Beast appears and accuses Beauty's father of being a 'Thief!' (*BB* 147). The white rose, emblematising the relation between Beauty and her father, becomes a token in a system of private ownership that is defined according to the terms of the male Beast and Beauty's father. The Beast sees the photograph of Beauty and the deal he offers is that Beauty's father will be forgiven his theft of the rose in exchange for bringing Beauty to dinner at the Beast's house. The objectification of Beauty as her father's property, his pet, continues as she now becomes an item of exchange between her father and the beast. Carter has a sly way of highlighting the assumed power of this male-defined economy in her narrator's comment just after the Beast has offered Beauty's father the deal: '"Take her her rose, then, but bring her to dinner", he growled; *and what else was there to be done?*' (*BB* 147; my italics). Beauty's father accedes to an agreement based on the idea of an impersonal, unalterable law of contract. Carter's sly question emphasises his accession and questions its grounds. Outside of this system, quite a number of other things might be done.

The complete powerlessness of Beauty in the face of this apparently inexorable, male-dominated system is emphasised in Carter's description, in the first place, of why Beauty goes through with her first meeting with the Beast and, in the second place, of exactly why she has to remain with the Beast while her father goes to London:

> she stayed, and smiled, because her father wanted her to do so ... when ... the Beast ... suggested ... that she should stay here, with him ... while her father returned to London ... she forced a smile. For she knew with a pang of dread, as soon as he spoke, that it would be so and her visit to the Beast must be, on some magically reciprocal scale, the price of her father's good fortune. (*BB* 148)

Bettelheim may have seen the relationship between Beauty, on the one hand, and her father and the Beast, on the other, as characterised by 'gentleness and loving devotion' (Bettelheim 1977: 303), a gentleness and love that ease the transition from the girl into the woman. But Carter sees the relationship in much more mercenary terms, as one in which Beauty is passed around between males and never given the chance of self-determination. Carter simultaneously makes the point that recognition of the systematic objectification of Beauty in a masculine world is deflected by what may be termed corrupt emotional practice on the part of males. The Beast is not a certain kind of male ogre: he doesn't imprison Beauty or rape her. But, not content with trading for her with her father, he exploits her sentiment. When she has returned to him at the end of the story the Beast performs an act of pure emotional blackmail:

> 'I'm dying, Beauty,' he said in a cracked whisper of his former purr. 'Since you left me, I have been sick. I could not go hunting, I found I had not the stomach to kill the gentle beasts, I could not eat. I am sick and I must die; but I shall die happy because you have come to say goodbye to me.' (BB 152–3)

The Beast here exploits what is, in fact, Beauty's very conventional 'femininity', her sentimental susceptibility to sickness in the male and her stereotypical recoil from destruction. But the Beast doesn't just exploit Beauty's conditioned femininity: a part of his manipulation is that he appropriates to himself the 'feminine' aversion to violence that masculine culture has itself attributed to the female. His sob-story is just too much for Beauty:

> She flung herself upon him, so that the iron bedstead groaned, and covered his poor paws with her kisses.
> 'Don't die, Beast! If you'll have me, I'll never leave you.' ... Her tears fell on his face like snow ... And then it was no longer a lion in her arms but a man. (BB 153)

A combination of economic dependency and conditioned emotional susceptibility condemns Beauty to continuing impairment and possession by the male. In Carter's reading the fable allegorises the stunting of women's growth to individual, adult identity. Carter herself commented that the Beauty and the Beast fable is 'an advertisement for moral blackmail: when the Beast says that he is dying because of Beauty, the only morally correct thing for her to have said at that point would be, "Die, then"' (Haffenden 1985: 83).

But in 'The Courtship of Mr Lyon' she doesn't say that. Mr Lyon's complacent, self-regarding satisfaction with his appropriation of Beauty is captured as we hear him say, after Beauty has agreed never to leave him, '"Do you know" ... "I think I might be able to manage a little breakfast today, Beauty, if you would eat something with me"' (*BB* 153). The very last line of 'The Courtship of Mr Lyon' is a parody of the ideological representation of conventional bourgeois marriage. It is a representation that, in all its sentimental idealisation, masks the real power relations which Carter's tale has exposed: 'Mr and Mrs Lyon walk in the garden; the old spaniel drowses on the grass, in a drift of fallen petals' (*BB* 153).

If 'The Courtship of Mr Lyon' highlights what is corrupt about the image of gender relations in the Beauty and the Beast tale, then 'The Tiger's Bride' seeks to alter the image from within a telling of the tale itself. The role of women as items of exchange in a patriarchal system is accented even more sharply in 'The Tiger's Bride' than in 'The Courtship of Mr Lyon'. The mother of the Beauty in 'The Tiger's Bride' had been 'bartered for her dowry to such a feckless sprig of the Russian nobility that she soon died of his gaming' (*BB* 155). Beauty and her profligate father go to Italy where, in some remote region they visit, the father is invited to play a game with the Beast of the tale – a tiger who wears 'a mask with a man's face painted most beautifully on it' (*BB* 156). Beauty's father ends up gambling and losing to the beast even his daughter:

> my father ... was left with nothing.
> 'Except the girl.'
> Gambling is a sickness. My father said he loved me yet he staked his daughter on a hand of cards ... You must not think my father valued me at less than a king's ransom; but at *no more* than a king's ransom ...
> The Beast's man informed me that he, the valet, would call for me and my bags tomorrow ... and conduct me forthwith to the Beast's palazzo. (*BB* 156–7)

Yet it is noteworthy that the Beauty of 'The Tiger's Bride' does not seem to have been *suddenly* disillusioned by having been, as she describes it, 'Lost to the Beast!' (*BB* 158). It is as if, under her

father's tutelage, she already knew that her status as an object, as
a commodity, was her only status in the world; that her flesh was
the only purchase she had upon the world. Before quoting the
passage that makes this plain, however, I must note that she also
recalls recalling – at the time she had to go to the Beast – how, as
a child, her nurse had used the image of a 'tiger-man' whose
'hinder parts were all hairy' to 'scare' her 'into good behaviour'
(*BB* 158). She also recalls recalling how, as a child, she had learned
of things she knew she must not tell her nurse. She had learned
from the 'giggling nursemaids ... the mysteries of what the bull
did to the cows' (*BB* 158). As a child she had also heard superstitions about how 'the waggoner's daughter', who was so ugly
that no man would ever have wanted her, had given birth to a son
'born of a bear' (*BB* 158). These recollections, at the time she had
to go to the Beast – of a childhood knowledge of sex together with
superstitions about sex and an imposed fear of the animal – combined with, as I say, an awareness of her status as a commodity.
This combination of knowledge, superstition, fear and awareness
further combined with self-assertion:

> Old wives' tales, nursery fears! I knew well enough the reason for the
> trepidation I cosily titillated with superstitious marvels of my childhood
> on the day my childhood ended. For now my own skin was my sole
> capital in the world and today I'd make my first investment. (*BB* 159)

This girl/woman/Beauty is not being easily and lovingly transferred from girlhood into womanhood. She is making the shift
apprehensively: her mind filled with factual knowledge of sex on
the one hand, the contrasting rhetorics of fear of animality and of
superstition about sex on the other; together with an awareness of
her own role as a flesh-object in a commodity system and a determination to play the game for all it was worth, since that was the
hand she'd been dealt.

Once she has arrived at the Beast's palace Beauty learns that
what he expects of her is to see 'the pretty young lady unclothed
nude without her dress' (*BB* 160). She at first agrees to satisfy his
demand, on certain terms: 'You may put me in a windowless room,
sir, and I promise you I will pull my skirt up to my waist, ready
for you. But there must be a sheet over my face, to hide it' (*BB*
161). Beauty is here asserting her own knowledge of the codes of

masculine objectification of the female, as if she were saying: 'If I'm going to be an object, then I'm *really* going to be one'. Her very assertion of her knowledge is something that defines her autonomy and incipient resistance. Whilst she is waiting to fulfil her promise Beauty is given 'a lady's maid' (*BB* 161) to accompany her. This maid turns out to be 'a marvellous machine' (*BB* 162); a machine made up as a caricature of a woman:

> the door swings open and out glides a soubrette from an operetta, with glossy, nut-brown curls, rosy cheeks, blue, rolling eyes; it takes me a moment to recognise her, in her little cap, her white stockings, her frilled petticoats. She carries a looking glass in one hand and a powder puff in the other and there is a musical box where her heart should be; she tinkles as she rolls towards me on her tiny wheels. (*BB* 162)

This animated doll, like the pet spaniel with a choker of turquoises in 'The Courtship of Mr Lyon', instances the position of women in patriarchy. Such women are not even servants; they are mimicries of the human. The Beast's valet notes that 'We have dispensed with servants ... We surround ourselves instead, for utility and pleasure, with simulacra and find it no less convenient than do most gentlemen' (*BB* 162). Beauty recognises this simulacrum of a woman, though it takes her a moment to do so. It is herself or, in its constructed inhumanness, it is a literalisation of her position in relation to her father and to the Beast:

> This clockwork twin of mine ... thrusts towards me her little mirror.
> I saw within it not my own face but that of my father, as if I had put on his face when I arrived at the Beast's palace as the discharge of his debt. (*BB* 162)

Beauty then decides that she will not, in fact, play her part in the discharging of her father's debt. She refuses to be an object in a patriarchal contract. She will not undress for the Beast. This decision is part of a gradual unpacking, on Beauty's part, of the role in society that she had been allotted as a girl/woman. And not just as a girl/woman. Her refusal involves an assertion of her status as something other than working-class, other than a 'maid'. There is an implication here that male-dominated society doubly oppresses the working-class female; that Beauty's resistance is founded in part in her bourgeois origins. Beauty sees that her culturally defined self was no self at all, merely an imitation of a self. As a girl she had been disallowed the rationality that – in Carter's vision of things – defines the human by a patriarchy that, in that very disallowance, itself lacked reason. As she realises the insubstantiality of her humanity as culturally defined, her fear of the beasts grows less. As she goes riding with Beast and valet, she begins to define herself outside of culture and in terms of the animal:

> I knew my two companions were not, in any way, as other men, the simian retainer and the master for whom he spoke, the one with clawed forepaws ... I knew they lived according to a different logic than I had done until my father abandoned me to the wild beasts by his human carelessness. This knowledge gave me a certain fearfulness still; but, I would say, not much ... I was a young girl, a virgin, and therefore men denied me rationality just as they denied it to all those who were not exactly like themselves, in all their unreason ... the six of us – mounts and riders, both – could boast amongst us not one soul, either, since all the best religions in the world state categorically that not beasts nor women were equipped with the flimsy, insubstantial things when the good Lord opened the gates of Eden and let Eve and her familiars tumble out ... I ... meditated on the nature of my own state, how I had been bought and sold, passed from hand to hand. That clockwork girl who powdered my cheeks for me; had I not been allotted only the same kind of imitative life amongst men that the doll-maker had given her? (*BB* 165)

After this development in Beauty's awareness, the Beast begins, at least, to show himself as partaking in an order of being that also lies outside the patriarchal. He does not insist that Beauty fulfil her allotted part in the contractual obligation arranged with her father. He does insist, however, as his valet tells Beauty, that if she will not let the Beast see her naked, then she must see the Beast without *his* mask of humanity. It is here that one of the clearest contrasts with 'The Courtship of Mr Lyon' occurs. In 'The Courtship of Mr Lyon' Beauty is not only defined as but defines herself as victim in the patriarchal game that she finds herself caught up in: 'when she saw the great paws lying on the arm of his chair, she thought: they are the death of any tender herbivore. And such a one she felt herself to be, Miss Lamb, spotless, sacrificial' (*BB* 148). In 'The Tiger's Bride' Beauty, having begun to define herself outside the prescriptions of patriarchal culture, refuses the role of victim. She refuses to be a lamb. The tiger reveals his animality beneath the human mask and she, asserting herself, does the same. Her stripping now does not place her as the object of the masculine gaze. It incorporates into her subject position an animality which cultural construction of what she is has sought to mask. Carter here exposes a key contradiction in the cultural construction of femininity. The exposure involves the issue of class. In masculine culture it is specifically bourgeois women who have been classed as non-animal, while working-class women have been more associated with the animal. Cultural construction of femininity has thus sought both to mask and paradoxically to insist upon women's animality in a kind of divide-and-rule strategy. Both bourgeois and working-class femininity are demeaned by the simultaneous masking of and insistence upon animality. By showing the bourgeois Beauty's dismissal of her mask, Carter is breaking the patriarchal frame that had sought to oppress simultaneously bourgeois and working-class women through applying contradictory definitions of animality. Beauty experiences freedom, for the first time in her life, as she begins to run with – not from – the tigers:

> The valet held out his master's cloak to screen him from me as he removed the mask. The horses stirred.
> The tiger will never lie down with the lamb; he acknowledges no pact that is not reciprocal. The lamb must learn to run with the tigers.
> A great, feline, tawny shape whose pelt was barred with a savage geometry of bars the colour of burned wood ...
> The valet moved forward as if to cover up his monster now the girl had acknowledged him, but I said: 'No.' ...
> I ... now unfastened my jacket.... Yet I was clumsy and blushed a little, for no man had seen me naked and I was a proud girl. Pride it was, not shame, that thwarted my fingers so ...
> I showed his grave silence my white skin, my red nipples, and the horses turned their heads to watch me, also, as if they, too, were courteously curious as to the fleshly nature of women ... I felt I was at liberty for the first time in my life. (*BB* 166)

Beauty completes the jettisoning of patriarchal definition by dressing up the clockwork maid in her own clothes, winding her up and returning her to her father, 'to perform the part of my father's daughter' (*BB* 167). Beauty returns to the Beast. In her interview with John Haffenden, Carter identified the wolves that appear in another story in *The Bloody Chamber*, 'The Company of Wolves', as representing, in part, libido (Haffenden 1985: 84). The tiger here does the same. When Beauty returns to find the Beast in 'The Tiger's Bride', Carter's tale once again seeks to exorcise a cultural definition of the female as passive victim, a definition which attributes libidinal desire only to the male and associates the female with being merely the inert object of that desire. Not, of course, that women have not both participated in and resisted patriarchal definitions of themselves. But there is an important patriarchal idea of the female as passive which Carter is deconstructing here. In Carter's tale the male is represented as being as much trapped within the patriarchal scenario as the female. Here, the female, equal to the male in fleshly nature *and* in appetite, dismisses nursery superstitions about the uniquely threatening animality of the male:

> He was pacing backwards and forwards ... the tip of his heavy tail twitching as he paced out the length and breadth of his imprisonment between the gnawed and bloody bones.
> He will gobble you up.
> Nursery fears made flesh and sinew; earliest and most archaic of fears, fear of devourment. The beast and his carnivorous bed of bone and I, white, shaking, raw, approaching him as if offering, in myself, the key to a peaceable kingdom in which his appetite need not be my extinction. (*BB* 168)

The ending of 'The Tiger's Bride' contradicts the endorsement of patriarchal power in the original Beauty and the Beast fable as it envisages a liberation from cultural misrepresentations of male and female through an exposure of an animal equality between the sexes:

> He dragged himself closer and closer to me, until I felt the harsh velvet of his head against my hand, then a tongue, abrasive as sandpaper. 'He will lick the skin off me!'
> And each stroke of his tongue ripped off skin after successive skin, all the skins of a life in the world, and left behind a nascent patina of shiny hairs. My earrings turned back to water and trickled down my shoulders; I shrugged the drops off my beautiful fur. (*BB* 169)

Patricia Duncker has argued that traditional fairy tales enshrine a sexist economy which Carter cannot fundamentally alter:

> the infernal trap inherent in the fairy tale, which fits the form to its purpose, to be the carrier of ideology, proves too complex and per-

vasive to avoid. Carter is rewriting the tales within the strait-jacket of their original structures. The characters she re-creates must to some extent, continue to exist as abstractions. Identity continues to be defined by role, so that shifting the perspective from the impersonal voice to the inner confessional narrative as she does in several of the tales, merely explains, amplifies and re-produces rather than alters the original, deeply, rigidly sexist psychology of the erotic. (Duncker 1984: 6)

Merja Makinen argues persuasively, on behalf of Carter, against a view like this:

> the question of the form of the fairy-tale: is it some universal, unchangeable given or does it change according to its specific historic rendition? Narrative genres clearly do inscribe ideologies (though that can never fix the readings), but later re-writings that take the genre and adapt it will not necessarily encode the same ideological assumptions. Otherwise, one would have to argue that the African novels that have sought to decolonize the European cultural stereotypes of themselves must always fail ... This is clearly not true. When the form is used to critique the inscribed ideology, I would argue, then the form is subtly adapted to inscribe a new set of assumptions. (Makinen 1992: 4–5)

I would agree that Carter successfully inscribes an old form with a new set of assumptions in *The Bloody Chamber* tales. They are assumptions that Duncker misses when she writes:

> The disarming of aggressive male sexuality by the virtuous bride is at the root of ... Beauty and the Beast ... 'The Tiger's Bride' argues a variation on the original bargain; the heroine is sold to the highest bidder in the marriage pact, but she too strips off all artifice, the lies inherent in borrowed garments, and reveals herself as she is, the mirror image of his feline predatory sexuality ... I would suggest that all we are watching, beautifully packaged and unveiled, is the ritual disrobing of the willing victim of pornography ... Carter envisages women's sensuality simply as a response to male arousal. She has no conception of women's sexuality as autonomous desire. (Duncker 1984: 6–7)

Such a reading fails to take account of, for example, Beauty's assertiveness when, having seen the Beast naked, she refuses to let him be covered up again and proceeds to show herself naked. She has the choice there. To let the Beast cover himself again would have been to endorse patriarchy by confirming that she has no animal self to expose. However, she is not the mirror image of his sexuality but the distinct and equal complement to the sexuality he displays. This is, of course, a heterosexual economy. But Carter's picturing of the autonomy of women's sexual desire within heterosexual terms does not preclude the existence of other, non-heterosexual relationships where women manifest autonomous desire. Nor, in her reading, does Duncker take into account Beauty's explicit rejection of patriarchy and her assertion of her own will and her own desires and drives when she sends back the mechanical maid to act out her old role as her father's daughter. As Makinen writes:

> Read the beasts as the projections of a feminine libido, and they become exactly that autonomous desire which the female characters need to recognise and reappropriate as a part of themselves (denied by the phallocentric culture). Isn't that why at the end of 'The Tiger's Bride' the tiger's licking reveals the tiger in the woman protagonist, beneath the cultural construction of the demure? Looked at again, this is not read as woman re-enacting pornography for the male gaze, but as woman reappropriating libido. (Makinen 1992: 12)

But reappropriating libido on Carter's, not on the Marquis de Sade's, terms. Avis Lewallen reads *The Bloody Chamber* tales, not least 'The Tiger's Bride', as operating within a purely Sadeian frame of reference. Having noted that the heroine of 'The Tiger's Bride' at the last recognises 'her own sexuality' (Lewallen 1988: 149), Lewallen goes on to say that:

> The question of choice, or lack of it, is echoed throughout the tales, and this is the Sadean framework – fuck or be fucked, both in the literal and in the metaphorical sense. Within this logic, to choose to fuck, given the options, seems a positive step, but the choice in fact is already prescribed. As Patricia Duncker puts it, 'we are watching ... the ritual disrobing of the willing victim of pornography'. (Lewallen 1988: 149)

Surely, this is to miss the reciprocity that Carter is so careful to stress in her telling of 'The Tiger's Bride'. It is a misreading, at root, of Carter's critique of Sade's 'fuck or be fucked' paradigm in *The Sadeian Woman*. Beauty in 'The Tiger's Bride is not based on Juliette in Sade. Beauty and the Beast in 'The Tiger's Bride' are modelled on Carter's image of the humane in *The Sadeian Woman*, where human beings interact as individually both subject and object, neither aggressor nor victim. In 'The Tiger's Bride' Beauty won't be fucked, as victim, by the Beast, as aggressor; nor will she, as aggressor, fuck the Beast, as victim. They will be fucking each other, equally, having disrupted the social conventions that prescribe fuck or be fucked as the only model of human relations. Running with the tigers means self-assertion, but not at the cost simply of devouring the other.

Carter certainly identifies an animal dimension to human beings that lies beneath social representations of that animality. In all of the tales in *The Bloody Chamber* it is existing social constructions that repress and misrepresent an animal energy shared equally between the sexes. One of the morals of all these tales is that we have to strip away existing cultural definitions of sexuality in order to reach a base level from which to begin building representation anew. It might be said, of course, that Carter, in arguing that the male *and* the female have equal 'natural' impulses, libidinal drives, is herself indulging in no more than a representation of nature and of sexuality. Since we can never know what nature 'truly' is, all we can ever have are representations of sexuality, Carter's not excluded. This would be a postmodern perspective on the matter. But Carter's empirical materialism leads her to see both women and men as creatures of the flesh and as equally rooted in and driven by fleshly impulses. To deny women the same fleshly ontology as men would be to fall into the patriarchal 'angel in the house' syndrome of misrepresentation of women, which of course has its equally constraining counter-misrepresentation of women who act out fleshly impulses as whores. It is patriarchal culture – in a duplicitous attempt to contain the female – which has generated the idea of male libido as threatening to devour sexually unmotivated females or as needing to protect itself against sexually motivated ones. By deconstucting one term of the opposition – in granting Beauty her own desire – Carter erases the opposition itself. She uses the image of animals to signify a libido that has been culturally repressed in some women and which needs recognising and articulating in order that they may define autonomous subject positions for themselves. A recognition of the materiality of the flesh is not the same as attributing particular essences to the flesh.

Carter's use of animals to figure a libido common to both the female and the male reappears in 'The Company of Wolves'. This tale is based largely upon the fairy tale of Little Red Riding Hood. The gender politics of the original tale and its successive pictorial illustrations have been analysed by Jack Zipes, who observes that most illustrations of the tale imply that Red Riding Hood 'willingly makes a bargain with the wolf, or, in male terms, "she asks to be raped"' (Zipes 1986: 239).

> Ultimately, the male phantasies of Perrault and the Brothers Grimm can be traced to their socially induced desire and need for control – control of women, control of their own sexual libido, control of their fear of women and loss of virility ...
> In the case of the Red Riding Hood illustrations and the classical texts by Perrault and the Grimms, the girl in the encounter with the wolf gazes but really does not gaze, for she is the image of male desire. She is projected by the authors Perrault and Grimm and generally by male illustrators as an object without a will of her own. The gaze of the wolf will consume her and is intended to dominate and eliminate her. The gaze of the wolf is a phallic mode of interpreting the world and is an attempt to gain what is lacking through imposition and force. Thus, the positioning of the wolf involves a movement toward convincing the girl that he is what she wants, and her role is basically one intended to mirror his desire. In such an inscribed and prescribed male discourse, the feminine other has no choice. Her identity will be violated and fully absorbed by male desire either as wolf or gamekeeper. (Zipes 1986: 257–8)

Carter's 'The Company of Wolves' tells the story of a girl who sets out through a forest taking her grandmother presents of food and liquor. She meets a young man and they agree to take different routes through the forest and see which one of them gets to the grandmother's house first. The man is, of course, a werewolf. He arrives at the house and eats the grandmother. The girl arrives a little later. The ritual of the original story is broadly observed until the wolf-man says 'All the better to eat you with'. At this point the girl reverses expectation. She declares her own activity and her refusal to be victim or merely object:

> What big teeth you have!
> She saw how his jaw began to slaver and the room was full of the forest's *Liebestod* but the wise child never flinched, even as he answered: All the better to eat you with.
> The girl burst out laughing; she knew she was nobody's meat. She laughed at him full in the face, she ripped off his shirt for him and flung it into the fire, in the fiery wake of her own discarded clothing. (*BB* 219)

Very quickly, the tale ends: 'See! sweet and sound she sleeps in granny's bed, between the paws of the tender wolf' (*BB* 220).

What Carter is doing in this retelling is taking the idea of the equality of libidinal impulse in human beings to ground a representation of human beings' interaction which escapes the Sadeian model of fuck or be fucked. The opposition of subject versus object, active versus passive, is transcended so that each individual in the encounter may be at once both. Just as the girl refuses to be 'meat', refuses to play the part simply of object of consumption or victim, so the wolf, traditionally solely the aggressor, is described at the last as 'tender'. Maggie Anwell has deftly summarised the way in which 'The Company of Wolves' fictionalises a model of subject relations that bypasses the egocentricity and the mutually exclusive dualisms of a Cartesian model of individual identity; a model which, as I have already argued, Carter opposed in more theoretical terms in *The Sadeian Woman*:

> Now she voluntary sheds her clothes, including her shawl, 'the colour of sacrifices, the colour of her menses'. As the werewolf gives the standard reply, 'All the better to eat you with', she bursts out laughing. She knows far better than he that she is 'nobody's meat'. She has discarded the role of sacrificial victim along with her shawl, and is clear in her acceptance of her own sexuality. We may note that this is not an aggressive 'masculinised' sexuality: she is neither Justine, martyred by passive acceptance of her fate, nor Juliet, equating sexuality with violence. Instead, we are left with an image of her successful negotiation: 'See! sweet and sound she sleeps in granny's bed, between the paws of the tender wolf.' (Anwell 1988: 80–1)

But if some women's recognition and expression of their own libidos serves to break patriarchal constructions of them as libidinally passive, then it also opens the way into an arena of new problematics. Or, to put it another way, it might be said that if women have libidinal drives equal to men and if they are not constructed merely as victims, then the question arises whether there are questionable dimensions to female libidinal drive. This is an issue taken up directly by Merja Makinen in her *Feminist Review* essay on Carter's *Bloody Chamber* tales.

First of all, Makinen notes that in *The Bloody Chamber* tales Carter is not only deconstructing patriarchal models of femininity, she is entering into a dialogue with feminist discourse itself, acknowledging that that discourse does not describe a stable, unitary perspective. Makinen argues, in effect, that some feminist perspectives on human sexuality do not themselves escape certain patriarchal constructions of female identity:

> I believe Carter is going some way towards constructing a complex vision of female psycho-sexuality, through her invoking of violence as well as the erotic. But that women can be violent as well as active sexually, that women can choose to be perverse, is clearly not something allowed for in the calculations of such readers as Duncker, Palmer and Lewallen. Carter's strength is precisely in exploding the stereotypes of women as passive, demure cyphers. That she therefore evokes the gamut of violence and perversity is certainly troubling, but to deny their existence is surely to incarcerate women back within a partial, sanitized image only slightly less constricted than the Victorian angel in the house. (Makinen 1992: 9)

Seeing that Carter has her female characters confronting not just male libido but their own, is more enlightening than preserving the idea of women as cyphers: 'Reading Carter's fairy-tales as her female protagonist's confrontation with desire, in all its unruly "animalness", yields rich rewards' (Makinen 1992: 11). The various and destabilising tendency of Carter's treatments of desire is what fascinates Makinen. Of three of the tales in *The Bloody Chamber*, for example, 'The Erl-King', 'The Snow Child' and 'The Lady of the House of Love', she writes:

> If the wild felines have signified the sensual desires that women need to acknowledge within themselves, the three fictive figures signify the problematics of desire itself. 'Erl-king' is a complex rendering of a subjective collusion with objectivity and entrapment within the male gaze. The woman narrator both fears and desires entrapment within the birdcage. The erl-king, we are told, does not exist in nature, but in a void of her own making (hence his calling her 'mother' at the end). The disquieting shifts between the two voices of the narrator, first and third person, represent the two competing desires for freedom and engulfment, in a tale that delineates the very ambivalence of desire. 'Snowchild' presents the unattainability of desire, which will always melt away before possession. No real person can ever satisfy desire's constant deferral. 'Lady of the House of Love', with its lady vampire, inverts the gender roles of Bluebeard, with the woman constructed as an aggressor, with a man as the virgin victim. But with this construction of aggressor, comes the question of whether sadists are trapped within their nature: 'can a bird sing only the song it knows or can it

learn a new song?' And, through love and the reciprocal theme – he kisses her bloody finger, rather than her sucking his blood – this aggressor is able to vanquish ancestral desires, but at a cost. In this tale the overwhelming fear of the cat tales, that the protagonist might be consumed by the otherness of desire, is given a new twist. (Makinen 1992: 11)

Makinen, too, notes that Carter's preferred analysis of subject relations avoids what I have spoken of as the oppositional paradigm of the Cartesian and Enlightenment view of individual identity: 'In all of the tales, not only is femininity constructed as active, sensual, desiring and unruly – but successful sexual transactions are founded on an equality and the transforming powers of recognising the reciprocal claims of the other' (Makinen 1992: 9). But this vision of successful sexual transactions is achieved through a recognition of the complexity of female sexuality and not through a (patriarchal) simplification of it:

I would argue that just as it is the debates around the marginalized and pathologized 'perversities' that are breaking up the phallocentric construction of sexuality, so Carter's texts are beginning to sketch the polymorphous potentialities of female desire. (Makinen 1992: 13–14)

This is all difficult ground, particularly for a male critic. But Carter was a dangerous writer. Nowhere are the dangers that Carter engaged and advertised in *The Bloody Chamber* more apparent than in the collection's title-story. 'The Bloody Chamber' is Carter's telling of Perrault's tale of a wealthy man, Bluebeard, who has married several wives, all of whom have disappeared. Bluebeard now marries the daughter of a neighbouring family. When Bluebeard is away on business he leaves his new wife the keys to his home, with the instruction that she should not use the key to open one particular room. However, her curiosity gets the better of her and she enters this forbidden room only to discover the remains of Bluebeard's previous wives. Bluebeard returns, discovers what his new wife has done, and decides that she too must die. She pleads for a little time and in that time, fortunately, her brothers come and rescue her, killing Bluebeard in the process.

Angela Carter's version of the tale is told in the first person by a woman who had married '[t]he richest man in France' (*BB* 116) – a Marquis, the equivalent of Bluebeard – and then escaped from him. The woman narrator tells the story of how she married the Marquis when, at seventeen, she was barely more than a girl. Her mother had 'defiantly beggared herself for love' (*BB* 111), lost her husband in 'the wars' (*BB* 111) and had to sell even her wedding ring to pay for her daughter, who is a pianist, to study music at the Paris Conservatoire. This mother is a fabulously formidable woman. Her daughter tells us how, in her younger years, she had 'outfaced a junkful of Chinese pirates; nursed a village through a visitation of the plague, shot a man-eating tiger with her own hand' (*BB* 112). The narrator tells us how her mother had queried her about the Marquis:

> 'Are you sure you love him?'
>   'I'm sure I want to marry him,' I said.
>   And would say no more. She sighed, as if it was with reluctance that she might at last banish the spectre of poverty from its habitual place at our meagre table. (*BB* 111)

Carter thus introduces what is a consistent theme throughout *The Bloody Chamber* tales, the potential distinction between love and marriage and the way in which marriage can have an economic dimension that lodges power with the male. Not heeding her mother's reservations, the girl marries the Marquis and the girl as narrator of the tale recounts how her marriage defined a leaving behind of the feminine and an assimilation to the world of the masculine. Right after her wedding, she leaves Paris by train for the Marquis' castle, bedazzled by the value of the wedding ring and other things he has bought her:

> This ring ... the wardrobe of clothes from Poiret and Worth, his scent of Russian leather – all had conspired to seduce me so utterly that I could not say I felt one single twinge of regret for the world of tartines and maman that now receded from me ... as the train began to throb again. (*BB* 115)

The girl, ceasing 'to be her' mother's 'child in becoming' the cigar-smoking Marquis' 'wife' (*BB* 111), is realigned within the order of the father: 'the cigar glowed and filled the compartment with a remembered fragrance that made me think of my father, how he would hug me in a warm fug of Havana, when I was a little girl' (*BB* 116).

One of the reasons why the girl failed to regret leaving Maman was that she was subject, *as* a girl, to a whole structure of myth and legend about the fulfilments to be derived from partnership with the male. It was a kind of cultural conditioning which not only held out the promise of fantastic fulfilment but at the same time insisted on the inevitability of this definition of fulfilment:

> His kiss, his kiss with tongue and teeth in it and a rasp of beard had hinted to me ... of the wedding night, which would be voluptuously deferred until we lay in his great ancestral bed in the sea-girt, pinnacled domain that lay, still, beyond the grasp of my imagination ... that magic place, the fairy castle whose walls were made of foam, that legendary habitation in which he had been born. To which, one day, I might bear an heir. Our destination, my destiny. (*BB* 112)

Carter points to the fact that such myths of feminine fulfilment are not merely masculinely inspired but patriarchally assumed when she has her narrator describe the Marquis' wedding present, which the girl wore on going to the opera before leaving Paris; a present that symbolises the connection between male economic power and the power to own, constrict and objectify the female:

> everyone stared at me. And at his wedding gift.
> His wedding gift, clasped round my throat. A choker of rubies, two inches wide, like an extraordinarily precious slit throat ... That night at the opera comes back to me even now ... the white dress; the frail child within it; and the flashing crimson jewels round her throat, bright as arterial blood. (*BB* 114–15)

What Carter's tale will, of course, emphasise is that the bottom line of this kind of proprietorial objectification of the female is the murder chamber in the Marquis' castle, where women have literally been denied subject-status and have been turned into objects, dead meat.

If patriarchy rules by ownership it rules simultaneously by the masculine gaze, a topic which had begun to be explored in detail by the late 1970s when Carter was writing 'The Bloody Chamber'. Carter provides a striking vignette of what was thought about the masculine gaze in the seventies in her narrator's account of the 'grand ... matrimonial bed' (*BB* 118) in the Marquis' castle. This bed has been constructed by the Marquis with a range of mirrors surrounding it. While the mirrors will, of course, reflect the man, they have been placed *by* him, at *his* initiative and *for* his purposes. Power lies with the constructor of the bed and its mirrors. It is a man's bed designed to satisfy a man's fantasies:

> And there lay the grand, hereditary matrimonial bed ... surrounded by so many mirrors! Mirrors on all the walls, in stately frames of contorted gold, that reflected more white lilies than I'd ever seen in my life before. He'd filled the room with them, to greet the bride, the young bride. The young bride, who had become that multitude of young girls I saw in the mirrors, identical in their chic navy blue tailor-mades, for travelling, madame, or walking ...
>   'See', he said, gesturing towards those elegant girls. 'I have acquired a whole harem for myself!' (*BB* 118)

In this passage the heroine as young girl objectifies herself first of all in the way she refers to herself in the third person. This is an analogue of the image of herself in the mirror which she comments on as if it were outside or different from herself. She comments on the images in the mirrors noting the chicness and elegance of the girls. There is an odd kind of self-alienation in this objectification of herself as other, her self-objectification on the masculine terms of the mirrors, which recalls John Berger's observation that the 'function ... of the mirror' in classical European paintings which exemplify the masculine gaze was 'to make the woman connive in treating herself as, first and foremost, a sight' (Berger 1972: 51). The multitude of mirrors and hence of girls emphasises her objectification: she loses individuality and becomes an item in a series of multiply reproduced items, a specimen of female sex in the Marquis' harem.

Not that, at this stage, the girl is arriving at any fully formed, conscious objection to the Marquis. There is a clever double narratorial perspective throughout this tale. The retrospective perspective of the woman narrator, who knows the full depravity of the Marquis, manages to capture the innocent perspective of herself as girl and her gradual, incremental loss of that innocence. The pattern may be illustrated by quoting from the scene where the girl discovers the Marquis' collection of pornography:

> The flames flickered along the spines inside the glass-fronted case that held books still crisp and new. Eliphas Levy; the name meant nothing to me. I squinted at a title or two: *The Initiation*, *The Key of Mysteries*,

The Secret of Pandora's Box, and yawned. Nothing, here, to detain a seventeen-year-old girl ...
  Nevertheless, I opened the doors of the bookcase idly to browse. And I think I knew, I knew by some tingle of the fingertips, even before I opened that slim volume with no title at all on the spine, what I should find inside ... Yet I had not bargained for this ... My mother ... had told me what it was that lovers did; I was innocent but not naive ... I knew enough for what I saw in that book to make me gasp. (*BB* 120)

In accordance with the plot of the original story, the Marquis is called away, or pretends to be called away, from the castle. He leaves all his keys to rooms in the castle with the girl, saying that she may use all of them bar one. After he has left she phones her mother and bursts into tears on hearing her mother's voice. No, nothing is really the matter, she reassures her mother. Then she goes into the room which the Marquis had forbidden her to enter. She finds a 'torture chamber ... Wheel, rack and Iron Maiden' (*BB* 131). Still, a part of her strives to avoid engaging with terminal horror: 'I ... almost persuaded myself that I might have stumbled only upon a little museum of his perversity, that he had installed these monstrous items here only for contemplation' (*BB* 131). Then, as she lights more candles, she finds the bodies. The girl's innocence is purged and she immediately thinks of how she may escape the castle; escape the patriarchal circuit of power that arrogates to itself an absolute, even divine authority:

The candles flared, as if in a draught from a door to elsewhere. The light caught the fire opal on my hand so that it flashed, once, with a baleful light, as if to tell me the eye of God – his eye – was upon me. My first thought, when I saw the ring for which I had sold myself to this fate, was, how to escape it. (*BB* 132)

The Marquis in 'The Bloody Chamber' holds essentially to the vision of subjectivity advanced by the Marquis de Sade, a vision that is based, as I have observed earlier, on an antagonistic dualism of self and other in which the egoistical, transcendent self can realise itself only through negation: through an impulse towards the negation of others which is at root a drive towards the negation of the self. The death wish informing the Marquis' conception of his own absolute subjectivity accounts for the despair that the woman narrator recalls perceiving in him:

When I came back into the bedroom carrying the bunch of keys that jangled at every step like a curious musical instrument, he was sitting on the bed in his immaculate shirtsleeves, his head sunk in his hands.

And it seemed to me he was in despair.

Strange. In spite of my fear of him ... I felt there emanate from him, at that moment, a stench of absolute despair, rank and ghastly, as if the lilies that surrounded him had all at once begun to fester ...

The atrocious loneliness of that monster! (*BB* 138)

Escape from the obliterating egoism of the Marquis is figured by Carter in a manner that marks a radical modification of the original story. It is not other men, her brothers, who rescue the girl from this man but a woman, her mother, who had been alarmed by her daughter's tears over the phone and who has travelled down to the Marquis' castle. She is let in to the castle by the blind young man whom the girl had recently asked to be employed as a piano-tuner and who, having been told of the girl's predicament, is in sympathy with her. The mother's arrival unravels the patriarchal skein that has been wound about her daughter:

The puppet master, open-mouthed, wide-eyed, impotent at the last, saw his dolls break free of their strings, abandon the rituals he had ordained for them since time began and start to live for themselves; the king, aghast, witnesses the revolt of his pawns.

You never saw such a wild thing as my mother ... one hand on the reins of the rearing horse while the other clasped my father's service revolver and, behind her, the breakers of the savage, indifferent sea, like the witnesses of a furious justice ... without a moment's hesitation, she ... took aim and put a single, irreproachable bullet through my husband's head. (*BB* 142)

In this image of the rescuing and avenging mother, Carter usurps a masculine trope and puts it at the service of the feminine. In this sense, her tale carries a different ideological message from the original. But Carter's story suggests that it was not only the girl who had been caught by patriarchy and who is liberated from it. The 'dolls' or 'pawns' breaking free of the 'puppet master' include the blind piano-tuner. Almost the last lines of 'The Bloody Chamber' tell us that, after the Marquis' death, the girl and the piano-tuner set up house together. It is a model of what in Carter's terms is a fit relationship between the sexes because it escapes the cruel Cartesian–Enlightenment–Sadeian dualism of subject versus object; aggressor or dominator versus victim or dominated. The point is put symbolically by the piano-tuner's blindness. He is not diminished as a man by his symbolic blindness. He is symbolically magnified as a man by virtue of the fact that in his blindness he does not fix and objectify his partner through the masculine gaze. The image of the blind piano-tuner exists in a kind of dialogue with the image of the blasted Rochester at the end of Charlotte Brontë's *Jane Eyre*. The blindness of the piano-tuner is not identical with the symbolic castration suffered by Rochester. The piano-tuner's sight can be replaced by enhanced senses of touch and hearing – enhancement which may displace the specularism of patriarchal logic and enable a redefinition of masculinity. Carter's pianist heroine in 'The Bloody Chamber' and the piano-tuner may achieve a harmonious relationship free of the oppressions of one by another.

The very last lines of 'The Bloody Chamber', however, highlight a feature of the story as a whole that a number of commentators have seen as profoundly problematic. As the Marquis was preparing to execute the girl, he pressed the key with which the girl had opened the bloody chamber against her forehead. The girl had dropped the key in the blood in the chamber and it bore an indelible red mark. This last detail follows the terms of the original story. But when, in Carter's tale, the Marquis pressed the key against the girl's forehead the red mark transferred itself permanently to her forehead. The last lines of 'The Bloody Chamber' say this:

> No paint nor powder, no matter how thick or white, can mask that red mark on my forehead; I am glad he cannot see it – not for fear of his revulsion, since I know he sees me clearly with his heart – but, because it spares my shame. (*BB* 143)

It is the question of the girl's or woman's 'shame' that is seen as problematic. Patricia Duncker and Avis Lewallen read it as the woman's shame at her own complicity in the masculine power structures that so nearly destroyed her. Duncker observes: 'she carries the mark of her complicity and corruption forever, the complicity of women who have been made in man's image, who have desired to be possessed ... who meet the reward of that complicity in the Bloody Chamber' (Duncker 1984: 11). Lewallen agrees with this but goes on to protest that '[t]o be branded as guilty, despite recognition of the manipulation to which she has been subject, seems somewhat unfair' (Lewallen 1988: 152). Yet it might be argued that it is not entirely unfair. While it is true that Carter has demonstrated the immense amount of manipulation to which the girl was subjected, either indirectly through cultural conditioning or directly through the Marquis, she has also been careful to note at least some element of responsibility on the girl's part for having been taken in by, at least, the Marquis' money. The narrator recalls how she was overawed by the power of his money: 'Oh, the wonder of it; how all that might of iron and steam had paused only to suit his convenience. The richest man in France' (*BB* 116). The Marquis' gift of the wedding ring and a 'wardrobe of clothes from Poiret and Worth' are also specified as having played their part in conspiring 'to seduce' her 'utterly' (*BB* 115). Later, once she has discovered the dead bodies of the former wives, the girl is shown to have been aware of the materiality of the transaction by which she gave herself and her body to the Marquis: 'My first thought, when I saw the ring for which I had sold myself to this fate, was, how to escape it' (*BB* 132). It might be argued that, as far as her presentation of the attractiveness of the Marquis' money, and as far as her presentation of the woman's later sense of guilt at having been open to that attraction, are concerned, Carter is only being psychologically realistic. It might be argued that to want to excuse the girl *all* responsibility in this matter would be going too far. Such an argument might say, for instance, that it would be equally possible for a man to reflect upon and to feel shame about the extent to which he had responded, culpably, on some past occasion to the power of money. On these terms, then, it might be possible to argue that, as far as responding to the power of money goes, Carter's depiction of the woman's guilt is not entirely unfair.

However, it can also be argued that what makes the difference between men and women in relation to money is that the position of women in the market of sexual relations is different from that of men. And Carter's presentation of the seductive power of the man's money cannot be separated from what Duncker calls her standardly pornographic representation of female masochism, the masochism of the woman narrator as girl, and of the former wives of the Marquis:

Carter's 'Bloody Chamber' uses all the iconography of the Gothic; the remote castle, the virgin at the mercy of the tormented hero-villain, the enclosed spaces, hidden atrocities, women voraciously, masochistically eager for the corruption of sexuality. All the pervading themes of pornography are there too: domination, control, humiliation, mutilation, possession through murder. All perpetrated on willing, eager victims. The marriage bargain becomes explicit, the bride as the bought woman, acting out the 'ritual from the brothel.' Carter's tale carefully creates the classical pornographic model of sexuality, which has a definite meaning and endorses a particular kind of fantasy, that of male sexual tyranny within a marriage that is grossly unequal; the child bride responsive to her husband's desire, ready to be 'impaled' among the lilies of death, the face with its 'promise of debauchery', a rare talent for corruption. Here is the sexual model which endorses the 'normal and natural sadism of the male, happily complemented by the normal and natural masochism of the female.' [n. Andrea Dworkin, *Pornography: Men Possessing Women* (1981)] (Duncker 1984: 10)

Robert Clark has argued that in her engagement with pornographic subject matter Carter merely 'fall[s] back into reinscribing patriarchal attitudes' (Clark 1987: 147). There are several passages in the tale which could illustrate this. When she is at the opera the girl sees herself in a mirror wearing the choker of rubies that the Marquis has given her:

When I saw him look at me with lust, I dropped my eyes but, in glancing away from him, I caught sight of myself in the mirror. And I saw myself, suddenly, as he saw me, my pale face, the way the muscles in my neck stuck out like thin wire. I saw how much that cruel necklace became me. And, for the first time in my innocent and confined life, I sensed in myself a potentiality for corruption that took my breath away. (*BB* 115)

Here is a woman signalling the pleasure she derived from having been subjected to the masculine gaze. 'I was not afraid of him; but of myself' (*BB* 123) the narrator again tells us; while, a little later, when the Marquis has left the girl alone in the Castle, we hear that 'I longed for him. And he disgusted me' (*BB* 125). But the most notable passage which seems to reinscribe a patriarchal view of women as responding with a natural masochism to male pornographic abuse comes when the Marquis first examines the girl's body:

He stripped me, gourmand that he was, as if he were stripping the leaves off an artichoke – but do not imagine much finesse about it; this artichoke was no particular treat for the diner nor was he yet in any greedy haste. He approached his familiar treat with a weary appetite. And when nothing but my scarlet, palpitating core remained, I saw, in the mirror, the living image of an etching by Rops from the collection he had shown me when our engagement permitted us to be alone together ... the child with her sticklike limbs, naked but for her button boots, her gloves, shielding her face with her hand as though her face were the last repository of her modesty; and the old, monocled lecher who examined her, limb by limb. He in his London tailoring; she, bare as a lamb chop. Most pornographic of all confrontations. And so my purchaser unwrapped his bargain. And, as at the opera, when I had first seen my flesh in his eyes, I was aghast to feel myself stirring. (*BB* 118–19)

As a man, I am not competent to judge the psychological veracity or otherwise of this image of positive female response to male pornographic attention. What I would note is that 'The Bloody Chamber' needs to be read in the light of Carter's observation in *The Sadeian Woman* that while standard pornography 'has an in-built reactionary mechanism' (*SW* 16), and while standard pornography 'reinforces the archetypes' of women's 'negativity and ... does so simply because most pornography remains in the service of the status quo' (*SW* 17), then, in contrast, a 'moral pornographer might use pornography as a *critique* of existent relations between the sexes' (*SW* 19, my italics). Robert Clark declares that this belief 'seems mistaken, the ideological power of the form being infinitely greater than the power of the individual to overcome it' (Clark 1987: 152–3). But it is possible to read the passage from 'The Bloody Chamber' which I have just quoted, along with other, comparable passages from the tale, as more successful attempts at moral pornography than Clark allows. Again, as a man, I think I am not an appropriate commentator on this particular matter. So I will quote at some length from Elaine Jordan who has, in any case, provided one of the best discussions of Carter as moral pornographer:

Carter's writing may simply be consumed but can also produce *wincing* from this fascination of the girl with being acquired and seduced by a knowing and powerful man who 'wants her so much' – a wincing recoil of the reader who has been at all seduced by the aroma, texture, dynamics, of erotic difference. 'Was it I who wanted this? Was it this that I wanted?' The rhetorical figure that's been on my mind as I've

tried to characterise Carter's writing has been zeugma, the yoking together of different objects and effects within the same syntax – a comic
and explosive device. Fascination and recoil are parts of the entice-
ments of pornography, either way. One feminist position is to condemn
any truck with such available fascinations altogether. Another is to face
the fascination – to spring forward *from* recoil, from wincing at an
acknowledged desire. (*Who* is it that acknowledges? Either the sadistic
or the masochistic subject, of whatever gender. To whatever degree.)
(Jordan 1992a: 124)

The idea of springing forward from recoil seems to me to touch
the heart of Carter's strategy in 'The Bloody Chamber': the idea
that neither female nor male can simply blank out the fact of
pornography. 'Recoil' here, it must be emphasised, is not just a
matter of confronting the 'enemy' and declaring that 'we must not
recoil'; and it is not to be reduced to an indignant moral posture
of outraged avoidance. It is a process which *includes* the fascination
that is being reacted against and which then springs forward to a
new position. A kind of dialectic producing a third term. Recognition and engagement with the fact of pornography need to be an
explicit part of any attempt to overcome it:

> If I read Robert Clark right, he believes that sexuality is *only* made
> significant by prohibition, so that Carter's experiment with 'moral
> pornography' as a critique of current sexual relations is doomed to be
> part of what it criticizes: 'the illicitly desiring self pulls forwards, the
> censoring pulls back preaching an exemplary sermon'. What then shall
> we do with our illicit desires? Flagellate ourselves? The notion of recoil
> can have an opposite value, one which does not deny or prohibit the
> energies of desire as they exist: a springing movement which may be
> experienced as active and productive, rather than a helpless captivation.
> Although the attitude of mind is perhaps already sufficiently wide-
> spread, I take the term recoil, or wincing, with its implication of self-
> overcoming ('Was it I? Was it this?') from my notes of a particularly
> lively account by Charles Scott of Foucault's *Madness and Civilization*
> and *The Order of Things*, notes which continue:
>
> > Genealogy is effective history, and curative science. It is not a com-
> > ing to truth or health (concepts which can be used punitively and
> > coercively), but to a knowledge of one's own contingent process, as
> > in psychoanalysis. The curative aspect is in a knowledge that finds
> > itself repeating and departing from the inheritance it describes. This
> > is not true insight inspecting a false knowledge: it stays on the
> > boundary, on the dangerous edge, as a therapeutic listening, the very
> > opposite of a discipline of confinement.

> Repeating and departing from the inheritance described struck me as a
> good account of the processes of Carter's writing, and the strongest
> answer to the charge that she merely reinscribes patriarchy. Where else
> can you start from, if not from where you actually are? (as Voltaire
> wrote, and it still seems to me good political practice). Where we are
> may include fascinations from which a rational and ethical self recoils.
> (Jordan 1992a: 124–5)

But that self must not recoil in the sense of horrified avoidance,
lest it wish to forfeit the advantages which reason gives. Withdraw-
ing or avoiding would vitiate reason's claim to be able to negotiate
human life in general. And, specifically, to negotiate plural energies in the self. One of Carter's most potent strategies in the telling
of this tale is having a narrator who is not just recounting things
she has experienced but is recounting simultaneously her awareness of and growing reflective distance upon those things. Take, for
example, her statement: 'I was aghast to feel myself stirring.' If she
had said something like 'and I felt myself stirring' then the observation would arguably be straightforwardly pornographic. But the
record of her own shock, her own aghastness, opens up a point of
critique which allows for a critical distance upon what might
otherwise be gratuitously pornographic. The text acknowledges
the depth and power of ideological inscriptions which cause a
female to respond in certain ways while at the same time exposing
and criticising those inscriptions. What the text does not do is to
deny or to evade the inscriptions. A rational and ethical self is
central to Carter's programme in *The Bloody Chamber* collection,
and it cannot sustain itself by evasion and repression. The centrality
of reason in Carter's portrayal throughout the volume of the need
to examine and reconstruct gender identity emerges particularly
clearly in the concluding tale of the volume.

'Wolf-Alice' is not based on any single fairy tale but incorporates features of several. As such, the tale acts as a kind of summary
of the collection's preoccupations and perspectives as a whole. The
story is of a girl who has been raised by wolves and who is, therefore, free of all the structuring of identity that comes with human
socialisation. She is 'not a wolf … although suckled by wolves'
but, equally, '[n]othing about her is human' (*BB* 221). Some
humans kill her 'foster mother' (*BB* 221) and deposit the wolf-girl
in a convent where attempts are made to civilise her. She learns a

few simple 'humanising' tricks, such as drinking from a cup and wearing clothes. But when the Mother Superior tried to teach her to give thanks in the chapel for having been rescued from the wolves, she would not go along with it, reverting instead to her animal state, pawing the floor and defecating in a corner. This is too much for the nuns. The wolf-girl is thrown out, 'delivered over to the bereft and unsanctified household of the Duke' (*BB* 222). The Duke is another creature who is estranged from the human order as it stands. He is a particularly unsavoury werewolf who scavenges only human carrion from the local churchyard. If she is 'not wolf or woman' (*BB* 223), he is only a 'parody' (*BB* 223) of a wolf and a man: wolves themselves 'would have angrily expelled him from the pack' (*BB* 223). Carter suggests his in-humanness by the fact that he casts no reflection in mirrors: 'nothing can hurt him since he ceased to cast an image in the mirror' (*BB* 222). As werewolf he is defined only by appetite:

> At night, those huge, inconsolable, rapacious eyes of his are eaten up by swollen, gleaming pupil. His eyes see only appetite. These eyes open to devour the world in which he sees, nowhere, a reflection of himself; he passed through the mirror and now, henceforward, lives as if upon the other side of things. (*BB* 222)

So the two misfits inhabit the same space together, both shunned by conventional human society: she seen as irredeemably animal in nature and his household characterised as 'unsanctified'. He takes no notice of her and she, in her animal innocence, is not appalled by him:

> Then her sensitive ears pricked at the sound of a step in the hall; trotting at once back to her kitchen, she encountered the Duke with the leg of a man over his shoulder. Her toenails clicked against the stairs as she padded incuriously past, she, the serene, inviolable one in her absolute and verminous innocence. (*BB* 225)

Carter stresses the status of the girl as a human female who is innocent in the sense that she does not suffer from human constructions of what the human female is:

> She grew up with wild beasts. If you could transport her, in her filth, rags and feral disorder, to the Eden of our first beginnings where Eve and grunting Adam squat on a daisy bank, picking the lice from one

another's pelts, then she might prove to be the wise child who leads them all ... but how can the bitten apple flesh out its scar again? (*BB* 223)

Carter's tale is an allegorical dream of the unbitten apple and of how things might have been had the apple been eaten in a different way, had humanity not fallen into the construction of itself and of reality that it did fall into. It is also an allegory of what things might still be like if the whole business to do with the eating of the wretched apple were simply thrown overboard. Thus the tale tells of the girl's independent discovery of her humanity. She develops a sense of time and its regularities from her menstrual periods, which start while she is in the Duke's Castle: 'you might say she discovered the very action of time by means of this returning cycle' (*BB* 225). She slowly discovers her own self through seeing her reflection in a mirror. Carter's picturing of the emergence of individual identity through the recognition of the self in a mirror reflection, recalls Lacan's idea that individual, self-conscious identity is born of reflection and representation in signs (Lacan 1977). When Lacan writes on the mirror stage in the human infant's growth he does not assume that human selfhood precedes representation but that it is born out of re-presentation. The self is founded on a reflexive image that in itself is not the self, but only a representation. The paradox about Lacan's idea of the construction or acquisition of selfhood through representation and signs – principally, of course, through language as the dominant sign-system – is that it is at once a condition of loss. What is lost is unselfconscious unity with the world, such as Wolf-Alice possessed when she lived with wolves: 'She inhabits only the present tense, a fugue of the continuous, a world of sensual immediacy as without hope as it is without despair' (*BB* 221). What is gained is a self or ego that amounts to a self-contradictory existence in that it exists by virtue of things – representations, signs – that stand in for something which they themselves are not. Carter has her wolf-girl moving to a recognition of her self in the mirror's reflection while, in the process, regretfully discovering that there is nothing behind the mirror's representation:

> This habitual, at last boring, fidelity to her very movement finally woke her up to the regretful possibility that her companion was, in fact, no more than a particularly ingenious variety of the shadow she cast on

sunlit grass ... She poked her agile nose around the back of the mirror; she found only dust, a spider stuck in his web, a heap of rags. A little moisture leaked from the corners of her eyes, yet her relation with the mirror was now far more intimate since she knew she saw herself in it. (*BB* 226)

The regret at finding there is nothing substantial behind the mirror is also a liberation. There is no essential, patriarchal authority to dictate what form the self so constituted must take. Wolf-Alice's emergent subjectivity precipitates her into the realm of subject–object relations that characterises the human condition. She begins to place her own subjectivity as the perspectival focus of the situations she finds herself in:

> now the world around her was assuming form. She perceived an essen-
> tial difference between herself and her surroundings that you might
> say she could not put her *finger* on – only, the trees and grass of the
> meadows outside no longer seemed the emanation of her questing nose
> and erect ears, and yet sufficient to itself, but a kind of backdrop for
> her, that waited for her arrivals to give it meaning. She saw herself
> upon it and her eyes, with their sombre clarity, took on a veiled, intro-
> spective look ...
>
> She goes out at night more often now; the landscape assembles itself
> about her, she informs it with her presence. She is its significance. (*BB*
> 225, 227)

Yet for all that Wolf-Alice generates an order of subject–object relations, Carter characterises this order as something different from the Cartesian dualism of subject versus an object that the subject merely dominates or negates. The Duke himself is a kind of parodic distillation of the effective inhumanity of the Cartesian paradigm. He is related to the Count in *The Infernal Desire Machines of Doctor Hoffman*, or to the Marquis de Sade in *The Sadeian Woman*, or to the Marquis in 'The Bloody Chamber'. The Duke is inhuman in his solitary, egoistic, consuming drive: 'His eyes see only appetite. These eyes open to devour the world' (*BB* 222). The deathliness of that drive is figured in 'Wolf-Alice' by the fact that the Duke sustains himself by eating corpses. What restores him to real humanity is that Wolf-Alice does not fulfil the role of victim or meat to his appetite but actively takes care of him, enters into a relationship with and not against him. She loves him after he has been shot and wounded while on one of his nighttime excursions. The subjectivity she has generated is not based on obliteration of but on communication with the other. The tale defines the medium within which this kind of inter-subjectivity may fulfil itself as 'reason'. It is a reason that is different from that male 'unreason' masquerading as reason which 'denied rationality' to the young girl in 'The Tiger's Bride' (*BB* 165). As the following quotation shows, it is a reason that is characterised by Carter as inherent in the symbolic instrument – the mirror – by which autonomous subjectivity is realised through self-representation. This reason is redefined in relation to the masculinism of Cartesian and Enlightenment notions of reason. For it is rationality which not only enables the girl to realise autonomous subjectivity but frees the man from definition as mere consumer and enables him to enter the representational realm of the genuinely human, which is here seen in terms not of exclusion but of mutual and reciprocal relationship:

> She prowled round the bed, growling, snuffing at his wound ... Then, she was pitiful as her gaunt grey mother; she leapt upon his bed to lick, without hesitation, without disgust, with a quick, tender gravity, the blood and dirt from his cheek and forehead.
> The lucidity of the moonlight lit the mirror propped against the red wall; the rational glass ... impartially recorded the scene.
> As she continued her ministrations, this glass, with infinite slow-ness, yielded to the reflexive strength of its own material construction. Little by little, there appeared within it, like the image on photographic paper that emerges, first, a formless web of tracery, the prey caught in its own fishing net, then a firmer yet still shadowed outline until at last as vivid as real life itself, as if brought into being by her soft, moist, gentle tongue, finally, the face of the Duke. (*BB* 227–8)

The rational humaneness that both Wolf-Alice and Duke reach by virtue of Wolf-Alice's caring is identified in this tale as a genuine humanity that is to be contrasted with what is, in fact, the incomplete humanity of the people who have shunned and persecuted them. The tales of *The Bloody Chamber* end again, as so often with Carter's fiction, with an image of what might be. Not a utopian image, but a model of something as yet unrealised. The central demythologising orientation of these tellings of fairy tales in *The Bloody Chamber* was to resurface – ambitiously and powerfully reinvented – in Carter's only novel of the 1980s, *Nights at the Circus*.

SIX

Nights at the Circus

In 1980, in an essay entitled 'The Language of Sisterhood', Carter observed that

> A good deal of harmless fun has been poked at certain neologisms coined by the Women's Movement in its sexually egalitarian or some-times even female supremacist zeal. The militant who wanted to change her name to 'Personchester'. Ho ho ho. *S/he* to replace the offensively sectarian yet ubiquitous use of *he* as an impersonal pronoun? What? Have the girls no sense of proportion? ... *Herstory. That* always provokes the big belly laugh. (Carter 1980: 226)

If certain people laughed at 'herstory' then the sisterhood itself tended 'toward a study of myth because of the paucity of historical references to that statistically rather more than half the human race to which we belong' (Carter 1980: 227). And the sisterhood turned not just to a study of myth but to a rewriting of it, since that was a way of reclaiming a past from which standard history had largely banished women. Such rewriting has, Carter asserts, produced specifically feminine narrative forms; forms character-ised above all else by miscegenation:

> we feel a compulsive need to rewrite those myths, since myth is more malleable than history, in order to accommodate ourselves in the past. In this way, cross-disciplinary bastards are born.
> Therefore a book like Adrienne Rich's *Of Woman Born* looks, at first sight, like some monstrous hybrid, a legendary obstetrical auto-biography which, because of its impurity of form, its lateral interpre-tation of the chronology of gynecology, necessitates a new area of

speculation to accommodate it: so the nascent discipline of women's studies accretes its set texts. It is, after all, very rarely possible for new ideas to find adequate expression in old forms. (Carter 1980: 228)

While Carter is here partly describing certain features of her own writing in the 1970s, the formal blending of which she speaks is again very apparent in *Nights at the Circus* (1984). Several commentators have discussed the form of *Nights at the Circus* in terms of the carnivalesque. Paulina Palmer writes that the novel

> represents a skilfully contrived exercise in intertextuality. Shakespeare, Milton, Poe, Ibsen and Joyce are some of the writers to whom she alludes, with the effect of creating a polyphonic interplay of European cultural attitudes and moments. The voices of these writers interact in, to cite the Russian critic Mikhail Bakhtin, a medley of 'paradoxically reconstructed quotations'. This medley unites the serious and the comic, the high and low. It subverts any single, unified utterance, in typical carnivalistic manner. (Palmer 1987: 197)

Elaine Jordan also notes that *Nights and the Circus* 'is a carnival of writing, containing "the protocols and styles of high culture in and from a position of debasement"' (Jordan 1990: 38). This carnivalesque aspect of *Nights at the Circus* might easily be described as its postmodern aspect. In *Rabelais and his World* Mikhail Bakhtin says that the carnival spirit, in its hostility to all that is 'completed', exposes the 'gay relativity of prevailing truths and authorities' (Bakhtin 1984: 10–11). Robert Wilson, in a discussion of one of Carter's short stories, makes an explicit connection between postmodernism and Bakhtinian ideas:

> Post-modernism designates a nexus of intersecting discourses ... It exemplifies the fruitfulness of post-structuralist metaphors that project splintered, instable textual mosaics in which all categories, both genres and periods, will display the decay of boundaries ... It also shows the relevance of those other metaphors about boundaries that characteristically play important roles in Bakhtin's thinking: metaphors in which alien languages confront each other in public fora, in which different speakers, bearing with them dissimilar axiological worlds, exchange utterances, seeking meanings that will never reside exclusively in either's speech. (Wilson 1989: 112–13)

The idea that Carter's writing in *Nights at the Circus* is carnivalesque captures something of the slipperiness and subversiveness of the novel. But the danger with seeing the novel as formally entirely carnivalesque would, by definition, be that the novel then became thematically entirely carnivalesque and that it could be seen as endorsing an *unregulated* subversion of established codes and conventions, as legitimating a chaos of relative perspectives. In my reading, the fantastic in *Nights at the Circus* is, in principle, like the fantastic in Carter's other fictions. Obviously not realist in mode it is, however, deployed and regulated from a rational, materialist, feminist base. And this base is not only an explicit part of the content or theme of *Nights at the Circus*, it also helps direct the novel at a formal level. For all the superficially 'carnival-esque' features of the work it has also to be said that *Nights at the Circus* is, at a deeper level, formally or generically quite tradi-tional. Or, perhaps it would be better to say that it invokes and depends upon – even as it re-imagines – highly traditional narra-tive forms. In the first place, the novel is structured – as, again, so much of Carter's fiction is structured – according to an eighteenth-century narrative mode. Carter commented to John Haffenden that 'the idea behind *Nights at the Circus* was very much to entertain and instruct, and I purposely used a certain eighteenth century fictional device – the picaresque, where people have adventures in order to find themselves in places where they can discuss philo-sophical concepts without distractions' (Haffenden 1985: 87). This eighteenth-century fictional device is invoked, it seems to me, in something other than a postmodern spirit. It is not invoked to be parodied or to be relativised as a narrative device. It is invoked straight, as it were, because Carter is using the device to explore issues and to say something about those issues in a way that she herself believes in. The issues raised and the responses to those issues explored through the fiction are neither ironised nor relativised. In the second – and in some respects more important – place, there is a sense in which *Nights at the Circus* falls simul-taneously within the tradition of the historical novel. Except that it might be more appropriate to call *Nights at the Circus* an 'her-storical' novel. Carter may have said herself that it is rarely possible for new ideas to find adequate expression in old forms. Yet a part of the ambition and achievement of *Nights at the Circus* is that it does not settle just for hybridity and fragmentariness but success-fully appropriates and reinvents entire traditional forms in its expression of new ideas.

In what sense is *Nights at the Circus* a kind of historical novel? In what senses does it offer an alternative history, a herstory? At a minimal level it must be noted that, unlike the futuristic settings of much of her previous fiction, the setting of *Nights at the Circus* is firmly historicised. Placed at the end of the nineteenth century, the year 1899, the novel does not simply mix the real and the surreal. It mixes reference to specifically *historical* facts and personages with fantastic characters and events.

What is certainly true is that it is the fantastic dimension of the narrative that initially dominates the reader's attention. The plot itself is not only fantastic but fantastically convoluted and in order to keep a sense of bearings throughout the whole of my discussion of *Nights at the Circus* I must first provide a fairly detailed summary of it. The story – sometimes told by a third-person narrator, sometimes told in the first person by a character within the story – relates the picaresque adventures of a celebrated female trapeze artist, Fevvers. She is called by this name because she has, quite literally, wings. More on that later, of course. The first part of the novel pictures Fevvers – together with her foster mother and companion, Lizzie – telling the story of Fevvers' early life to an American journalist, Jack Walser, who has come to write a piece that will debunk the phenomenon of Fevvers and her wings. We hear that Fevvers, abandoned as a baby on the doorstep of a brothel in the East End of London, was brought up by a community of prostitutes. In her early years in the brothel, Fevvers played a little ornamental Cupid in the drawing-room where the women received the male customers. When the brothel closed, Fevvers began her life's wanderings. She found employment as a freak exhibit in a perverted sex show – a 'museum of woman monsters' (*NC* 55) – set up in a house in Kensington by one Madame Schreck. Then she was abducted by one of the patrons of Madame Schreck's house, a man calling himself Christian Rosencreutz. Rosencreutz, who was much involved in the cabbalistic arts, had identified Fevvers, because of her wings, as Azrael or Gabriel; basically he wanted ritually to kill her in order to extract from her some mysterious essence which would help him stay forever young. Fevvers, needless to say, managed to escape. This is the first of a number of escapes from weird and/or lustful men that she will make during the course of the book. We hear that after this first

escape, Fevvers decided that she would earn a living by performing in the circus on the high wire. This returns us to the opening
of Part I where Fevvers, now famous as a trapeze artist, is being
interviewed by Jack Walser.

The second part of the novel – set a short time after the interview recorded in Part I – has Fevvers performing as an attraction
in a circus run by the American Colonel Kearney. The circus is at
St Petersburg, and is aiming to travel to Japan via Siberia. The
journalist Walser, still anxious to gather more information on
Fevvers, has joined the circus, disguised as a clown. Several
episodes, involving various members of the circus, ensue, during
which quite a deal of attention is given to the clowns. At one stage
their leader, the great clown Buffo, loses his reason and chases
Walser (dressed as a human chicken) with murderous intent before
being overpowered and led away. In another episode, a troupe of
apes – 'Monsieur Lamarck's Educated Apes' (NC 99) – renegoti-
ate the terms of their contract with Colonel Kearney and decide
to catch the train for Helsinki rather than go on to Siberia. Amidst
all these wild and wonderful happenings we are told that Walser
has fallen in love with Fevvers and that Fevvers is also developing
some serious affection for Walser. This middle part of the novel
ends with Fevvers again threatened by a predatory male – the
Grand Duke. Again she escapes and is on the road again. Or
rather, not the road, but the rails, since she joins the train that
will take the circus to Siberia.

Which is the setting of the concluding part of the novel. The
circus has reached Siberia when the train transporting it is blown
up by a band of outlaws and Fevvers breaks a wing. Fevvers and
Lizzie and some other members of the circus are captured and
taken away by the outlaws. Walser, who was buried deep in the
wreckage of the train, is dug out some time after the abduction of
Fevvers and Lizzie by a group of women who have just escaped
from a Siberian penitentiary and are going off to found a lesbian
commune somewhere in the wilderness. The shock of the explosion
has unhinged Walser's mind and he runs off, without memory and
identity, into the snow: 'Like the landscape, he was a perfect blank'
(NC 222). Meanwhile, Fevvers and Lizzie discover that their
captors are peasants who have been forced into being outlaws because they killed some government officials who had violated their

womenfolk. They want forgiveness from the Tsar and have captured Fevvers because they have heard that she has had a liaison with the Prince of Wales (a false rumour put about by Colonel Kearney). They want Fevvers to persuade Queen Victoria to intercede with the Tsar on their behalf. While Fevvers and Lizzie and the others are held captive in a shed, a whirlwind spirits away both the outlaws and the circus clowns (who had gone outside to entertain the outlaws). Setting off in the snow to seek rescue, the remnant of the circus troupe run into Walser who, we discover, has run into a Shaman and been living with the native Siberian tribespeople. Banishing the Shaman, Fevvers finds that Walser's personality and reason have returned, though his identity is now something more than it was before the wrecking of the train. The novel ends in good Hollywood style with the happy union of Walser and Fevvers.

With a fable like this – comic, absurdly comic, in its mad extravagance as well as in its resolution – it is not unreasonable to ask what on earth historicism has to do with it. Well, there is the fundamental period setting: the very end of the nineteenth century. This is not a gratuitous or romantic choice of period. Carter herself observed that *Nights at the Circus*

> is set at exactly the moment in European history when things began to change. It's set at that time quite deliberately, and [Fevvers] is the new woman. All the women who have been in the first brothel with her end up doing these 'new women' jobs, like becoming hotel managers and running typing agencies, and so on, very much like characters in Shaw. (Katsavos 1994: 13)

When Fevvers first spreads her wings she is described by Ma Nelson, the mistress of the brothel Fevvers was brought up in, as 'the pure child of the century that just now is waiting in the wings, the New Age in which no women will be bound down to the ground' (*NC* 25). More, as I have said, on Fevvers and her symbolism later in this discussion. The basic point for now is that Fevvers is associated with the issue of emergent women's rights, and the period of the late nineteenth century, as Carter remarks, was a critical phase in the dawning of consciousness about and agitation for women's rights. The late nineteenth century laid the ground for what would be, in part at least, consolidated and crystallised and turned into British parliamentary legislation in the twentieth century. The issue then at centre-stage was, of course, women's suffrage. In 1865 John Stuart Mill was elected Member of Parliament for Westminster, having put the matter of women's suffrage in his election address. Mill's campaigning for women's rights was profoundly influenced by the woman he had married in 1851, Harriet Taylor. From the point of Mill's election as MP the issue of women's suffrage came to occupy an important place in parliamentary business in each successive parliament. Numerous bills or amendments to bills were proposed with the intention of conferring the franchise upon women; all were defeated by one parliamentary ruse or another. Perhaps most disappointing to radicals was the Liberal W. E. Gladstone's refusal to accept an amendment to the Reform Bill of 1884 which would have granted women's suffrage. It was not, of course, until 1918 that women of a certain age (thirty and over) finally gained the vote.

Nights at the Circus carefully, not obtrusively, sketches in this historical context for its fantasy. There are, in the first place, several general allusions to actual historical personages from the period. When Fevvers, recently returned to London from a triumphant tour on the Continent, is first talking to Walser about her life and career she mentions the late Victorian music hall comedian Dan Leno: 'here's the prodigal daughter home again to London ... London – as dear old Dan Leno calls it, "a little village on the Thames of which the principal industries are the music hall and the confidence trick"' (*NC* 8). In the account of her Continental tour several French names associated with experimental work in the 1890s are dropped, such as the painter Henri Toulouse-Lautrec, the dramatist Alfred Jarry, and the novelist Colette, before reference is indirectly made to the work of Sigmund Freud:

> On that European tour of hers, Parisians shot themselves in droves for her sake; not just Lautrec but *all* the post-impressionists vied to paint her; Willy gave her supper and she gave Colette some good advice. Alfred Jarry proposed marriage ... In Vienna, she deformed the dreams of that entire generation who would immediately commit themselves wholeheartedly to psychoanalysis. (*NC* 11)

Back in London, Fevvers gains the attention – though no more – of the infamously lecherous Prince of Wales:

Fevvers ... goes on kissing her hand to the tumultuous applause as the curtain falls and the band strikes up 'God Save the Queen'. God save the mother of the obese and bearded princeling who has taken his place in the royal box twice nightly since Fevvers' first night at the Alhambra, stroking his beard and meditating upon the erotic possibilities of her ability to hover and the problematic of his paunch vis-à-vis the missionary position. (*NC* 18)

More important, however, are the specifically political references sprinkled throughout the text. Such as when Fevvers remarks to Walser that the prostitutes of her childhood home were all sympathetic to the women's movement:

'we were all suffragists in that house; oh, Nelson was a one for "Votes for Women", I can tell you!'
    'Does that seem strange to you? That the caged bird should want to see the end of cages, sir?' queried Lizzie, with an edge of steel in her voice. (*NC* 38)

Or there is Rosencreutz, whose real name Fevvers secretly reveals to Walser before citing 'Rosencreutz' as the type of those parliamentary men who consistently succeeded in the later years of the nineteenth century in opposing the extension of the franchise to women:

'You must know this gentleman's name!' insisted Fevvers and, seizing his notebook, wrote it down ... On reading it:
    'Good God,' said Walser.
    'I saw in the paper only yesterday how he gives the most impressive speech in the House on the subject of Votes for Women. Which he is against. On account of how women are of a different soul-substance from men, cut from a different bolt of spirit cloth, and altogether too pure and rarefied to be bothering their pretty little heads with things of *this* world, such as the Irish question and the Boer War.' (*NC* 78–9)

Then there is Lizzie. Lizzie is fondly drawn in a serio-comic spirit as the epitome of the English radical tradition. At the end of the novel Fevvers explains that she had never made a good prostitute in Ma Nelson's house because of

her habit of lecturing the clients on the white slave trade, the rights and wrongs of women, universal suffrage, as well as the Irish question, the Indian question, republicanism, anti-clericalism, syndicalism, and the abolition of the House of Lords. With all of which Nelson was in full sympathy but, as she said, the world won't change overnight and we must eat. (*NC* 292)

Whilst in Russia Lizzie had persuaded Walser to include some of her own letters in the journalistic packets he was sending back to Britain. It turns out that these were not just personal communications but news of Russian internal politics to Russian dissidents in exile; dissidents who would eventually produce the Revolution of 1917:

> Those letters we sent home by you in the diplomatic bag were news of the struggle in Russia to comrades in exile, written in invisible ink ... Liz *would* do it, having made a promise to a spry little gent with a 'tache she met in the reading-room of the British Museum. (*NC* 292)

The historical roots of Lizzie's radicalism are with the English radical movement of the 1790s, a movement associated with the names, among others, of William Godwin and Mary Wollstonecraft. This historical background to Lizzie's thought is briefly alluded to after Lizzie has been hearing how the women planning to set up a lesbian community had intended to procreate:

> These women planned to found a female Utopia in the taiga and asked a favour of the Escapee; that he should deliver 'em up a pint or two of sperm ... With this request, he had complied. I could see he was a perfect gentleman.
> 'What'll they do with the boy babies? Feed 'em to the polar bears? To the *female* polar bears?' demanded Liz, who was in a truculent mood and clearly thought herself back in Whitechapel at a meeting of the Godwin and Wollstonecraft Debating Society. (*NC* 240–1)

The most important thing about the fantasy dimension of *Nights of the Circus* is that, for all its flamboyant craziness, it makes sense *specifically in relation to* the historical context that is sketched in by Carter. It is not gratuitous or surrealist fantasy, but fantasy whose symbolic meaning can be recovered in rational historical terms. Take Fevvers. A woman with wings is a literal non-sense. This woman has a symbolic dimension that is self-consciously acknowledged in the narrative itself. As, for example, when Ma Nelson identifies Fevvers, after she has first spread her wings, as the herald of a 'New Age in which no women will be bound down to the ground' (*NC* 25) and when, following that spreading of her wings, she has Fevvers pose in the brothel not as Cupid but as the Winged Victory: 'That night, we threw away the bow and arrow and I posed, for the first time, as the Winged Victory, for, as you can see, I am designed on the grand scale' (*NC* 25). Later in the novel Fevvers will refer to herself as 'the New Woman' (*NC* 281). At one level, then, Fevvers symbolises that gathering of confidence among women in the late nineteenth century which led to the gains in self-possession and autonomy made by women in the twentieth century. In 1899 hardly anyone had seen a mentally and emotionally newly constituted woman, in the same way as no one had seen a woman with wings. The difficulty we might have in coming to terms with the notion of a woman who literally possesses wings enacts the difficulty that was felt in the late nineteenth century – and, indeed, may still be felt today – in coming to terms with mentally and emotionally 'new' or reconstructed women. The literalness of Fevvers' wings enforces, at one level, a psychological point.

Lest, however, we reduce Fevvers to the status of being *only* a symbol, it must be emphasised that the novel insists that Fevvers is not only symbolic but at once a real, material woman. 'What is revealed in her routine', Mary Russo observes, 'is at one level economic: the Victorian working girl is not the angel (in the house), and the novel is in many ways about working girls' (Russo 1994: 177). Fevvers is a 'working girl' and she possesses a kind of gloriously vulgar earthiness (Carter once described her as 'Mae West with wings'; Haffenden 1985: 88). When Fevvers is telling the story of her early life to Walser, she gets hungry and orders food. Once it has arrived:

> She gorged, she stuffed herself, she spilled gravy on herself, she sucked up peas from the knife; she had a gullet to match her size and table manners of the Elizabethan variety. Impressed, Walser waited with the stubborn docility of his profession until at last her enormous appetite was satisfied; she wiped her lips on her sleeve and belched. (*NC* 22)

Likewise, the novel stresses Fevvers' hunger for money as one of the driving forces of her personality: 'You'd never think she dreamed, at nights, of bank accounts, or that, to her, the music of the spheres was the jingling of cash registers' (*NC* 12). This hunger for money sometimes leads Fevvers into serious and potentially extremely dangerous misjudgements. As when she is tempted by the promise of a 'diamond rivière' (*NC* 181) to go alone to the Grand Duke's palace: 'She wanted to *eat* diamonds' (*NC* 182). So she goes but quickly finds herself 'getting out of [her] depth' (*NC*

191) and in 'deadly danger' (*NC* 190), a danger from which she only barely manages to escape. The point of the novel's emphasis on the sheer humanity of this woman with wings, this woman who had posed as the Winged Victory in Ma Nelson's brothel, is that it is part of Carter's appropriation of one of Western patriarchy's most persistent images of woman. Lorna Sage has observed that

> The image of the woman with wings has served throughout the centuries as a carrier of men's meanings, and at the turn of the century in particular this time-honoured icon had a new lease of life ... Victory – like all traditional allegories – became pretty well anybody's property. In 1900 she was leading General Sherman's horse in New York; in 1911, she settled on the bonnet of Rolls Royces in the form of the Silver Lady ... She was already working ... as a cigar label. (Sage 1994a: 47–8)

The problem with patriarchy's use of woman as the Winged Victory, or, indeed, its use of any other symbolic woman, is that in such use the female has no unique personality, no individuality. Lorna Sage refers to Marina Warner's 1985 study *Monuments and Maidens: The Allegory of the Female Form*, which makes this case in considerable detail:

> The point about nearly all of those larger-than-life female figures, [Warner] says, was that they had no character (she is using the Statue of Liberty to make her point):
>
>> We can all take up occupation of Liberty, male, female, aged, children, she waits to enfold us in her meaning. But a male symbol like Uncle Sam relates to us in a different way ... The female form tends to be perceived as generic and universal ... We can all live inside Britannia or Liberty's skin, they stand for us regardless of sex, yet we cannot identify with them as characters. Uncle Sam and John Bull are popular figures, they can be grim, sly, feisty, pathetic, absurd, for they have personality. Liberty, like many abstract concepts expressed in the feminine, is in deadly earnest and one-dimensional ... *Liberty is not representing her own freedom.*
>
> Nor was Victory representing her own triumph. What Carter does is give Fevvers the mobility, particularity, weight, and humour of a character, and so give her back her gender. Fevvers uses signs as well as being one. Yeats in the Leda poem ['Leda and the Swan'] produces a grand rhetorical question: 'Did she put on his knowledge with his power ... ?' Well, annoyingly enough, yes, in this version. Fevvers' other name, we recall, is Sophia, which means wisdom. (Sage 1994a: 48–9)

The classical Greek model for so many female Winged Victory icons is the marble statue known as the Winged Victory of Samothrace. But that statue is damaged, missing its head and arms. Fevvers in *Nights at the Circus* is, as Carter has noted, 'the Winged Victory ... except that she does have a head!'; she's 'a metaphor come to life' (Haffenden 1985: 93). And with that head and life there comes, in Carter, as Sage indicates, a gender, a personality and autonomous motivation. Fevvers is a reappropriation on behalf of women of what had been appropriated – the figure of woman – on behalf of men. With the reappropriation comes a rehistoricisation and re-humanisation of what men simply dehistoricised, transcendentalised and dehumanised. Abstractions of things like Victory and Liberty as constructed from a masculine perspective don't tend to spill gravy and belch. The music of the spheres in masculine idealisation isn't characteristically associated with the making of cash.

Carter's use of Fevvers to rehumanise and rehistoricise figures of the female has several parallels with her treatment of Charles Baudelaire's black mistress Jeanne Duval, in the title story of the 1985 collection *Black Venus*. Carter spoke of Fevvers as 'a metaphor come to life'. In 'Black Venus' Carter takes the woman Jeanne Duval who was turned into a metaphor by Baudelaire and *restores* her to life. In his poetry Baudelaire transformed Jeanne Duval into the figure of his own satanically inspirational muse. As a muse figure she shared the characteristics of what Warner calls 'abstract concepts expressed in the feminine': she had no unique, self-willed, material reality. Carter quotes from Baudelaire's *Fleurs du mal* (1857) as she first describes Baudelaire's poetic colonisation of Jeanne Duval before going on to point out how this colonisation deprived Duval of any real presence and how Duval herself did not wish any of the things ascribed to her in Baudelaire's construction of her as muse:

> He thinks she is a vase of darkness; if he tips her up, black light will spill out. She is not Eve but, herself, the forbidden fruit, and he has eaten her!
>
> > Weird goddess, dusky as night,
> > reeking of musk smeared on tobacco,
> > a shaman conjured you, a Faust of the savannah,
> > black-thighed witch, midnight's child ...

Indeed, the Faust who summoned her from the abyss of which her eyes retain the devastating memory must have exchanged her presence for his soul; black Helen's lips suck the marrow from the poet's spirit, although she wishes to do no such thing. (*BB* 237)

Not only imaginatively colonised as a woman by Baudelaire, Duval is at once the product of that literal, masculine European colonisation of other peoples and other parts of the world:

Robbed of the bronze gateway of Benin ... of the esoteric wisdom of the great university of Timbuktu ... The Abyssinia of black saints and holy lions was not even so much as a legend to her ... The splendid continent to which her skin allied her had been excised from her memory. She had been deprived of history, she was the pure child of the colony. The colony – white, imperious – had fathered her ...

Her granny spoke Creole, patois, knew no other language, spoke it badly and taught it badly to Jeanne, who did her best to convert it into good French when she came to Paris ... but ... her heart wasn't in it, no wonder. It was as though her tongue had been cut out and another one sewn in that did not fit well. (*BB* 238–9)

Compounded with Baudelaire's imaginative imperialism, this shattered history of Duval's amounted to an obliteration of her autonomy, an obliteration of her identity itself – an identity which Carter reinscribes by stressing, as she did with with Fevvers in *Nights at the Circus*, Duval's sheer humanity. In 'Black Venus', Baudelaire's poetic idealisation and misrepresentation of Duval extend into his daily treatment of her. The beginning of the story pictures the two of them living out depressing autumn days in Paris. Baudelaire's will to dream survives even these. His romanticising impulse involves a patronisation of Duval:

On these sad days, at those melancholy times, as the room sinks into dusk, he ... will ramble on: 'Baby, baby, let me take you back where you belong, back to your lovely, lazy island where the jewelled parrot rocks on the enamelled tree ... My monkey, my pussy-cat, my pet ... think how lovely it would be to live there.' (*BB* 231–2)

This kind of nonsense is immediately debunked: 'But, on these days, nipped by frost and sulking, no pet nor pussy she; she looked more like an old crow with rusty feathers in a miserable huddle by the smoky fire which she pokes with spiteful sticks' (*BB* 232). Again, Carter stresses the necessary materialism of a woman for whom the practical exigencies of life contradict romantic fantasy: 'she dressed up in the set of clanking jewellery he'd given her, paste, nothing she could sell or she'd have sold it ... A slumbrous resentment of anything you could not eat, drink or smoke ... was her salient characteristic' (*BB* 233–4).

Carter thus rehumanises Duval but she cannot give her back an uncompromised African history. What she does do is picture Duval's survival and the money she made out of Baudelaire after his death. Just as Fevvers plainly understands that autonomy is not some transcendent condition but something which has to be purchased, so Duval purchases an autonomy that mocks its financial origin in the person who wilfully cooperated in her dispossession. Duval takes ship for the Caribbean with a man 'who called himself her brother' (*BB* 243):

> They'd salted away what the poet managed to smuggle to her, all the time he was dying ...
> She was surprised to find out how much she was worth.
> Add to this the sale of a manuscript or two, the ones she hadn't used to light her cheroots with ... Later, any memorabilia of the poet, even his clumsy drawings, would fetch a surprising sum ...
> Her voyage was interrupted by no albatrosses. She never thought of the slaver's route, unless it was to compare her grandmother's crossing with her own, comfortable one. You could say that Jeanne had found herself ... She decided to give up rum, except for a single tot last thing at night, after the accounts were completed. (*BB* 243)

Carter's disdain for masculine constructions of the female, whether as Winged Victory, as muse or whatever, surfaces in her interview with Kerryn Goldsworthy in 1985, where she refers specifically to the 'Black Venus' story:

> Jeanne Duval didn't want to be a muse; as far as one can tell, she had a perfectly horrid time being a muse. She felt that she should take Baudelaire for as much as she could get. He treated her, as they say, Quite Well, except that he appears not to have taken her in any degree seriously as a human being. I mean you can't take a muse seriously as a human being, or else they stop being a muse; they start being something that hasn't come to inspire you, but a being with all these problems ...
> I think the muse is a pretty fatuous person. The concept of the muse is – it's another magic Other, isn't it, another way of keeping women out of the arena. There's a whole book by Robert Graves

dedicated to the notion that poetic inspiration is female, which is why women don't have it. It's like haemophilia; they're the transmitters, you understand. But they don't suffer from it themselves. (Goldsworthy 1985: 11–12)

An aspect of Carter's appropriation of masculine iconography in *Nights at the Circus* is her refusal of the idea that there is such a thing as essential womanly nature. Fevvers claims that she was not born in the normal way of human individuals but was hatched. She compares herself with Helen of Troy, whom classical legend describes as issuing from an egg brought forth by her mother Leda after Leda had been 'embraced' by Zeus in the form of a swan: 'I never docked via what you might call the *normal channels*, sir, oh, dear me, no; but, just like Helen of Troy, was *hatched*' (*NC* 7). Carter finds in this notion of 'hatching' a metaphor for the idea that gendered identity is something that is not given but is made and can be remade. Ricarda Schmidt comments that Fevvers' notion of having been hatched means that she 'fantasizes a beginning for herself outside the Oedipal triangle, outside the Law of the Father' (Schmidt 1990: 67) – and outside all the essentialist determinations prescribed by that Law. The anti-essentialism of this metaphor of hatching means, of course, that men can be re-made just as much as women. The principle is implicit in Fevvers' imagining of the way in which she will reconstruct Walser's masculinity:

> Let him hand himself over into my safekeeping, and I will transform him. You said yourself he was unhatched, Lizzie; very well – I'll *sit* on him, I'll hatch him out, I'll make a new man of him. I'll make him into the New Man, in fact, fitting mate for the New Woman. (*NC* 281)

Fevvers is the New Woman because she has been constructed as the New Woman. Her slogan as the winged trapeze artist reads: 'Is she fact or is she fiction?' (*NC* 7). This is a question repeatedly asked of her by members of her audience and, not least, when he first meets her, by Walser. But the teasing question is misconceived, because she is both fiction *and* fact. She has been constructed and has constructed herself; she's been composed or written into being and in that sense is fictional. But that composition, that 'fiction', is now true and the fact. She's the new, the reconstituted woman. As such she is the product, in significant part, of Lizzie's radicalism. 'I raised you up' says Lizzie to Fevvers at one point, 'to fly to the heavens' (*NC* 282). Lizzie's radical act of raising was inescapable from the exercise of reason. As Fevvers herself comments towards the end of the book: 'I am a rational being and, what's more, took in my rationality with her [Lizzie's] milk' (*NC* 225). However witch-like Lizzie may sometimes appear (she seems able to alter the pace at which time passes), she is not, in fact, a witch. Fevvers is at pains to stress that anything that Lizzie can do has a rational explanation:

> Lizzie, at her cards, shook her old grizzled head. No tricks. Why not? For the things my foster-mother can pull of when she sets her mind to it, you'd not believe! Shrinkings and swellings and clocks running ahead or behind you like frisky dogs; but there's a logic to it, some logic of scale and dimension that won't be meddled with, which she alone keeps the key of, like she keeps the key of Nelson's timepiece stowed away in her handbag and won't let me touch.
>
> Her 'household' magic, she calls it. What would you think, when you saw the bread rise, if you didn't know what yeast was? Think old Liz was a witch, wouldn't you! And, then, again, consider matches! Lucifers; the little wooden soldiers of the angel of light, with whom you'd think she was in complicity if you'd never heard of phosphorous. (*NC* 199)

Lizzie's radical feminism is founded in the dynamics of reason and Fevvers' character as the New Woman is imbued with the rationality fed her by Lizzie. Fevvers' strong identification with rationality as a value is evident when she is describing Ma Nelson's house to Walser:

> It was one of those old, square, red-brick houses with a plain, sober facade and a graceful, scallop-shaped fanlight over the front door ... You could not look at Mother Nelson's house without the thought, how the Age of Reason built it; and then you almost cried, to think the Age of Reason was over before it properly begun, and this harmonious relic tucked away behind the housing of the Ratcliffe Highway, like the germ of sense left in a drunkard's mind. (*NC* 25–6)

But the reason exercised by Lizzie and the other women in Ma Nelson's house was not the Enlightenment reason of egocentricity, exclusion and oppression. The original Age of Reason may be over but reason has, nevertheless, evolved in this 'germ of sense'. Reason is identified in *Nights at the Circus* as the reason of mutuality, communication and exchange which we have seen Carter defining in her 1970s novels and in *The Sadeian Woman*: 'Life within those walls', Fevvers observes, 'was governed by a sweet and loving reason. I never saw a single blow exchanged between any of the sisterhood who reared me, nor heard a cross word or a voice raised in anger' (*NC* 39).

If the figure of Fevvers stands as an appropriation of a significant part of masculine iconography involving women, then her story as a whole in *Nights at the Circus* stands at once as an appropriation of conventional his-story, masculine history. Towards the end of the novel, when Fevvers is speaking of Walser as someone she can turn into a 'New Man' (*NC* 281), she says to Lizzie:

> Think of him, not as a lover, but as a scribe, as an amanuensis ... And not of my trajectory, alone, but of yours, too, Lizzie; of your long history of exile and cunning which you've scarcely hinted to him, which will fill up ten times more of his notebooks than *my* story ever did. Think of him as the amanuensis of all those whose tales we've yet to tell him, the histories of those women who would otherwise go down nameless and forgotten, erased from history as if they had never been, so that he, too, will put his poor shoulder to the wheel and help to give the world a little turn into the new era that begins tomorrow. (*NC* 285)

The important thing about the fact that Fevvers thinks of the reconstructed Walser as writing an alternative history, is that the point applies to *Nights at the Circus* itself. The novel is historical to the extent that it contains references to actual personages and events. It is a *hers*torical novel to the extent that it gives details on and voices to women involved in historical events – details and voices typically left out of conventional history, or, for that matter, left out of conventional historical novels. The mixture of historical realism and the extraordinary in this woman's story may be seen to parallel – in an admittedly extreme form – the processes that go on in the making of conventional history. In 1974, in a book entitled *On Style in History*, the historian Peter Gay discussed the question of the relationship between facts and interpretation in the writing of history. He observed amongst some historians a scepticism about the reality of historical fact and an ensuing relativism in respect of historical interpretation:

> Since the mid-nineteenth century, historians have reiterated that progressive historians write progressive history and bourgeois historians

bourgeois history, and that, like their controlling assumptions, the style
of these historians is the expected, indeed the inescapable, style of their
party or their class. And they have reinforced their skeptical epistemology with a relativist metaphysics, questioning the objective existence
of facts as distinct from the historian who interprets them. Historical
facts, Carl Becker wrote, are not out there, in the world of the past, but
in here, in the mind of the historian. And the popular conclusion has
been summarily put by E. H. Carr: 'The belief in a hard core of facts
existing objectively and independently of the interpretation of the
historian is a preposterous fallacy, but one which it is very hard to
eradicate. (Gay 1975: 197–8)

Gay does not go along with this conclusion. He believes in objective
facts. The 'pressure towards objectivity', he writes,

is realistic because the objects of the historian's enquiry are precisely
that, objects, out there in a real and single past. Historical controversy
in no way compromises their ontological integrity. The tree in the
woods of the past fell in only one way, no matter how fragmentary or
contradictory the reports of its fall, no matter whether there are no
historians, one historian, or several contentious historians in its future
to record and debate it.
    If this sounds like naive Realism, I can only plead that I mean it to
be Realism, though not of the naive variety. (Gay 1975: 210)

It is not naive because Gay allows for the constitutive role played
by the act of interpretation, but he will not go the whole way and
assert that the act of interpretation is all there is. Such a move
would not answer to the sense of outrage that might be felt if, for
example, some relative of one of those who died in the 1995 bomb-
ing of a federal building in Oklahoma City were told that the
event and the loss were not objective facts. The importance of
interpretation does not preclude the existence of objective facts,
however hard it may sometimes be to recover those facts. What
the importance of interpretation does mean is that history is a
never-finalised process:

I am not suggesting that this process will ever end; the landscape of
the past is too remote, too obscure, or, in modern history, too over-
crowded for that. In fact, such a conclusive interpretation – the map
that will never need revision – is unrealizable in principle. One commonplace way of stating that principle is to say that every generation
must rewrite the histories of its predecessors. The commonplace is
true, but not for the reason usually offered on its behalf. It holds true,

rather, because events have posterities that may continue to the end of time – or, at least, the end of all historical writing. The meaning of an event for its posterities, as distinct from its contemporary meaning or its causes, is perpetually open to revision. As new generations reappraise the French Terror or the Great Depression, these events acquire new meanings, and these in turn become subject to inquiry and interpretation. History, in a word, is unfinished in the sense that the future always uses its past in new ways. (Gay 1975: 212)

The fantastic dimension in *Nights at the Circus* – underpinned by the factual frame of historical reference, the objective reality of the women's movement and so on – parallels Gay's notion of new uses and meanings being given to events of the past. The fantastic story of *Nights at the Circus* articulates meanings associated with historical events that are not articulated in conventional history. It is a rewriting of the historical events from a feminine perspective and in that sense *Nights at the Circus* is a 'herstorical' rather than a 'historical' novel.

The herstoricism of *Nights at the Circus* never loses sight of the material realities of women's lives at the end of the nineteenth century. It never carnivalises its preoccupation with women's suffering and disempowerment. The novel offers, in fact, within its narrative, a critique and mockery of the principle of carnival. That principle is dramatised, appropriately enough, by the circus clowns and their leader Buffo. Buffo is described as 'the Lord of Misrule himself' (*NC* 175). His act enacts the subversion of order and form, including his own:

At the climax of his turn, everything having collapsed about him as if a grenade exploded it, he starts to deconstruct himself. His face becomes contorted by the most hideous grimaces, as if he were trying to shake off the very wet white with which it is coated: shake! shake! shake out his teeth, shake off his nose, shake away his eyeballs, let all go flying off in a convulsive self-dismemberment. (*NC* 117)

This convulsive self-dismemberment is seen as adding up to nothing in the real, practical, political world. 'Angela Carter's clown', Christopher Norris writes, 'is an adept of deconstruction before the letter, of a gestural writing that effaces all signs of origin and exists only in the moment of its own production' (Norris 1987: 52). Buffo, in a phrase that alludes ironically to Lear's words in Shakespeare's *King Lear* ('Nothing will come of nothing', I.i.89), asserts that 'Nothing' is precisely what he celebrates: '*Nothing* will come of nothing. That's the glory of it' (*NC* 123). The problem is that King Lear questions the value of nothingness while Buffo nihilistically delights in it. Fevvers and Lizzie may see that gendered identity is something that can be reconstructed. But they do not lose the sense that there is a connection between the idea that identity is malleable and the empirically verifiable, material facts of people's lives. Their sense of the reconstruction of identity is worked out within a frame of rational interaction and cooperation between people. Buffo makes no such connection in his celebration of the idea that 'We' clowns 'can invent our own faces! We *make* ourselves' (*NC* 121). The idea of the constructedness of identity operates, in Buffo's imaginings, in a non-material, ahistorical realm. He effectively transcendentalises the principle of the construction of identity and in so doing defines nothing but nothing:

> 'Yet', he went on, 'am I this Buffo whom I have created? Or did I, when I made up my face to look like Buffo's, create, *ex nihilo*, another self who is not me? And what am I without my Buffo's face? Why, nobody at all. Take away my make-up and underneath is merely not-Buffo. An absence. A vacancy. (*NC* 122)

Buffo's clowns are seen – when as a group they undertake a 'Dance of disintegration' (*NC* 125) – as invoking chaos. That invocation is seen in the novel as not having any practical social or humanitarian use. 'Don't you know how I hate clowns, young man?', Fevvers asks Walser, 'I truly think they are a crime against humanity' (*NC* 143). Clowning and carnivalesque disruption of established order are not the means of bettering specifically the situation of women. At the opening of the Russian section of the novel, Carter describes the deprived life of a baboushka who looks after a little boy called Ivan:

> 'There was a pig' said the baboushka to little Ivan, who perched, round-eyed, on a three-legged stool beside her as she blew on the charcoal underneath the samovar ...
> The toil-misshapen back of the baboushka humbly bowed before the bubbling urn in the impotently submissive obeisance of one who pleads for a respite or a mercy she knows in advance will not be forthcoming ...
> All Russia was contained within the thwarted circumspection of her movements; and much of the essence of her abused and withered femaleness. (*NC* 95–6)

Later, the little boy is described as being fascinated by the circus clowns. The fascination is with something that can never aid the suffering woman back home:

> Little Ivan's relations with the clowns went thus: first, he was afraid of them; then, he was entranced by them; at last he wished to become as they, so that he, too, could terrify, enchant, vandalise, ravage, yet always stay on the safe side of being, licensed to commit licence and yet forbidden to act, so that the baboushka back at home could go on reddening and blackening the charcoal even if the clowns detonated the entire city around her and nothing would really change. Nothing. The exploded buildings would float up into the air insubstantial as bubbles, and gently waft to earth again on exactly the same places where they had stood before. The corpses would writhe, spring apart at the joints, dismember – then pick up their own dismembered limbs to juggle with them before slotting them back in their good old sockets, all present and correct, sir.
>
> So then you'd know, you'd seen the proof, that things would always be as they had always been; that nothing came of catastrophe; that chaos invoked stasis. (*NC* 151–2)

Much later in the novel, when Fevvers and her company are short of food, they eat what had been the clowns' dog: 'Fido or Bonzo or whatever he was called didn't go far amongst seven but he staved off the pangs so this last relic of the gigantic uselessness of the clowns served some function, in the end' (*NC* 249). Lastly, on the matter of Buffo and the clowns, I have to mention that Carter builds in to her portrayal of the clowns a portrayal of the gigantic uselessness of religion and all its otherworldliness. Buffo is presented as a type of Christ as he sits at the table with his clowns in a parody of the Last Supper: 'was he not the very Christ, presiding at the white board, at supper, with his disciples?' (*NC* 176).

The mocking of the ahistoricism of the clowns emphasises Carter's and her novel's sympathy with the worldly, the material and the his/herstorical. It is a type of mockery that is repeated in respect of the Shaman and his tribespeople with whom Walser lives for a while. The solipsism of the tribespeople's world-view is described with a degree of scorn:

> This world, dream, dreamed idea or settled conviction extended upwards, to the heavens, and downwards, into the bowels of the earth and the depths of the lakes and rivers, with all whose tenants they lived on intimate terms. But it did not extend laterally. It did not, could not,

take into account any other interpretation of the world, or dream, which was not their own one ... 'history' was a concept with which they were perfectly unfamiliar, as, indeed, they were with any kind of geography except the mystically four-dimensional one they invented for themselves.

They knew the space they saw. They believed in a space they apprehended. Between knowledge and belief, there was no room for surmise and doubt. They were, at the same time, pragmatic as hell and, intellectually speaking, permanently three sheets in the wind. (*NC* 253)

And not just scorn, but also burlesque comedy. The absurdity of the Shaman's belief in what constitutes mystical truth is the subject of a scene where Walser, still somewhat deranged and half remembering having been chased as the human chicken by a homicidal Buffo, is eating a meal with the Shaman:

Normally, Walser shared the Shaman's suppers, but, today, as an experiment, the Shaman decided to feed Walser the same diet he offered to the idols in the austere and windowless village god-hut, the quasi-anthropomorphs in front of whom he practised the mysteries of his religion. They thrived on a porridge made of crushed barley mixed with pine nuts and broth from boiled capercailzie. Walser supped up suspiciously, then pushed the porridge round and round the wooden bowl with his horn spoon. The dried herbs crackled above the stove. Walser's eyes fused.

'Hamburgers,' he ruminated aloud. The Shaman pricked up his ears. Walser rambled off down a gastronomic memory lane; who can tell what litany the Shaman thought he was reciting?

'Fish soup.' Walser's face was the mirror of his memory; he grimaced. He tried again. 'Christmas dinner ...'

His face convulsed and he whimpered. The words, 'Christmas dinner', reminded him of something most fearful, of some hideous danger; they reminded him of the main course, they reminded him of ... 'Cock-a-doodle-do!'

He cried aloud, assailed by the dreadful if incomprehensible memories, then fell into a haunted silence until another happier thought came to him:

'Eel pie and mash.'

At that, he beamed and rubbed his stomach with his hand. Raptly attentive, the Shaman, the reader of signs, poured him more broth, and waited for further revelations.

'Eel pie and mash, me old cock,' said Walser appreciatively. (*NC* 256)

There is another mockery of the self-serving character of the tribespeople's metaphysical ideas, their innocence of history, when the narrator of the novel describes their eating of a baby bear:

The bear's executioner was elected from amongst the villagers by the spirits, who manifested their choice in dreams or by other extra-terrestrial means ... The entire village crowded into the god-hut to watch the ceremony, lamenting vigorously and apologising profusely: 'Poor bruin! We're so sorry, bruin! How we love you, poor little bruin! How bad we feel because we must do away with you!' Then the bear's head would be cut off and the rest of it roasted over an open fire ...

Bruin, now free of his fleshy envelope, would carry messages to the dead; those who ate him would partake of the strength and valour of the bear; and, besides, since death was not precisely mortal in this theology, bruin would soon be up and about again, to be born again, captured again, reared again, killed again in a perpetually recurring cycle of return.

And, golly! didn't he taste good!

After the flesh was boiled away, his skull would be tossed on the heap in the god-hut that, were it to have been counted out, would have announced the extreme antiquity of these customs. But nobody ever counted the heap because none of them knew in what way the past differed from the present. (*NC* 258)

Carter's rational–empirical estimation of the world, her sense that there are facts and material realities outwith personal or cultural interpretation, emerges when she describes the Shaman and the tribespeople's idea of the world as one which simply failed to connect with *real* reality:

And even when his eyes were open, you might have said the Shaman 'lived in a dream'. But so did they all. They shared a common dream, which was their world, and it should rather be called an 'idea' than a 'dream', since it constituted their entire sense of lived reality, which impinged on *real* reality, only inadvertently. (*NC* 253)

Carter's empiricism frequently caused her to react against sentimental mythologising, whether it be a mythologising of Mother goddesses or of undeveloped, non-Western societies. In her interview with John Haffenden this reaction comes over as humorous practical sense:

Shamans are actually very good at what they do, because they themselves believe in it, but that doesn't make it true. So the question of illusion – what is real and what is not real – comes up again there, in a tribal group which has a different epistemology. Of course every social system tends to denaturize people, it's one of the things about living in groups; since you can't live on your own and retain your social identity, it's just one more bit of the difficulty of being! I used that tribal society in *Nights at the Circus* just because there is now so much sentimentality about primitives, and sometimes I feel it too; but, Jesus, it can't be any fun having toothache in a tribal society – they would press a pregnant bat to the cavity. (Haffenden 1985: 88–9)

Carter's mockery of the Shaman and the tribespeople is, when it comes down to it, really a mockery and an attack upon Westerners who do not actually attempt to relate to or with the non-Western but who seek merely to reconstruct it in their own ideal images. As I have noted before, Carter herself has sometimes been described as a writer in that branch of postmodern writing known as magic realism. It is a label she manages to reject, in the Shaman episode of *Nights at the Circus*, in the context of criticising a world-view that makes no distinction between fact and fiction:

> The Shaman listened the most attentively to what Walser said after a dream because it dissolved the slender margin the Shaman apprehended between real and unreal, although the Shaman himself would not have put it that way since he noticed only the margin, shallow as a step, between one level of reality and another. He made no categorical distinction between seeing and believing. It could be said that, for all the peoples of this region, there existed no difference between fact and fiction; instead, a sort of magic realism. (*NC* 260)

Yet if Carter mocks the ahistoricism of the Shaman and the tribespeople in the same manner as she questioned the ahistorical implications of clowning, then we should always remember that it is not simply conventional masculine history to which she is committed as the alternative. Indeed, she sees conventional history as sharing a great deal in common with the nature of carnival. Buffo and the clowns become tokens of the British Empire and of British imperial history. Buffo's circus performance at one stage involves an 'exceedingly large coffin draped with the Union Jack' (*NC* 117) and there is a wonderfully parodic image of patriotic Britishness when the women who have escaped the Siberian penitentiary see the clowns as they are being led away by the outlaws:

> it was the motley band who brought up the procession that made the women cross themselves, for these were men of all shapes and sizes, some small as dwarves, some long and lanky as clothespoles, less than a dozen of them, in the ragged remains of what had once been bright clothing in the strangest styles. Some had huge red noses, others big black rings round their eyes, but the paint was peeling from all the

faces, so they looked piebald. Two of these men, wizened and old and
inclined more to the stature of dwarves than of giants, provided the
music for the party – but the fiddle was small, as if shrunken, and the
other augmented his tambourine with a metal triangle hanging behind
his back, at which he kicked up with every step he took. And they were
playing ... 'Rule Britannia!' (*NC* 220)

Buffo, we are told, was 'a great patriot, British to the bone' and
'as widely travelled as the British Empire in the service of fun'
(*NC* 118). The conjunction of clown and Empire deprives imperialism of any serious claim over our hearts and minds. It renders
imperial history absurd. Carter views American democratic capitalism, captured in Colonel Kearney's enterprise of taking the circus across Russia, in a comparable absurdist light. After Kearney
has agreed to take on Walser as a clown in his circus, he declares:

'Surely I can rely on a fellow Amurrican to see the glory of it! All
nations united in the great Ludic Game under the banner of Liberty
itself. D'you see the grand plan, young man? Old Glory across the
tundra, crowned heads bow to the democratic extravaganza! Then,
think of it, tuskers to the land of the Rising Sun, young man! Hannibal's
tuskers stopped short after the Alps but mine, mine shall go round the
en-tire world! Never before, in the en-tire history of thrills and laughter,
has a free Amurrican circus circumnavigated the globe!'
     What a visionary he was!
'And, after this unprecedented and epoch-making historical event,
I'll land you safe and sound back home in the good old U.S. of A.
Yessir!' (*NC* 102–3)

Carter's point is that American democratic history is a travesty; it
is not history as it might be. Kearney boasts that as a youth he
could 'set [his] mind to anything provided it weren't of any use'
(*NC* 100). Carter cannot resist making fun of the specifically
masculine absurdity of Kearney's American ideology when she has
Kearney lose consciousness after having drunk too much while
trying to seduce Fevvers:

Removing the bourbon bottle from his fist, she poked curiously into
the aperture of his fly, which he'd just fumbled open before he passed
out, and withdrew a string of little silk American flags ...
     'How did it go?' inquired Lizzie in their own drawing-room, thick
with the scent of hot-house flowers ...
     'Couldn't get 'is star-spangled banner up,' replied Fevvers. (*NC* 171)

The images of British imperialism and American capitalism, though comic, have also a grotesque side that registers the disgust Carter feels for their masquerade of history. Throughout the novel, Lizzie is represented as holding an almost Marxist view of history. And at one point, while explaining her leftist, rationalist view of life to a young idealist who had gone on about some future utopia towards which the human soul was moving through history, she observes:

> 'I'd certainly agree with you that this present which we contemporaneously inhabit is *imperfect* to a degree. But this grievous condition has nothing to do with the soul, or, as you might also call it, removing the theological connotation, "human nature". It isn't in that Grand Duke's nature to be a bastard, hard though it may be to believe; nor does it lie in those of his employees to be slaves. What we have to contend with, here, my boy, is the long shadow of the *past historic* ... that forged the institutions which create the human nature of the present in the first place.
>
> 'It's not the human "soul" that must be forged on the anvil of history but the anvil itself must be changed in order to change humanity.' (*NC* 240)

The anvil of traditional history must itself be changed if new possibilities for human lives are to be released. There must be an alternative or a reconceived history or herstory within which people may grow. In such a new his/herstory Fevvers the New Woman may be able to realise herself and Jack – Jack-the-Lad – Walser can do what, we are told at the very end of the novel, he has done: 'Walser took himself apart and put himself together again' (*NC* 294). At the end of their story, Walser and Fevvers, in love, make love with Fevvers on top because her wings make it impossible for her to adopt another position. The scene alludes to an old favourite of Carter's: the story of the rape of Leda by Zeus in the guise of a swan, a story already alluded to at the opening of *Nights at the Circus*, as we have seen, in Fevver's comment that 'like Helen of Troy' she was 'hatched' (*NC* 7). The difference at the end of *Nights at the Circus* is that this scene inverts the classical stereotype of a male figure with wings overwhelming a woman. But it is not *just* an inversion, as if the feminism of this novel were inscribed within what Carter termed a 'female supremacist' mode (Carter 1980: 226). The relationship between Walser and Fevvers is based not on the principle of dominator and dominated but on the idea of love between equals. The cancelling of the traditional patriarchal icon of male dominance is necessary to emblematise this new relationship. Carter is indicating that a new his/herstory is possible because of this new kind of relationship between a woman and a man.

And while it is primarily, it is not *only* a heterosexual model that Carter uses to image the possibilities of a new his/herstory. There is in *Nights at the Circus* the further story of two of the female circus artistes, Mignon and the Princess of Abyssinia. Mignon is the partner of the 'Ape-Man' and she is not treated well: 'From the monkey house, echoing on the night air, came a rhythmic thud as the Ape-Man beat his woman as though she were a carpet' (*NC* 115). Mignon escapes the Ape-Man and she and the Princess of Abyssinia start a loving relationship in which they 'seemed, as a pair, to transcend their individualities' (*NC* 202–3). The new his/herstory will be large enough to accommodate sexual orientations not articulated in patriarchal history. The Princess, though she had never been to Abyssinia, is black, and establishing a role for her in this plot is a way of indicating that the new his/herstory will embrace, as one might expect, both sexual *and* racial differences.

In the closing paragraphs of *Nights at the Circus* Fevvers starts laughing:

> Her laughter spilled out of the window and made the tin ornaments on the tree outside the god-hut shake and tinkle ...
>
> Fevvers' laughter seeped through the gaps in the window-frames and cracks in the door-frames of all the houses in the village; the villagers stirred in their beds, chuckling at the enormous joke that invaded their dreams, of which they would remember nothing in the morning except the mirth it caused. She laughed, she laughed, she laughed.
>
> It seemed this laughter of the happy young woman rose up from the wilderness in a spiral and began to twist and shudder across Siberia. It tickled the sleeping sides of the inhabitants of the railhead at R.; it penetrated the counterpoint of the music in the Maestro's house; the members of the republic of free women experienced it as a refreshing breeze....
>
> The spiralling tornado of Fevvers' laughter began to twist and shudder across the entire globe, as if a spontaneous response to the giant

comedy that endlessly unfolded beneath it, until everything that lived and breathed, everywhere, was laughing. (*NC* 294–5)

How are we to read this laughter? At one level, it is simply personal. Fevvers is ecstatically happy to have found someone to love who loves her in return. But we must also remember that *Nights at the Circus* is a his/herstorical novel. The twentieth century that it looks forward to had, by the time Carter wrote the novel, already substantially happened. I read Fevvers' laughter as, in part, the delight of the victor, the delight that Carter herself has retrospectively and that her character has prophetically, in knowing that the war for women's rights, even if not ultimately won, would score up notable victories in the twentieth century. The celebratory laughter touches all human beings because the gaining of women's rights is a gaining of the rights of being human.

If *Nights at the Circus* hints at some kind of connection between masculinist values and the carnivalesque, it is a perspective which is elaborated, alongside other things, in the last novel Carter wrote before her death, *Wise Children*.

SEVEN

Wise Children

Wise Children (1991) is about English culture. And it is about a Shakespeare who has been constructed as one of the originating myths of English culture. As the novel several times reminds us, Shakespeare's head appears on the Bank of England £20 note. *Wise Children* refers to Shakespeare's tragedies, but its heart is with the comedies. It rewrites the dark underside of the comedies just as it reinvents their happy endings. The novel is about the way in which English imperialism and patriarchy appropriated Shakespeare and cast him as a founding myth in their own image. It is about the ways in which aspects of Shakespeare can be re-read and used as an alternative model for English cultural identity; one which stands outside the inheritance of patriarchy and imperialism.

The central action of the novel takes place on a single day in the very late 1980s. The day is 23 April, traditionally Shakespeare's birthday, which is also the festival day of England's patron saint, St George. The novel's narrator, Dora Chance, tells of the events of the day after it is over and she intersperses her record with extensive accounts of her own life and of the lives of other members of her family in the preceding years. Dora, who has an identical twin sister, Nora, is seventy-five. They are the illegitimate daughters of an eminent actor, Sir Melchior Hazard. The family relationships in the novel are complicated but in their complication lies one of the basic allusions to Shakespeare's work. Though Dora and Nora's biological father is Melchior, they are officially known as the daughters of Melchior's fraternal twin, Peregrine or

'Perry'. Melchior and Peregrine are sons of the marriage of Estella and Ranulph Hazard. Thirty or more years older than Estella, Ranulph Hazard was one of the 'great, roaring, actor-managers' of the late Victorian stage, and he met Estella in 1888 when she played Cordelia to his King Lear (*WC* 14). But though they were sons of the marriage of Ranulph and Estella, it is not certain that Melchior and Peregrine are the biological sons of Ranulph. Illegitimacy or shades of illegitimacy, different kinds of illegitimacy, run in the family, as we shall see. Melchior, whose birthday is the same as Shakespeare's and whose hundredth birthday it is on the 23 April recorded by Dora in her story, has had three wives. The first, Lady Atalanta Hazard (née Lynde; also referred to, in her old age, by Dora and Nora as 'Wheelchair'), is the mother of two daughters, Saskia and Imogen. But while legally Melchior is their father, their biological father is Peregrine. There are no children from Melchior's second marriage to Delia Delaney (née Daisy Duck, formerly the second wife of an American film producer nicknamed 'Genghis Khan'). From Melchior's third marriage to a young woman known as 'My Lady Margarine' – who had played Cordelia to his Lear, just as Estella had played Cordelia to Ranulph's Lear – there issued two further fraternal twins, Tristram and Gareth Hazard. Dora's and Nora's mother, 'Pretty Kitty', was a foundling who died very shortly after they were born, 'when the Zeppelins were falling' (*WC* 2) during the First World War. They were adopted by the owner of the house where 'Pretty Kitty' had been lodging, a woman calling herself Mrs Chance but who allowed Dora and Nora only to call her 'Grandma', 'out of respect for the dead' (*WC* 26). Dora and Nora have had no children of their own but live with Melchior's discarded first wife, Wheelchair, and they are close to their goddaughter, a black girl called Tiffany, who is the daughter of Brenda, a neighbour of Dora and Nora in the London district of Brixton.

Dora and Nora are not only illegitimate in that they were born out of wedlock, they are also culturally illegitimate when measured against their father's, Melchior's, status as 'a pillar of the legit. theatre' (*WC* 11), the venerable, famed Shakespearian actor of his day. *Their* career was as 'song and dance girls'. 'We can', says Dora, 'still lift a leg higher than your average dog, if called for' (*WC* 2). Melchior's (apparent) father, Ranulph, the actor-manager, had also been a pillar of the mainstream Victorian theatre. And Shakespeare was *his* thing, too: 'Shakespeare was a kind of god for him. It was as good as idolatry' (*WC* 14). So much so that he was filled with a proselytising zeal, and when his new young wife was offered the part of Hamlet in a production in New York (he being too old to play the Prince) he had jumped at the chance of playing Hamlet's father: 'all agog to give America the tongue that Shakespeare spake' (*WC* 16). The production was successful and would have 'run ad infinitum except the twins [Melchior and Peregrine] announced that they were on the way and a female Hamlet is one thing but a pregnant prince is quite another' (*WC* 16). Nevertheless, once the twins were born, Ranulph and Estella took Shakespeare on a world tour. The description of the tour draws a parallel between Ranulph's proselytising on behalf of Shakespeare and England's imperial occupation of – and renaming of – territories across the globe:

> he saw the entire world as his mission field ... the old man was seized with the most imperative desire, to spread and go on spreading the Word overseas. Willy-nilly, off must go his wife and children, too, to take Shakespeare where Shakespeare had never been before.
> In those days, there was so much pink on the map of the world that English was spoken everywhere ... Off to the ends of Empire they went ... an entire dried-out township in New South Wales was re-named Hazard ... A street in Hobart, Tasmania ...
> A theatre, long since demolished, named the Hazard, in Shanghai. Then Hong Kong. Then Singapore. (*WC* 17, 19)

In the twentieth century, Melchior's perspective on Shakespeare was again, like his father's, that of the colonialist imagination, an imagination that is mercilessly mocked and parodied in the novel. Melchior even went to Hollywood in the 1930s to make a film of *A Midsummer Night's Dream*, motivated by a desire for revenge on the Americans for their independence, revenge on the first of the ones that got away. Dora – who, with Nora, had also had a part in the film – relates a point of crisis in the making of the film:

> Think what was at stake. The entire production was at stake. His Hollywood future – that is, his chance to take North America back for England, Shakespeare and St George. (*WC* 133)

Melchior made a speech to his cast about plundering Hollywood on behalf of the English:

'welcome, to all of you come together here ... to ransack all the treasur-
ies of this great industry of yours to create a glorious, an everlasting
monument to the genius of that poet whose name will be reverenced as
long as English is spoken ... who left the English language just a little
bit more glorious than he found it, and let some of that glory rub off
on us old Englishmen too, as they set sail around the globe, bearing
with them on that mission the tongue that Shakespeare spoke!' (*WC*
135)

When he agreed to marry Delia Delaney, the woman who had
been the wife of the film's producer, 'Genghis Khan', we hear
from Dora that he fantasised about appropriating, on a par with
Julius Caesar himself, the entirety of Hollywood:

I think he thought that he was marrying, not into Hollywood but
Hollywood itself, taking over the entire factory, thus acquiring control
of the major public dreaming facility in the whole world. Shakespeare's
revenge for the War of Independence. Once Melchior was in charge of
this fabulous machine, he would bestride the globe. (*WC* 148)

The 'imperial Hazard dynasty that bestrode the British theatre
like a colossus for a century and a half' (*WC* 10) is, then, associated with the hegemony of English imperialist culture. And the
gendered bias of that hegemony is also dramatised through the
Hazard dynasty. Kate Webb, in a fine essay which anticipates
several of the points I make in this chapter about *Wise Children*,
notes that the 'Hazard family is a patriarchal institution' (Webb
1994: 282). It is a patriarchy that, like the imperialism with which
it is associated, is ceaselessly attacked in the novel for its hypoc-
risy, its lovelessness and its irresponsibility. Throughout their lives,
until his hundredth birthday, Melchior never 'officially recognised'
(*WC* 5) Dora and Nora as his natural offspring. Indeed, he 'flatly'
denied his paternity (*WC* 30). He might still have tried to love
them, but he didn't. When their uncle Perry bought them a phono-
graph, Dora and Nora heard a song: 'A song, our song, a song that
made us a promise our father never kept, though others did: "I
can't give you anything but love, baby"' (*WC* 33). Again, at the
opening of the very last chapter, when, both in their seventy-fifth
year, they cross the Thames from Brixton to their father's house
in Regent's Park to attend his one-hundredth birthday party ('the
river lies between Brixton and glamour like a sword. I wonder why
they call it Old *Father* Thames'; *WC* 194), Dora recalls having on

past occasions sauntered by her father's house 'just for a little look ... love locked out, ducky' (*WC* 194). The substitute, but no less real, family that Dora and Nora found and find themselves within, down in Brixton, almost makes a point of constructing itself without father-figures:

> It was Cyn's eldest, Mavis, who got off with a GI which resulted in our Brenda, whom we took care of when she had *her* bit of trouble and brought home our precious little Tiffany, the first Black in the family.
> 'Family,' I say. Grandma invented this family. She put it together out of whatever came to hand – a stray pair of orphaned babes, a ragamuffin in a flat cap. She created it by sheer force of personality. I only wish she'd lived to see our little Tiffany. There is a persistent history of absent fathers in our family. (*WC* 35)

The absence of their father places Dora and Nora out of the line of inheritance not simply of his personal possessions, but outside of the dominant cultural ideology which he emblematises. There is a music-hall comedian by the name of Gorgeous George – echoing St George of England – whom Dora and Nora went to see when they were in their early teens. He sang 'Rose of England' and displayed a map of the British Empire tattooed on his body, of which Carter's description is pure parody:

> he stripped off only to reveal a gee-string of very respectable proportions ... and it was made out of the Union Jack. Amply though the garment concealed his privates, now you could see the Cape of Good Hope situated in his navel and observe the Falkland Islands disappear down the crack of his bum when he did his grand patriotic ninety-degree rotation ...
> We gazed enraptured on the flexing pecs. 'Rule, Britannia' accompanied his final turn, which revealed how most of his global tattoo was filled in a brilliant pink, although the limelight turned it into a morbid, raspberry colour that looked bad for his health. (*WC* 67)

It is from the imperialist, patriarchal England that Dora and Nora are disinherited, though it is a disinheritance that they scorned and which, as it all turned out, is a blessing. Of Gorgeous George:

> as regards the pink bits on his bum and belly, we knew already in our bones that those of us in the left-hand line were left out of the picture; we were the offspring of the bastard king of England, if you like, and we weren't going to inherit any of the gravy, so the hell with it. (*WC* 67–8)

One of the blessings of Dora's and Nora's disinheritance is their disengagement from the masculine cult of war, which is also seen in the novel as a symptom of patriarchal and imperial power. The point is emphasised grotesquely in a further description of Gorgeous George:

> George made a few passes with his golf club, and simulated bayonet practice with it in his patriotic bathers for a bit, with a few more imitation drum rolls and stern cheers from the crowd. And some had tears in their eyes, I swear, and shouted: 'Good old George! Hurrah for George!' But we girls were bemused: what kind of a show was this? Hadn't Grandma told us that wars were a way to get the young men out of the picture, leave all the women for the ugly old codgers who wouldn't have got any, otherwise? So we knew what wars were for and, to tell the truth, from George's joke, it looked as though he thought that that was what fathers always wanted, too. (*WC* 67)

Grandma, with her constructed, fatherless family had indeed offered a view of war distinct from patriarchal assumptions. 'When the bombardments began', during the Second War, Grandma would protest at the young men fulfilling the law of the father: 'Grandma would go outside and shake her fist at the old men in the sky' (*WC* 29). As Dora narrates the events of her own and Nora's lives in the decades before their father's one-hundredth birthday, her story returns periodically to the tragedies of war. Grandma had kept scrapbooks of their performances:

> The last scrapbook stops short in 1944, leaving us marooned for ever just turning thirty, on the cusp, caught up in one last pose, would you believe, done up as bulldogs. *Bulldog Breed*. For some bloody silly charity matinée, drumming-up cash to replace lost lovers, lost sons, boys dead on the Burma Road, the irreplaceable. (*WC* 78)

Grandma was killed in 1944, 'taken out by a flying bomb on her way to the off-licence' (*WC* 79). Dora sees tragedy as a masculine form. When she is recording her life of the 1930s, she writes: 'Only untimely death is a tragedy. And war, which, before we knew it, would be upon us; replace the comic mask with the one whose mouth turns down ... I refuse point-blank to play in tragedy' (*WC* 154).

The irresponsibility of the masculine line of the Hazards resurfaces in Melchior's son Tristram. Tristram, though he 'wasn't worth the paper she wiped her bum with' (*WC* 40), had formed a relationship with Dora and Nora's godchild Tiffany. Though Tiffany adored him, he treated her very badly, not least through having an affair with the much older family member, Saskia. But Tiffany gets pregnant by him, as Dora relates: 'Nora and I know what hoops the kept woman has to jump to work her passage and our little Tiff had looked very haggard and wan last time we saw her and kept excusing herself to go to the bathroom, too' (*WC* 40). The crisis between Tristram and Tiffany comes to a head when she appears, distraught and distracted – Ophelia-like, as Kate Chedgzoy has noted (Chedgzoy 1995: 81) – in the middle of a television game-show which he hosts. She runs away from the show and Tristram goes round to Dora and Nora's looking for her, where, as a father, his evasion and cowardice express themselves: "'I'm not ready to be a father", said Tristram. "I can't take the responsibility. I'm not mature enough." "No man ever is," announced Wheelchair, in her grande dame voice' (*WC* 44). The vapid irresponsibility of Tristram is figuratively merged with Melchior's magisterial irresponsibility when, in a scene from the game-show which Tiffany has wrecked, a video of which Tristram has brought round to Dora and Nora's, the two men clasped in absurd, bathetic union: 'Tristram looked as though he was propping old Melchior up, now, unless it was Melchior holding up his son; each clutched the other like drowning men at spars' (*WC* 45). When the police find the body of a young woman in the Thames, her face destroyed by the propellers of a police launch, it is presumed to be Tiffany.

Masculine irresponsibility is manifest also in Melchior's brother, Peregrine. If Carter attacked the principle of carnival in *Nights at the Circus*, then she does so again in her characterisation of Pere-grine. Perry is presented by Dora as an attractive avuncular figure, describing him as 'adventurer, magician, seducer, explorer, script-writer, rich man, poor man – but never either beggarman or thief' (*WC* 18). He was attractive *and* generous; when rich, always bring-ing Dora and Nora presents and giving them money. But he had a low 'boredom threshold' (*WC* 61). He could not settle for long. So he skipped in and out of Dora and Nora's lives, never consist-ently one thing:

> Over the years, Peregrine offered us a Chinese banquet of options as to what happened to him next. He gave us all his histories, we could choose which ones we wanted – but they kept on changing, so. That

was the trouble. Did he really meet up with Ambrose Bierce in a flophouse in El Paso and go off with him to fight in Mexico? (In confirmation of this, in *sole* confirmation, I'm bound to say, one personalised dedication in a copy of *The Devil's Dictionary*.) Was it true he'd posed as Ben Travers? I knew for a fact he'd worked in circuses. Unless it was on the halls. (*WC* 31–2)

In his ungroundedness, in the flux and interchangeability of his histories, Peregrine had no real history. Or, at least, he had not deigned to live *in* history. He is an allegory of the not-real; an allegory of the principle of carnival. Once, when she was talking with Melchior's first wife after her divorce from Melchior, Dora, who had fantasised about Lady Atalanta ('Wheelchair') marrying Peregrine, was told by Lady Atalanta: "'One doesn't *marry* a man like that, my dear," she said ... she knew a thing or two about Perry. Here today and gone tomorrow, not so much a man, more of a travelling carnival' (*WC* 169). And the carnivalesque is no solution to anything, as Carter pointed out in discussion with Lorna Sage, when she also observed that Bakhtin on carnival was someone she had read very late and only then because so many readers had declared that her work was carnivalesque in Bakhtin's definition of the term. But while she quite liked Bakhtin, she could not take him as an authority:

> she is characteristically sceptical about the vogue for the carnivalesque: 'It's interesting that Bakhtin became very fashionable in the 1980s, during the demise of the particular kind of theory that would have put all kinds of question marks around the whole idea of the carnivalesque. I'm thinking of Marcuse and repressive desublimation, which tells you exactly what carnivals are for. The carnival has to stop. The whole point about the feast of fools is that things went on as they did before, after it stopped.' (Sage 1992: 188)

Carter makes the same point at the end of a piece, 'In Pantoland', included in her posthumous, 1993 collection of short stories, *American Ghosts and Old World Wonders*:

> As Umberto Eco once said, 'An everlasting carnival does not work.' You can't keep it up, you know; nobody ever could. The essence of the carnival, the festival, the Feast of Fools, is transience. It is here today and gone tomorrow, a release of tension not a reconstitution of order, a refreshment ... after which everything can go on again exactly as if nothing had happened.

Things don't change because a girl puts on trousers or a chap slips on a frock, you know. Masters were masters again the day after Saturnalia ended; after the holiday from gender, it was back to the old grind. (*BB* 389)

Carnival is no reconstitution of order. If it has no purchase on gender relations in the real world, neither does it have any purchase on war. 'I do not wish to talk about the war', says Dora, as she tells her story. 'Suffice to say it was no carnival' (*WC* 163). Later in her narrative she records how she had said to Perry on the day of Melchior's hundredth birthday:

wars are facts we cannot fuck away, Perry; nor laugh away, either.
Do you hear me, Perry?
No. (*WC* 221)

Dora has another, similarly fruitless, go at Perry:

'Life's a carnival,' he said. He was an illusionist, remember.
'The carnival's got to stop, some time, Perry,' I said. 'You listen to the news, that'll take the smile off your face.'
'News? What news?' (*WC* 222)

Perry prefers to pretend it is possible to live outside history, just as Dora herself, unselfconsciously, had lived when she was young. She comments on how, in her old age,

I understood the thing I'd never grasped back in those days, when I was young, before I lived in history. When I was young, I'd wanted to be ephemeral, I'd wanted the moment, to live in just the glorious moment, the rush of blood, the applause. Pluck the day. Eat the peach. Tomorrow never comes. But, oh yes, tomorrow *does* come all right, and when it comes it lasts a bloody long time, I can tell you. (*WC* 125)

Now Dora lives in the empirically verifiable real world. It is not entirely nice, but it is not an illusion. While she was always fond of Perry, she was aware of a negative dimension to his disengagement from the real world, a darkness hinted at in the 'personalised dedication in a copy of *The Devil's Dictionary*' (*WC* 32) which she mentions as the sole evidence of his liaison with Ambrose Bierce. The satanic associations Peregrine bears balance the way that Melchior is associated, in Dora's recollection of how she and Nora once felt about him, with a higher plane of being: 'our father was in constant communication with the angels' (*WC* 87). In their equal irresponsibilities as polar opposites in a religiose metaphysic, Peregrine and Melchior confirm the unacceptability of that patriarchal metaphysic. For all that she loves Peregrine, Dora's narrative very occasionally lets slip a thoroughly negative estimate of him. The first is when, during an account of Peregrine's refusal to take a walk-on part in the Hollywood production of *A Midsummer Night's Dream*, the script of which he has written, Carter has Dora record: 'He liked to pull the strings and see the puppets move, he said' (*WC* 92). The line takes us back to the masculinist game-players, like Honeybuzzard and Uncle Philip, whom Carter has vilified from her earliest novels. Peregrine's endless capacity for irresponsible enjoyment of life is then caught by Dora when she expostulates after describing his happiness during their successful times in the 1930s: 'Peregrine, at ease, as ever, enjoying every minute, the bastard' (*WC* 94).

Peregrine evaded reality ('What news?') and so, in his own way, did Melchior. Melchior, rather, *repressed* his connection with and responsibility for Dora and Nora just as imperialism repressed the realities of subjected peoples. Repression is the key word. Melchior's attachment to legitimacy and 'high' culture is part of dominant, imperial masculine culture's attempt to repress the kind of 'low' culture with which Dora and Nora are associated. In *Wise Children* the central metaphorical vehicle for exploring this repression, at once personal and cultural, is Shakespeare. Legitimate, imperial, patriarchal Shakespeare as propounded by Ranulph and Melchior represses something that, *Wise Children* suggests, can be found in Shakespeare's work itself. Dora and Nora, as participants in 'low', popular culture, are tokens of that repressed something. A part of Carter's allegory is to insist that the illegitimate, 'low' cultural reality inhabited by Dora and Nora possesses a line of descent from Shakespeare just as much as a line of descent from Shakespeare can be claimed by the elitist Melchior. Symbolically, Dora and Nora's birthday falls, like Melchior's, on Shakespeare's birthday. They live in Bard Road, Brixton. The 'low' or the illegitimate they stand for may be found in Shakespeare's work itself, however much this aspect of it has been disallowed by Melchior. Carter expressed to Lorna Sage the inappropriateness of mainstream English culture's reading of Shakespeare solely in terms of high culture. She also noted in Shakespeare a political streak that she did not like, though it did not affect her overall sympathy with the demotic scope of his work:

> Shakespeare just isn't an intellectual, and I think this is one of the reasons why intellectuals get so pissed off with him. They are still reluctant to treat him as popular culture ... The extraordinary thing about English literature is that actually our greatest writer is the intellectual equivalent of bubble-gum, but can make twelve-year-old girls cry, can foment revolutions in Africa, can be translated into Japanese and leave not a dry eye in the house ... Shakespeare, like Picasso, is one of the great hinge-figures that sum up the past – one of the great Janus-figures that sum up the past as well as opening all the doors towards the future. I tend to agree that his politics were diabolical. I think I know the sort of person he was, the sort of wet war-hating liberal who was all gung-ho for the Falklands, who in taking sides would have said, you know, it's a sorry business, but once we have embarked on it ... signed William Shakespeare, Highgate Village. That sort of intellectual dishonesty seems to me to *reek* from all the political aspects of the plays, but the plays themselves add up to something else. You can play them any way you want. It must be obvious that I *really like* Shakespeare. (Sage 1992: 186–7)

The intellectual dishonesty of the political aspects of Shakespeare's plays embraces the essential conservatism that may be traced not only in, say, the tragedies and the history plays but also in the proto-imperialist dimension of works such as *The Tempest*. This dimension feeds directly into the high, patriarchal appropriation of Shakespeare. But there are, simultaneously, other possibilities in Shakespeare's work which Carter is drawn to in *Wise Children*. These possibilities are a part of Shakespeare's embedding in Renaissance English culture. They are possibilities in the realm of gender identity which are highlighted by Stephen Orgel in *Impersonations: The Performance of Gender in Shakespeare's England*, where he writes that:

> As proliferating studies in the history of sexuality have shown, the binary division of sexual appetites into the normative heterosexual and the deviant homosexual is a very recent invention; neither homosexuality nor heterosexuality existed as categories for the Renaissance mind. Indeed, the very idea that sexual preferences constitute categories – that people can be identified according to what kinds of sex they enjoy – and moreover that such categories are exclusive ones – that an interest in men necessarily precludes or conflicts with an interest in

women – is largely a piece of post-Enlightenment taxonomy. (Orgel 1996: 59)

Nor is it only a matter of the absence in Renaissance English culture of more recent patriarchal definitions of heterosexuality as the legitimate norm. Orgel writes that Renaissance theatre, specifically, 'is a world in which masculinity is always in question. In the discourses of patriarchy, gender is the least certain of boundaries' (Orgel 1996: 153). And cross-dressing in Renaissance theatre touches the 'dangerous possibility that is articulated in innumerable ways throughout this society, from gynecological theory to sartorial style, from the fear of effeminacy to the stage's translation of boys into women and women into boys: that women might not be objects but subjects, not the other but the self ' (Orgel 1996: 153). Carter alludes to the cross-dressing in Shakespeare's comedies when she has Ranulph's wife Estella play the part of the Prince in the New York production of *Hamlet*. But Carter's image of a woman playing the part of a man in a tragic, rather than a comic, context serves to subvert the pure 'masculinism' of the tragic genre. Carter's image of Estella playing Hamlet is itself an appropriation of the subjectivity that in patriarchal imagination is reserved for males. The patriarchal ideology of legitimacy and of 'high' cultural authority purveyed by the Hazard family line has, from the outset, been debunked by Estella's cross-dressing as a tragic hero. Throughout *Wise Children* Carter exposes the way in which the Hazard family itself contains all the elements of the illegitimate and the 'low' that its menfolk have insisted on repressing, just as they have repressed or occluded the same things in Shakespeare's own work. This is the significance of the 'complications' in the Hazard family tree; complications which, as I noted at the outset of this discussion, constitute one of the basic allusions to Shakespeare's work. Kate Webb has observed that the complications are not just those of unacknowledged paternity:

> Shakespeare may have become the very symbol of legitimate culture, but his work is characterised by bastardy, multiplicity and incest; the Hazard dynasty may represent propriety and tradition, but they, too, are an endlessly orphaned, errant, and promiscuous bunch ...
>
> *Wise Children* is like the proverbial Freudian nightmare – aided and abetted (as Freud was himself) by Shakespearian example. Dora's family story is crammed with incestuous love and oedipal hatred: there are

sexual relationships between parent and child (where this is not tech-
nically so, actor-parents marry their theatrical offspring – in two generations of Hazards, Lears marry Cordelias); and between sister and
brother (Melchior's children Saskia and Tristram). And there is oedipal hatred between child and parent (Saskia twice tries to poison her
father, and she and her twin sister Imogen are guilty either of pushing
their mother down a flight of stairs or at least of leaving her there, an
invalid, once she has fallen); and between parent and child ('All the
same, he [Ranulph] loved his boys. He cast them as princes in the
tower as soon as they could toddle'.) (Webb 1994: 282, 292–3)

The illegitimate 'other' that Melchior repressed lay at the heart of
his own life and family. We are back with a variant of the theme of
Heroes and Villains. Melchior's patriarchal insistence on the purity
of the high and the mainstream was an illusion, a point which is
symbolised by the 'crown from Lear' (*WC* 20) which he inherited
from his father and which he sets huge store by. The problem is
that the crown is not the one that his father wore in *King Lear*.
For his father had gambled away that crown in Tucson, Arizona,
of all places, and Estella had 'put together a new one for him out
of a bit of cardboard. She dabbed on some gold paint' (*WC* 20).
The token of kingly authority to which Melchior adhered was a
bit of cardboard, a sham, just like his outward show of pure cultural legitimacy.

Nor is it only within family terms that legitimacy is exploded in
Wise Children. The traditionally rigid insistence on demarcating
the 'high' from the 'low' is also shown to have broken down in late
twentieth century English culture. *Wise Children* traces the way in
which a major impetus behind this breakdown was provided by
American culture. When Melchior went to Hollywood in the 1930s
to take part in making a film of *A Midsummer Night's Dream* he
went, as I have indicated, with the silly fantasy of imposing 'high'
English culture on the ex-colony. He even arranged for Dora and
Nora to take with them some earth from Stratford-upon-Avon to
sprinkle on the set of the film. Unfortunately a cat used the pot of
earth as a urinal after they had reached Hollywood, and Dora and
Nora secretly replaced the English earth with Californian soil, so
that Melchior's symbolic sprinkling of the true, essential thing is
mockingly compromised. And the film of *A Midsummer Night's
Dream* itself, later described as a 'masterpiece of kitsch' (*WC* 111),
is, from the point of view of the purist, a travesty. Dora's

description of the making of the film is everywhere amusing. A small detail:

> that 'wood near Athens' was a deathtrap. A couple of bunnies were concussed by swinging dewdrops; a gnome missed his footing on a toadstool and fractured a fibula; we backed into one of the spiky conkers by mistake, laddered our tights, punctured our posteriors and Nora's went septic, off work for ten days on her front and *hors de combat* in the Forest of Arden, swearing and cursing and leafing through *Brides* magazine. (*WC* 143–4)

The 'debasement' of Shakespeare, as the proponents of 'high' culture would have it, parallels the fate of the British Empire. This is a decline symbolised by Gorgeous George, employed to play Shakespeare's Bottom in the film, who Dora on one occasion tripped over as he lay oblivious on the ground:

> Bottom was dead to the world ... and wouldn't be needing his ass's head. I got off his plus-fours, too, and his jacket, and so I inadvertently exposed the British Empire, all that pink on his torso, not to mention the lesser breeds without the law. I didn't want our nation's shame out in the open for all to see so I rolled him under an imitation bush, picked off a handful of imitation leaves and covered him up. (*WC* 157)

The culture of England, in the near forty-five years following the Second World War, is shown in *Wise Children* to have undergone a sea-change from the old imperial order. Tristram Hazard, the 'last gasp of the imperial Hazard family' (*WC* 10) is in the 1980s the television host of an 'S-M game show' (*WC* 16). Dora records the contrast between his job and the old high, imperial values of his line just after she has heard a wax cylinder recording of Ranulph playing Macbeth:

> Only a hundred years ago ... My own grandfather. Yet it was a voice from before the flood, from another kind of life entirely, so antique-sounding that it scarcely seems possible his granddaughters now sit in silk camiknickers in the basement of a house in Brixton, drinking tea and watching on television his great-grandson address an invisible audience out of a plastic box, in that between-two-worlds, neither Brit nor Yank, twang of the game-show host:
> 'Say it again for me! LASHINGS OF LOLLY!'
> Lo, how the mighty have fallen. An S-M game show? How low can you get? (*WC* 16)

Comparably, Melchior himself appears in 'TV ... commericals' (*WC* 8). The 'low' has *revealed* itself at the heart of the 'high'. And the 'low' is now courted by the 'high'. Dora and Nora get requests from 'Film Studies' Ph.D. students wanting to interview them about their parts in the film of *A Midsummer Night's Dream* (*WC* 8). The breakdown of divisions between 'high' and 'low' is celebrated in *Wise Children*, not bewailed. The decay of the cultural limits between 'high' and 'low', so that the culture can no longer define itself in terms of either but only in terms of some new thing, is not to be understood as a carnivalesque disruption of the boundaries between the elevated and the debased. That disruption was only ever temporary and was superseded, as Carter pointed out, by the reinstatement of established order. It is, rather, a real mixing and blending which involves a permanent erasure of the old boundaries and which demands a new definition of English cultural identity. This is a mixing and blending in the actual 'history' that Dora, in her old age, lives in; it is not an escape – *à la* Peregrine – from history. This is a mixing and blending which embraces the multiplicity of cultural phenomena, avoiding the iniquities of the old lines of demarcation and exclusion. The vision of the novel embraces rather than represses differences of sexuality in late-twentieth-century England. Gay sex, for example, is understood as part of a centred multiplicity of life in the culture. Dora notes with pleasure the activities of two men in the cinema when she goes to see a screening of her old film of *A Midsummer Night's Dream*:

> As we got up, we spotted a bloke in the next row down on his knees at trough in his boyfriend's fly. It was the only thing about the entire expedition that cheered me up, in fact, to think that *somebody* was having a bit of fun in all the damp, draughty emptiness. (*WC* 110)

The vision of the novel embraces English people of a different skin colour from traditional English people: 'our precious little Tiffany, the first Black in the family' (*WC* 35). Tiffany is part of the family 'invented' by Grandma (*WC* 35). That invented or constructed family stands in the novel as the archetype of a re-invented society that has broken free of the monomania of patriarchal exclusion. The society of that family is based on loving rather than repressive relations. It is a love – symbolised by Grandma's accommodatingness – defined outside the terms of imperious,

masculine imagination. It is love defined, as it had been in several
of Carter's previous novels, by reciprocity rather than by domination of one by another. It is love – there is no other word – which
defines community: a community grounded in the empirical reality of a history that stands in contrast with the irresponsibilities of
patriarchal repression of unwanted bits of history or of masculine
indulgence in a carnivalesque evasion of history.

Lorna Sage reports Carter saying that 'She has often been asked
... why there are so few mothers in her books, and has realised
that all along the houses have stood in for mother' (Sage 1992:
190). So it is with 49 Bard Road where Dora and Nora live. The
spirit of the house, in the very late 1980s when Dora is recounting
her story, was formed in the first place by Grandma Chance and
her accommodating love. If biological paternity is always in question in *Wise Children*, so, also, the culture of maternity envisaged
in the novel is separated from biological essentialism. As Gerardine
Meaney has pointed out: 'Maternity too moves out of the realm of
biological certainty: "Mother is as mother does" (223)' (Meaney
1993: 127). And 'Grandma' Chance 'does' as mother. When Dora
and Nora became really unsettled during their stay in Hollywood
in the 1930s, Grandma Chance suddenly appeared, bringing with
her the virtues of her household, to which fertile and creative
house all three returned:

> She seemed to fill up all the space available, so there wasn't any room
> left in the whole of southern California for insecurity. She had her
> oilcloth carrier with her, evidently her only luggage. Daisy's white cat
> ... now made its appearance ... It stopped short when it saw Grandma.
> It rubbed its head against her knee and started to purr. She bent down
> and picked it up.
> 'I feel the need of something to cuddle,' she said ...
> We took the white cat to Brixton with us, in the end. It didn't have
> any time for Daisy any more. It never showed much sign of either sex
> while it lived with Daisy but ... as soon as that cat arrived at Bard
> Road, it turned into a breeding machine. The founding mother of the
> Chance cat dynasty. (*WC* 160–1)

Dora records how desolated she and Nora were after Grandma's
death:

> Without Grandma in it, minding the fires, leaving the lights on for us
> at nights, up in the morning putting on the kettle ... the house was

nothing but a barn and we rattled around uncomfortably, piles of dirty dishes in the sink ... baked beans fossilising at their leisure in the bottoms of pans on the cold stove, etc. etc. etc. (*WC* 165)

But, immersed in Grandma's spirit, Dora and Nora did maintain the house ('Bless this house', says Dora at the outset of her narrative; *WC* 1), together with the family invented by Grandma; making one or two additions – such as Tiffany – along the way. The familial community – devoid of father-figures – invented by this woman recalls the sisterly community of the house in which Fevvers was brought up in *Nights at the Circus*. The communities of both of these houses far away from the 'legitimate' centre are similar in that they are founded on a model of mutual love and interrelationship which contrasts with authoritarian, exclusive patriarchal ideas of human relations. We recall Fevvers, remembering *her* house:

It was one of those old, square, red-brick houses ... you may still find in those parts of London so far from the tide of fashion that they were never swept away ... this harmonious relic tucked away behind the howling of the Ratcliffe highway, like the germ of sense left in a drunkard's mind ... Let me tell you that it was a wholly female world within Ma Nelson's door ... Life within those walls was governed by a sweet and loving reason. I never saw a single blow exchanged between any of the sisterhood who reared me, nor heard a cross word or a voice raised in anger. (*NC* 25–6, 38–9)

The anti-patriarchal model of human relations generated in Bard Road in *Wise Children* is a model that, Carter suggests, does not simply offer an alternative to patriarchal models, an alternative rooted in the real history of contemporary England. It is also capable of neutralising the pains wrought by the patriarchal law of repressive exclusion and evasion. The last chapter of *Wise Children*, set on Melchior's one-hundredth birthday, is a modern version of the conclusion to Shakespeare's later comedies, which, like all the comedies, play on the theme of reconciliation. But in their dramatisation of this theme the later comedies play specifically on the reconciliation of parent with child.

When they enter Melchior's house Dora and Nora, hitherto always excluded from the house, find Melchior a changed man, his capacity for exclusion eroded:

dammit, we fell in love with him, again, just as we'd done that August
bank holiday all those years ago, when he first broke our hearts when
he was scared and young and foolish. We saw that he was none of these
things, now ... Nora was chucking down buckets and he stretched out
his old, veined, freckled hand and touched her cheek hesitantly, tremu-
lously, so as to break your heart.
    'You shouldn't cry,' he said. 'Not at our birthday party.'
    That did it. Now I was at it too.
    'Dad,' said Nora, and I said, 'Dad.' He gave us another hug.
    'My lovely girls.' I don't know what changed him. Perhaps ... per-
haps, when he saw poor little Tiff distracted on the game show, he
thought of Pretty Kitty for the first time in decades. Perhaps ...
    We got ourselves another drink and hid behind a pillar to compose
ourselves. We were grinning away like Cheshire cats, we couldn't help
it. Not that he'd said anything. Not that anything had changed. But
we'd had a bit of love. (*WC* 200–1)

But things do change. This 'bit of love' is private to them. Later,
in a scene which recalls the pathos of Lear's reconciliation with
Cordelia, the matter goes public, official:

Nora signed me with her eyes. It was time for me and she to go public
about our paternity ... We pressed our cheeks against his hands. This
was too much for Melchior. He melted for all to see.
    'Oh, my beloved father – '
    The crystals rang with the last notes of Puck's glorious aria. Not a
dry eye in the house as Melchior raised his head and gave his girls a
watery, tremulous smile.
    'I am the one deserves to weep,' he said, and kisses us. (*WC* 217)

So Carter, paralleling in her writing of *Wise Children* the reconciling,
comedic sympathies of her characters Dora and Grandma, appropriates the tragic, masculine denouement of *King Lear* and resituates
it in a comedic conclusion to her novel.

At this one-hundredth birthday party Dora also gains an insight into the pain experienced by Melchior within his patrimony.
Dora discovers in his bedroom a portrait of his father, Ranulph, in
tragic costume. She realises it is an imitation of this costume which
Melchior has donned for his party, a costume which bespeaks the
son's attempt not merely to live up to the image of his father but,
much more important, the desperate desire in that attempt to fulfil the love he himself had been denied by the old patriarch. It is
a tragic costume:

The son put on the lost father's clothes and when I saw what he had done I could have cried because I'd never taken into consideration that he'd got problems of his own where family was concerned ... No love, no nothing. And, tonight of all nights, he'd chosen to become his own father, hadn't he, as if the child had not been the father of the man, in his case, but, during his whole long life, the man had waited to become the father of himself. (*WC* 224)

But *Wise Children* is a comedy; darkly serious, but comedic in its vision. '[F]or that which had been lost was found and so on', Dora wryly notes in comic vein (*WC* 218). So Perry, who has been lost for many years and who Dora never expected to see again, returns, and asks Melchior's forgiveness for the fact that he, Peregrine, and not Melchior, is the biological father of Melchior's daughters, Saskia and Imogen. Tiffany, presumed dead, turns out not to be, and now she no longer recalls the tragic Ophelia as she gives Tristram a piece of her mind:

'Pull yourself together and be a man, or try to,' said Tiffany sharply. 'You've not got what it takes to be a father. There's more to fathering than fucking, you know.' ...

'Not that your old man and mother aren't perfectly welcome to take a peek at the baby when it's born but don't you come sniffing around until you've dried off behind the ears, Tristram.'

He was too stunned to get up off his knees as Bren and Leroy stepped round him to embrace their daughter in a fusillade of flashes. (*WC* 211)

Not everyone in either a Shakespearian comedy or in Carter's updating of such comedy partakes in the positive feeling of the conclusion.

At the last, Dora and Nora inherit the two babies of Gareth, the other son of Melchior's marriage to 'My Lady Margarine'. The babies have been brought by Perry. In a family known for its longevity, Dora and Nora reconcile themselves to having to live to a hundred in order to bring the babies up. Dora tells the reader of her narrative:

They were twins, of course, three months old, by the look of them. '*Oooh*, Perry!' said Nora. 'Just what I always wanted.'

'Gareth's,' said Peregrine to Melchior. So it turned out the Hazard dynasty wasn't at its last gasp at all but was bursting out in every direction ...

Margarine grabbed hold of Perry: have you seen him? How is he? Who is the mother? Where is she?

But who she was or where they both were do not belong to the world of comedy. Perry told us, of course, because we were family, but I don't propose to tell *you*, not now, when the barren heath was bloomed, the fire that was almost out sprung back to life and Nora a mother at last at seventy-five years old and all laughter, forgiveness, generosity, reconciliation.

Yes.

Hard to swallow, huh?

Well, you might have known what you were about to let yourself in for when you let Dora Chance in her ratty old fur and poster paint, her orange (Persian Melon) toenails sticking out of her snakeskin peeptoes, reeking of liquor, accost you in the Coach and Horses and let her tell you a tale. (*WC* 226–7)

But the tale is an allegory so it doesn't have to be naturalistic. The baby twins, as Dora tells us, 'were boy and girl, a new thing in our family' (*WC* 227). The girl and the boy will be brought up in a family modelled outside patriarchy. A model enabling them to grow up as woman and man free of the oppressions and inequalities that patriarchy imposes on different genders, on different sexualities and on different races; a model free of the fiction that is patriarchy. A fiction serving the interests of the masculine but which comes to be constructed by both sexes, as Nora grasps in a conversation with Dora as they are returning home to Brixton after the party:

'We're both of us mothers and both of us fathers,' she said.

'They'll be wise children, all right.' ...

'Nora ... don't you think our father looked two-dimensional, tonight?' ...

'D'you know, I sometimes wonder if we haven't been making him up all along,' she said. 'If he isn't just a collection of our hopes and dreams and wishful thinking in the afternoons. Something to set our lives by, like the old clock in the hall, which is real enough, in itself, but which we've got to wind up to make it go.' (*WC* 230)

The wise child knows its own father. The wisdom explored in *Wise Children* is the capacity to know and to see through patriarchal definitions of fatherhood. Outside of the violations of love – between genders, sexualities and races – perpetrated by the fiction of patriarchy, Dora and Nora serenade the babies with the only thing they can offer them:

'We can't give you anything but love, babies,
    That's the only thing we've plenty of, babies – ' (*WC* 231)

Elaine Jordan has written that 'Carter's stories do not replace
realistic experience with literary fantasy, but offer other scenes,
other imaginations of what could be made real' (Jordan 1990: 29).
For Carter, fantasy or imagination is inseparable from the consti-
tution of the real. In the England of the 1990s the power of the
old, elitist, imperialist, patriarchal mind-set remains powerfully
and disablingly great. In *Wise Children* Carter refers back to an
age before the consolidation of English patriarchal imperialism to
find in a dimension of Shakespeare's work the seeds of an English
identity which is more accommodating than that later provided by
imperialism and patriarchy. There are hints, in the variety and
multiplicity of life on the streets of her beloved London and elsewhere, that an alternative English cultural model of reciprocity,
tolerance and equality may be in the making, as Carter would have
wished it.

References

Works by Angela Carter

BB *Burning Your Boats: Collected Short Stories*, with an Introduction by Salman Rushdie, London, Vintage, 1996; first published 1995 by Chatto & Windus.

DH *The Infernal Desire Machines of Doctor Hoffman*, London, Penguin, 1982; first published 1972 by Rupert Hart-Davis.

HV *Heroes and Villains*, London, Penguin, 1981; first published 1969 by William Heinemann.

L *Love*, London, Picador, 1988; first published 1971 by Rupert Hart-Davis; revised edition first published 1987 by Chatto & Windus.

MT *The Magic Toyshop*, London, Virago, 1990; first published 1967 by William Heinemann.

NC *Nights at the Circus*, London, Picador, 1985; first published 1984 by Chatto & Windus, The Hogarth Press.

PNE *The Passion of New Eve*, London, Virago, 1992; first published 1977 by Victor Gollancz.

SD *Shadow Dance*, London, Virago, 1995; first published 1966 by William Heinemann.

SL *Shaking a Leg: Journalism and Writings*, The Collected Angela Carter, edited by Jenny Uglow with an Introduction by Joan Smith, London, Chatto & Windus, 1997.

SP *Several Perceptions*, London, Virago, 1995; first published 1968 by William Heinemann.

SW *The Sadeian Woman: An Exercise in Cultural History*, London, Virago, 1979.

WC *Wise Children*, London, Vintage, 1992; first published 1991 by Chatto & Windus.

Other works

Abrams, M. H. (1993) *A Glossary of Literary Terms*, 6th edn, Fort Worth, Harcourt Brace Jovanich.

Alexander, Marguerite (1990) *Flights from Realism: Themes and Strategies in Postmodernist British and American Fiction*, London and New York, Edward Arnold.

Allott, Miriam (ed.) (1970) *The Poems of John Keats*, London, Longman, Annotated English Poets.

Anwell, Maggie (1988) 'Lolita Meets the Werewolf: "The Company of Wolves"', in Lorraine Gamman and Margaret Marshment (eds), *The Female Gaze: Women as Viewers of Popular Culture*, London, The Women's Press, 76–85.

Atwood, Margaret (1992) 'Magic Token through the Dark Forest', *The Observer*, 23 February, 61.

Bakhtin, Mikhail (1984) *Rabelais and His World*, trans. Helene Iswolsky, Bloomington, IN, Indiana University Press.

Barker, Paul (1995) 'The Return of the Magic Story-Teller', *Independent on Sunday* Review, 8 January, 14–16.

Berger, John (1972) *Ways of Seeing*, London, British Broadcasting Corporation and Penguin.

Bertens, Hans (1995) *The Idea of the Postmodern: A History*, London and New York, Routledge.

Bettelheim, Bruno (1977) *The Uses of Enchantment: The Meaning and Importance of Fairy Tales*, first published 1976 by A. Knopf; New York, Vintage, Random House.

Bloom, Harold (1963) *The Visionary Company: A Reading of English Romantic Poetry*, first published 1961 by Doubleday; New York, Anchor Books.

Bronfen, Elisabeth (1992) *Over Her Dead Body: Death, Femininity and the Aesthetic*, Manchester, Manchester University Press.

Butler, Judith (1990) *Gender Trouble: Feminism and the Subversion of Identity*, London, Routledge.

Callil, Carmen (1992) 'Flying Jewellery', *Sunday Times*, 23 February, sect. 7, 6.

Carter, Angela (1980) 'The Language of Sisterhood', in Leonard Michaels and Christopher Ricks (eds), *The State of the Language*, Berkeley, Los Angeles and London, University of California Press, 226–34.

——— (1988) 'Truly, it Felt Like Year One', in Sara Maitland (ed.), *Very Heaven: Looking Back at the 1960s*, London, Virago, 209–16.

Chedgzoy, Kate (1995) *Shakespeare's Queer Children: Sexual Politics and Contemporary Culture*, Manchester and New York, Manchester University Press.

Clark, Robert (1987) 'Angela Carter's Desire Machines', *Women's Studies*, 14, 147–61.

Davidson, Donald (1984) *Inquiries into Truth and Interpretation*, Oxford, Clarendon Press.

Day, Aidan (ed.) (1991) *Alfred Lord Tennyson: Selected Poems*, London, Penguin.

Descartes, René (1965) *A Discourse on Method*, first published 1637; published in Everyman's Library 1912; reprinted 1965, London, J. M. Dent.

Duncker, Patricia (1984) 'Re-imagining the Fairy Tales: Angela Carter's *The Bloody Chamber*', *Literature and History*, 10/1, Spring, 3–14.

Eagleton, Terry (1985) 'Capitalism, Modernism and Postmodernism', *New Left Review*, 152, July/Aug., 60–73.

Encyclopaedia Britannica (1910–11), 11th edn, 29 vols, New York, The Encyclopaedia Britannica Company.

Feyerabend, Paul (1987) *Farewell to Reason*, London, Verso.

Fowles, John (1987) *The French Lieutenant's Woman*, first published 1969 by Jonathan Cape; London, Pan Books with Jonathan Cape.

Frye, Northrop (1974) *Fearful Symmetry: A Study of William Blake*, first published 1947; Princeton, NJ, Princeton University Press.

Gay, Peter (1975) *Style in History*, first published 1974; London, Jonathan Cape.

Gerrard, Nicci (1995) 'Getting Carter', *The Observer* Life, 9 July, 20–3.

Goldsworthy, Kerryn (1985) 'Angela Carter', *meanjin* (Adelaide), 44/1, March, 4–13.

Habermas, Jürgen (1984) *The Theory of Communicative Action*, vol. 1, first published 1981 by Suhrkamp Verlag; translated and introduced by Thomas McCarthy, London, Heinemann Educational.

—— (1985) 'Modernity – An Incomplete Project', first published 1981 in *New German Critique*; reprinted in Hal Foster (ed.), *Postmodern Culture*, London and Sydney, Pluto Press, 3–15.

—— (1987) *The Philosophical Discourse of Modernity*, first published 1985 by Suhrkamp Verlag; translated by Frederick Lawrence and introduced by Thomas McCarthy, Cambridge, Polity Press.

Haffenden, John (1985) Interview with Angela Carter, in *Novelists in Interview*, London and New York, Methuen, 76–96.

Hamilton, Paul (1996) *Historicism*, London and New York, Routledge.

Harris, Daniel A. (1974) 'Androgyny: The Sexist Myth in Disguise', *Women's Studies*, 2, 171–84.

Harron, Mary (1984) 'I'm a Socialist, Damn it! How Can You Expect Me to be Interested in Fairies?', *The Guardian*, 25 September, 10.

Jackson, Rosemary (1981) *Fantasy: The Literature of Subversion*, London and New York, Routledge.

Jordan, Elaine (1990) 'Enthralment: Angela Carter's Speculative Fictions', in Linda Anderson (ed.), *Plotting Change: Contemporary Women's Fiction*, London, Melbourne and Auckland, Edward Arnold, 19–40.

—— (1992a) 'The Dangers of Angela Carter', in Isobel Armstrong (ed.), *New Feminist Discourses: Critical Essays on Theories and Texts*, London and New York, Routledge, 119–31.

—— (1992b) 'Down the Road, or History Rehearsed', in Francis Barker, Peter Hulme and Margaret Iverson (eds), *Postmodernism and the Rereading of Modernity*, Manchester and New York, Manchester University Press.

—— (1994) 'The Dangerous Edge', in Sage 1994b, 189–215.

Katsavos, Anna (1994) 'An Interview with Angela Carter', *Review of Contemporary Fiction*, 14, 3, Fall, 11–17.

Keynes, Geoffrey (ed.) (1966) *The Complete Writings of William Blake*, London, New York and Toronto, Oxford University Press.

Kristeva, Julia (1991) *Strangers to Ourselves*, translated by Leon S. Roudiez, New York, Columbia University Press.

Lacan, Jacques (1977) 'The Mirror Stage as Formative of the Function of the "I" as Revealed in Psychoanalytic Experience', in *Écrits: A Selection*, first published 1966 by Editions du Seuil; translated by Alan Sheridan, London, Tavistock, 1–7.

Lewallen, Avis (1988) '"Wayward Girls but Wicked Women?" Female Sexuality in Angela Carter's *The Bloody Chamber*', in Gary Day and Clive Bloom (eds), *Perspectives on Pornography: Sexuality in Film and Literature*, Basingstoke and London, Macmillan, 144–58.

Lloyd, Genevieve (1993) *The Man of Reason: 'Male' and 'Female' in Western Philosophy*, first published 1984 by Methuen; 2nd edn, London, Routledge.

Lovibond, Sabina (1989) 'Feminism and Postmodernism', *New Left Review*, 178, Nov./Dec., 5–28.

Lyotard, Jean-François (1984) *The Postmodern Condition: A Report on Knowledge*, first published 1979 by Editions de Minuit; translated by Geoff Bennington and Brian Massumi, Manchester, Manchester University Press.

Makinen, Merja (1992) 'Angela Carter's *The Bloody Chamber* and the Decolonization of Feminine Sexuality', *Feminist Review*, 42, Autumn, 2–15.

McDowell, Margaret B. (1991) 'Carter, Angela', in Lesley Henderson (ed.), *Contemporary Novelists*, Chicago and London, St James Press, 179–82.

McHale, Brian (1994) *Postmodernist Fiction*, first published 1987 by Methuen; London and New York, Routledge.

Meaney, Gerardine (1993) *(Un)Like Subjects: Women, Theory, Fiction*, London and New York, Routledge.

Moi, Toril (1984) 'Pornografi og fantasi: om kvinner, klaer og filosofi', *Vinduet*, 1/38, 17–24.

Morrison, Blake (1997) 'Polemics with a Giggle', *Independent on Sunday Review*, 6 July, 30–31.

Norris, Christopher (1987) *Derrida*, Fontana Modern Masters, Glasgow, Fontana.

Orgel, Stephen (1996) *Impersonations: The Performance of Gender in Shakespeare's England*, Cambridge, Cambridge University Press.

Palmer, Paulina (1987) 'From "Coded Mannequin" to Bird Woman: Angela Carter's Magic Flight', in Sue Roe (ed.), *Women Reading Women's Writing*, Brighton, Harvester Press, 179–205.

Richardson, Alan (1988) 'Romanticism and the Colonization of the Feminine', in Anne Mellor (ed.), *Romanticism and Feminism*, Bloomington and Indianapolis, Indiana University Press.

Roe, Sue (1994) 'The Disorder of *Love*: Angela Carter's Surrealist Collage', in Sage 1994b, 60–97.

Rose, Jacqueline (1996) *States of Fantasy*, Oxford, Clarendon Press.

Russo, Mary (1994) *The Female Grotesque: Risk, Excess and Modernity*, New York and London, Routledge.

Sage, Lorna (1977) 'The Savage Sideshow: A Profile of Angela Carter', *The New Review*, 4, 51–7.

—— (1992) 'Angela Carter Interviewed by Lorna Sage', in Malcolm Bradbury and Judith Cooke (eds), *New Writing*, London, Minerva Press, 185–93.

—— (1994a) *Angela Carter*, Writers and their Work Series, Plymouth, Northcote House in Association with the British Council.

—— (ed.) (1994b) *Flesh and the Mirror: Essays on the Art of Angela Carter*, London, Virago.

Schmidt, Ricarda (1990) 'The Journey of the Subject in Angela Carter's Fiction', *Textual Practice*, 3, 56–75.

Suleiman, Susan Rubin (1994) 'The Fate of the Surrealist Imagination in the Society of the Spectacle', in Sage 1994b, 98–116.

Todd, Janet (1986) *Sensibility: An Introduction*, London, Methuen.

Todorov, Tzvetan (1973) *The Fantastic: A Structural Approach to a Literary Genre*, translated by Richard Howard, Cleveland, Case Western Reserve University Press.

Vries, Ad de (1984) *Dictionary of Symbols and Imagery*, first published 1974; revised edn 1976, reprinted 1984, Amsterdam and London, North-Holland Publishing Company.

Warner, Marina (1992) 'Angela Carter', *The Independent*, 17 February, 25.

Waugh, Patricia (1984) *Metafiction: The Theory and Practice of Self-Conscious Fiction*, London and New York, Methuen.

—— (1992) 'Modernism, Postmodernism, Feminism: Gender and Autonomy Theory', in Patricia Waugh (ed.), *Postmodernism: A Reader*, London and New York, Edward Arnold, 189–204.

Webb, Kate (1994) 'Seriously Funny: *Wise Children*', in Sage 1994b, 279–307.

Wilson, Robert Rawdon (1989) 'SLIP PAGE: Angela Carter, In/Out/In the Postmodern Nexus', *A Review of International English Literature*, 20/4, October, 96–114.

Young, Robert (1990) *White Mythologies: Writing History and the West*, London and New York, Routledge.

Zipes, Jack (ed.) (1986) *Don't Bet on the Prince: Contemporary Feminist Fairy Tales in North America and England*, Aldershot, Gower.

Index

Printed in the United Kingdom
by Lightning Source UK Ltd.
110096UKS00001B/226-243